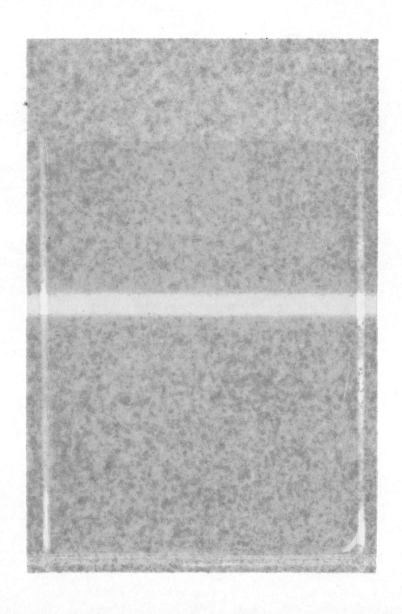

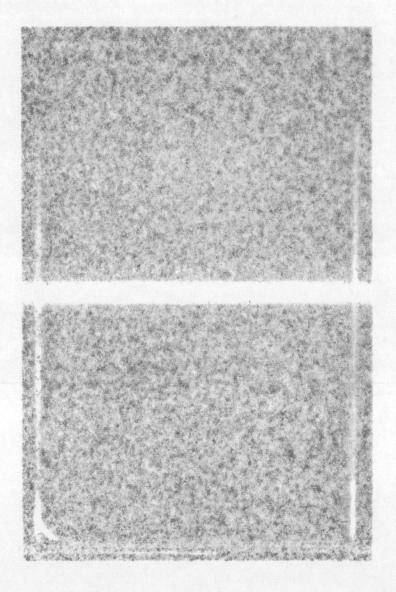

BAROQUE AND ROCOCO SILKS

Baroque and Rococo Silks

by

PETER THORNTON

TAPLINGER PUBLISHING CO., INC.
New York

First American Edition published by
TAPLINGER PUBLISHING CO., INC., 1965

Library of Congress Catalogue Card Number:
65–14391

Made and Printed in Great Britain

Acknowledgment

I have the privilege of being on the staff of the Victoria and Albert Museum, in London. Working in a large national museum brings with it several great advantages. In the first place one has continual access to the rich collections that are housed there. In my own case this has enabled me to become familiar with a wide range of textiles and to handle frequently a large selection of silks like those described in this book. In the second place one has the advantage of being able to make full use of the great resources of an extensive art library. Finally one has the inestimable advantage of working with or alongside a group of people who are all concerned with the same kinds of thing as oneself. I owe a very great debt to my colleagues, especially to those in the Department of Textiles, for what they have taught me, for the advice they have so freely and so often given me, for their gentle criticism of my wilder theories, and for the way in which they have helped me put so much in perspective. My gratitude is particularly great to George Wingfield Digby, Keeper of the Department of Textiles, under whom I worked for about seven years, for his patience, generosity and kindness to me during that time, to Donald King whose opinion I have always so greatly valued and of whose wide knowledge I have so often and unashamedly taken advantage, and to Natalie Rothstein with whom I worked closely for a number of years and whose indefatigable researches have done so much to extend our knowledge of eighteenth-century textiles and textile industries. I have had access to all the information she collected while working with me and not an inconsiderable amount of what I have written in the introduction to this book is based on her findings.

Working in a great national museum also brings another advantage. It more readily obtains for one an *entrée* to the collections of other museums and brings one into contact with their staffs. This can be very fruitful and I have taken frequent advantage of this facility — so much so that I now owe a debt of very considerable gratitude to many people but most particularly to Mr. Adolph Cavallo of the Museum of Fine Arts, Boston, Massachusetts, to Dr. Agnes Geijer of the State Historical Museum, Stockholm, to M. Robert de Micheaux and M. Felix Guicherd of the Musée Historique des Tissus at Lyons, to Dr. Gudrun Ekstrand of the Royal Armouries, Stockholm, to M. Ratouis de Limay, Conservateur en chef of the Library of the Union Centrale des Arts Décoratifs in Paris, to M. Valery Radot, one-time Conservateur en chef of the Cabinet des Estampes in the Bibliothèque Nationale, Paris, to Dr. Gudmund Boesen, Keeper of the Danish Royal Collections at Rosenborg Castle, Copenhagen, to M. Boris Lossky, Director of the Musée des Beaux Arts at Tours, and to Baron Ludwig Dory Jobahaza of the Historical Museum, Frankfurt-on-the-Main, all of whom have helped me a great deal on many occasions. I should also like to thank the Librarians and Archivists at Guildhall in the City of London, and in the cities of Lyons and Tours (including the staff of the Archives Departementales at Tours) for giving me access to and guiding me through the important collections of documents relating to my subject which are in their care.

My gratitude is also extended to the many owners, both private persons and public institutions, who have given me permission to reproduce the numerous photographs in this book. Their names are recorded under the appropriate items in the notes to the plates.

Since this book is primarily concerned with the *decoration* of seventeenth- and eighteenth-century silks, the illustrations play a most important part. For this reason I am particularly grateful to the Council of the British Academy for their generosity in voting me a grant from the Pilgrim Trust Research Fund towards the cost of the many photographs reproduced here. Not only did this grant ensure that I could include a sufficient number of illustrations for my purpose, but it gave me a certain encouragement which I much appreciated during the many months it took me to write this book.

PETER THORNTON

London, January 1963

Contents

CONTENTS

ILLUSTRATIONS

COLOUR PLATES

MONOCHROME PLATES
at the end of the book
are in two groups

Within these two groups the plates are arranged
approximately in chronological order.

DIAGRAMS A – D will be found on pages 86 and 87

FOREWORD

This book is about the figured silks woven in Europe during the Baroque and Rococo periods, that is, between about 1640 and 1770 or so. My primary aim has been to try and trace the general development of the patterns which appeared on the richer classes of silk material during this space of time. These comparatively large patterns were composed by professional silk-designers and, while the aesthetic merits of the individual compositions vary enormously, all of them have the right to be regarded as artistic creations. It is thus as works of art that they are considered here, reflecting, as they do, the various stages of general art-history and certain important aspects of the spirit of the sumptuous Age in which they were made.

I have tried very hard not to use technical terms that need tedious explanation. I have assumed that the reader knows more or less what a satin looks like and can tell it from, say, a taffeta or a damask or a velvet, but if he does not know, it doesn't really matter. The student of historic textiles will know about such things already and most other people don't care. The silk-designer of the period had of course to take very seriously into account the kind of weave in which his pattern was to be produced but, while this made a difference to the detail treatment of the motifs, the position of that pattern in the general stylistic development of silk-patterns during this period can still be recognized, in spite of such technical differences, as I hope to show. Whatever the technique in which a particular pattern was woven, the essential style of the composition was dictated almost entirely by fashion — and of course the limitations of the medium. For it should be remembered that these silks were all woven on a loom and the patterns with which they were decorated were produced entirely by and during the process of weaving the material — in contradistinction from processes like embroidery and fabric-printing which can only be carried out on a finished woven material.

The more general aspects of the subject and the historical background are discussed in the Introduction. The seven Chapters that follow are in effect a commentary on the stylistic development illustrated by the plates at the end of the book. Detailed notes to the plates have been supplied separately.

I feel I owe the reader an apology for the indecent number of footnotes that I have found it necessary to include. This is partly because a great deal of the information introduced in the main text comes from obscure sources, some of them unpublished, and it seemed only right to provide references for those who wish to study this subject more closely. To a larger extent it is because I have tried to avoid cluttering up the main text with evidence, justifications — and the odd red herring! And of course the virtue of footnotes is that one can skip them.

P. K. T.

INTRODUCTION

I. FASHION AND SILK-PATTERNS

The silks discussed in this book were the fashionable materials of their day. They were extremely expensive because they took a long time to make and because the raw materials had for the most part to be brought from far afield. Furthermore, many of these silks were embellished with silver or silver-gilt thread — sometimes both — and, although these threads only consisted of a thin strip of rich metal wound on a silken core, this greatly increased the cost. Only a comparatively small number of people could afford such luxurious materials but, all the same, there were enough of them to keep large silk-weaving industries at work in Europe throughout the seventeenth and eighteenth centuries.

People were at that period still prepared to spend a lot of money on their personal adornment, as evidence either of their wealth or of their good taste. They no longer took this characteristic to such extremes as had their forebears during the Middle Ages, when princes of both Church and State had paid immense sums for their superb vestments and robes, while their houses remained furnished in the most rudimentary fashion. The emphasis had gradually changed until, by the middle of the seventeenth century, considerable attention was being paid to interior decoration; yet most people still preferred first to ensure that their wardrobe was sufficiently magnificent before they started worrying about the furnishing of their houses. Even in the eighteenth century, when there were so many opportunities for buying fine furniture, silver, porcelain and so on, enormous sums were still lavished on dress. The cost of clothes during the seventeenth and eighteenth centuries lay almost entirely in the material. Tailoring and the making-up of dresses was still a rather elementary business and consumed only a small fraction of the total cost of a dress or a suit.

Most of the materials that we can buy in the shops today — with the obvious exception of the man-made fibres — were available in the eighteenth century. There was, if anything, a wider range of fine woollen cloth than we have now, there were various kinds of linen material, there were silks, there were cottons, and there were mixtures of the four basic fibres as well. Of these, silks were the most expensive. There were many classes of silk, and the price range was a wide one. At the lower end of the scale were the various plain materials, then came those with stripes and simple patterns, and finally there were the rich materials with complicated patterns. It is these that concern us here.

Since there were no fashion journals appearing regularly at that time, the cut of costume changed only comparatively slowly. *It was the patterns on the fashionable silk dress-materials that changed instead, and they changed each year.* It is possible to follow these changes and discover what kind of pattern was in fashion at each stage. This is the central theme of the chapters that follow this introduction. The last chapter is devoted to a brief study of the contemporary furnishing silks. It is brief, because we know far less about them at present. All the same, it seemed wrong to write a book about Baroque and Rococo silks without saying something about the splendid materials that played so important a part in the furnishing of the great houses of the time.

The demand for fresh patterns

There is plenty of evidence that the patterns of fashionable silks changed each year during the eighteenth century. Already in 1681, we find the Directors of the East India Company in London giving one of their factors 'this for a constant and generall Rule, that in all flowered silks you change ye fashion and flower as much as you can every yeare, for English Ladies and they say ye French and other Europeans will give twice as much for a new thing not seen in Europe before....'[1] Admittedly these instructions were for the guidance of the Company's servants in India who were weaving silks, mostly light-weight materials, for the European market, but there can be no doubt that the European silk-weavers followed the same rule.

Probably the most telling piece of evidence for this is the statement, made in a report drawn up in 1725 by the Corporation of Silk-weavers at Lyons, the principal centre of silk-weaving in France, that '*Les fabricans françois, persuadez que la nouveauté a des charmes, s'appliquent sans cesse à varier les nuances et les desseins de leurs étoffes, et pour le faire avec succez ils suivent la consommation, ils envoyent chaque année leurs dessinateurs à Paris pour examiner ce qui a plus d'avantage aux personnes du meilleur goût et sur les idées qu'ils prennent dans cette capitale ils travaillent à de nouveaux desseins lesquels ils tâchent de perfectionner ce qui a déjà paru le plus parfait et de conformer ce qu'ils inventent à ce qui a le plus flatté le goût du public*'.[2] Much the same was said by an English silk-designer about a

---

[1] Sir William G. Forrest, The Bengal and Madras Papers, Calcutta, 1928, Vol. I, 20th May 1681. The term 'flowered silks' was used by English silk-weavers in the seventeenth and eighteenth centuries to denote all silks woven on a draw-loom. It was only necessary to use so complex a loom for materials that were decorated with large patterns. In the case of silks at this period, the patterns woven on a draw-loom almost always consisted of floral compositions of some kind — hence the name 'flowered silks'. Thus the 'flowered branch' of the English silk industry numbered those weavers who produced the more ambitious and artistically interesting patterns. Simpler patterns, produced by a foot-operated mechanism on a simpler loom, were the concern of the 'foot-figured' branch. Simpler still were the materials woven by the 'plain' branch.

[2] This report, together with some related documents all dealing with the selling of freshly composed French designs to foreigners, is to be found in the Lyons Municipal Library (Archives of the Lyons Silk industry, HH 131). Reference is also made in these papers to '*L'aggrément de la nouveauté*', to '*les desseins les plus nouveaux*', and to the profits which the weavers could expect to make by selling *new* patterns. The spelling is sometimes curious.

quarter of a century later. 'For many years past', we are told, 'the manufacturers of silks have puzzled both their own and tortured the pattern-drawer's brains to contrive new fashions.'[1] These are the statements of professional people engaged in the silk-weaving industry, but what they say must have been common knowledge among those who cared about fashion. For instance, Casanova, author of the famous memoirs, said of the fashion in silk-patterns that '*elle change chaque année*' and that a material which was in fashion one year had lost a third of its value the year after.[2]

More direct evidence comes from the designs themselves. In Paris there are two important collections of eighteenth-century silk-designs among which are several inscribed with phrases like '*Nouveau du printemps 1725*' and '*Plante nouvelle du printemps 1733*'.[3] Even more revealing is the extremely important collection of designs for Spitalfields silks in the Victoria and Albert Museum, London.[4] With a few exceptions, these are all dated precisely and one can see at a glance how the general style of the

---

[1] This passage is quoted from a most useful little essay on '*designing and drawing Patterns for the Flower'd-silk Manufactory . . .*' which appeared in G. Smith's *Laboratory, or School of Arts,* published in London, but only in the 1756 edition (p. 42). I am greatly indebted to Miss Edith Standen of the Metropolitan Museum of Art, New York, for drawing my attention to this essay and for providing me with a photocopy of it which is now deposited in the Library of the Victoria and Albert Museum, London. The original is in the Library of the Metropolitan Museum. It is not known who wrote the essay although it is clear that he or she was a practising silk-designer at Spitalfields. There were very few designers in London at any period during the eighteenth century and I have elsewhere suggested that the author may have been a certain Anna Maria Garthwaite, several of whose designs are illustrated here (Plates 64B, 66A, 74A, 80B, 81A, 88A, 89A, 94A and 115A) and who was a prominent designer of flowered silks in the second quarter of the century. (See Peter Thornton, 'An 18th century Silk-designer's Manual', *Bulletin of the Needle and Bobbin Club,* New York, Vol. 42, 1958, Nos. 1 and 2.)

[2] *Mémoires de J. Casanova de Seingalt écrits par lui-même* (ed. Maillart), Garnier Frères, Paris, p. 274. The full passage reads '*Ce qui fait la richesse de Lyon, c'est le bon goût et le bon marché, et la divinité à laquelle cette ville doit sa prosperité, c'est la mode. Elle change chaque année; et tell étoffe que le goût du jour met aujourd'hui à trente, n'en vaut plus l'année prochaine que vingt ou quinze; et alors on l'envoie dans l'étranger, où elle est recherchée comme toute nouvelle.*'

[3] The two collections are: (a) In the Cabinet des Estampes, Bibliothèque Nationale, Paris. Vols. Lh.41 (which is labelled '1730' although it contains designs from the 1750's, one of them being dated), Lh.44–44d (which are said to contain designs from Tours but inscriptions show that many of them in fact were drawn by important Lyonnais designers). (b) In the Library of the Musée des Arts Décoratifs, Paris. Vol. DD97, the Martin Collection (17 volumes of designs, dating from the 1720's onwards, from both Lyons and Tours.); Vol. CC109, the Galais Collection (about 21 volumes of designs assembled by Galais, a designer at Tours, but, as a long inscription in the first volume indicates, comprising Lyons designs as well as many from Tours). There are further collections of designs in the Musée Historique des Tissus, Lyons (including Vols. A.320–36 and A.560), and at the Château Plessis-lès-Tours which comes under the jurisdiction of the Musée des Beaux-Arts, Tours. Comparatively few French silk-designs now bear dates; these have usually been trimmed away by collectors.

[4] In the Department of Prints and Drawings. There are some 840 designs in all, in two sets: (a) The Liddiard Set, containing designs from the silk-weaving establishment of James Leman, an important Spitalfields master-weaver and designer. The designs, many of them drawn by Leman himself, were composed between 1717 and 1722. (b) The Garthwaite Set which almost entirely consists of designs by Anna Maria Garthwaite, an independent silk-designer who worked for many of the leading Spitalfields silk-weavers and mercers of her day. They range in date from the 1720's until 1756. Among her drawings are a few '*patterns by different hands*' which include a handful of designs by the important French refugee designer, Christopher Baudouin. Another important set of designs belongs to Messrs. Vanners & Fennell Bros. Ltd. of Sudbury, Suffolk (photocopy in the Department of Textiles, Victoria and Albert Museum). This contains the early work of James Leman, the earliest designs being from the year 1706 and the last from 1716. This, together with the other two sets, provides us with an unbroken series of English silk-designs covering the years

patterns changed each year, so that one cannot confuse a pattern drawn in, say, the 1720's with one from the 1740's.

When did European silk-weavers first begin to turn out new patterns each year? We do not know. New designs were probably introduced fairly frequently already during the Renaissance, but there is no evidence that there *had* to be something new appearing *regularly* each year.[1] I think this was a seventeenth-century innovation and it was most probably the French who were responsible for it. Fashion, with its insistence on continual change, seems always to have come more naturally to the French than to anyone else. Already in the sixteenth century a charming story was current which told of a painter who, having painted the portrait of an Italian wearing Italian costume, that of a Spaniard wearing clothes in the Spanish style, and that of a German dressed in the German manner, decided to paint the Frenchman naked *'prévoyant le changement de façon d'habits que le Francoys pourroit faire le lendemain, suivant sa costume'*, and merely depicted him holding a piece of cloth, and brandishing a pair of scissors.[2] The Italians had long noted that Frenchmen liked to have new clothes as often as possible. Marino Cavalli, Venetian Ambassador to the French Court in 1546, mentioned in a report the huge profits then being made by Tuscan and Genoese silk-merchants in France, and stated that the French favoured lighter materials than the Venetians because they *'s'ennuieraient à porter le même habit longtemps'*.[3]

About the middle of the seventeenth century, references began to be made to the *newness* of this or that silk-design. There is, for instance, a *'dessein nouveau pour étoffes de brocart à fond d'or ou d'argent'* among some compositions by the Parisian designer of ornament, Paul Androuet Ducerceau, that were probably drawn in the 1660's,[4] and in the same decade the Queen of Denmark acquired from Paris a parcel of silks that included a *'brocardt vert nouveau patron de fleurs'*.[5] In 1678, the Parisian *Mercure Galant*, a journal

---

1706 to 1756. I do not believe there is a comparable series anywhere. Some designs by Leman, Garthwaite and Baudouin are reproduced here. (For biographical notes on these designers, see Peter Thornton and Natalie Rothstein, *The importance of the Huguenots in the London Silk Industry*, in the Proceedings of the Huguenot Society of London, Vol. XX, No. 1. 1958.)

[1] During the eighteenth century, new patterns in fact appeared twice a year. There was the 'Spring Trade' and the 'Winter Trade'. Much information of this kind may be obtained from the reports of the evidence given before the Select Committee of the House of Commons which met in 1765 and 1766 to look into the state of the London silk industry, at that time suffering from a trade recession. These appear in the House of Commons Journals for those two years and are hereafter referred to as the 'Reports'. See, in this instance, the 1766 report, p. 724; evidence of Mr. Sabatier who was a weaver of substance.

[2] Justin Godart, *L'Ouvrier en Soie. Monographie du Tisseur Lyonnais*, Lyons and Paris, 1899, p. 208.

[3] Francisque Michel, *Recherches sur le Commerce, la Fabrication et l'Usage des Étoffes de Soie, d'or et d'argent...*, Paris, 1860, Vol. II, p. 285 and, on this subject in general, the preceding pages.

[4] The design in question belongs to the same group as those illustrated in Plates 13A and B, the date of which is discussed on page 103.

[5] Sigrid Flamand Christensen, 'De Danske Kongers Kronologiske Samling paa Rosenborg', *Kongedragterne fra 17 og 18 Aarhundrede*, Copenhagen, 1940, Nr. 28, p. 78. This may be the silk illustrated in our Plate 12B.

devoted largely to questions of fashion in its widest sense, promised its readers a special supplement with the designs of the new spring silks.[1]

It is probably no accident that one begins to find references like these from about 1660 onwards and it will be noted that they all concern *French* silk-patterns.

It was at this very time that the French silk industry was given a major overhauling which enabled it to become within a comparatively short while the chief producer of woven silks in Europe. This was part of the drastic reorganization of French industry in general that took place in the 1660's, instigated and supervised by the great minister, Colbert. Special support was given to industries producing luxury goods. The Corporations of Silk-weavers at both Tours and Lyons, the two chief centres of the industry in France, received new charters in 1667, and complete prohibition was imposed during the same year on the wearing of foreign silks.[2] It seems more than likely that every encouragement was at the same time given to what appears to be a French national characteristic — the love of new fashions. If French society could be persuaded to demand new fashions *each year*, imagine how this would stimulate the silk-industry — and, incidentally, all other luxury trades! And if other nations could be persuaded that they too ought to want these new fashions, how much more lucrative would the industry become! The reasoning might not have been quite so objective as this but there can be little doubt that Colbert and the French silk-industry did everything possible to stimulate the demand for fresh patterns. In fact, there were all kinds of delays in implementing the new regulations of 1667 and the French silk-industry only really gained its full strength towards the end of the seventeenth century. By that time, however, the tradition of introducing new silk-patterns each year was firmly established.[3] The successive styles which resulted from this practice are the main subject of this book and are discussed, phase by phase, in the chapters that follow.

It should be added that the inclination to change the patterns frequently was probably helped by another factor. Europe was becoming increasingly wealthy during the second half of the seventeenth century although her wealth was to increase even more strikingly during the eighteenth century. This brought about a growing demand for silks and other luxury wares. It is fair to assume that as the consumption rose, so did the demand for fresh patterns — one did not want all one's suits or dresses to look alike — and, as the

---

[1] J. L. Nevinson, *L'Origine de la Gravure des Modes*, Actes du Ier Congrès International d'Histoire du Costume, Venice, 1952, p. 208.

[2] For a general survey of the reorganization of the French silk industry, see E. Pariset, *Histoire de la Fabrique Lyonnaise*, Lyon, 1901, Chapter II, especially pp. 80–114, and also Chanoine L. Bossebœuf, 'La Fabrique de Soieries de Tours', *Bulletin et Mémoires de la Société Archéologique de Touraine*, Vol. XLI, 1900, Chapter V.

[3] This is borne out most clearly by the earliest of the English silk-designs mentioned above (Note 4, p. 19). There is a quite unmistakable development in the general style of the designs already during the first decade of the eighteenth century indicating that this cannot have been a new departure by that time.

output increased to meet the growing demand, it must have become ever easier to spread the cost of introducing new patterns.

France the leader of fashion

Everyone knows that Louis XIV succeeded in making France, or rather Paris and the Court of Versailles, the arbiter of fashion for the whole of Europe. It is quite extraordinary how successful were his efforts in this direction, and the leadership which France thus established for herself during the third quarter of the seventeenth century has never really been lost to this day. France still sets the fashion in many fields, just as she did in the later decades of the seventeenth century and throughout the eighteenth century — the period that concerns us in the present study.

Her leadership was (and of course still is) particularly notable in the field of fashionable dress — in the choice of cut, trimmings, accessories, and dress-materials. People all over Europe clamoured for news of the latest French fashions, and many were the scathing references made to such behaviour by patriotic writers in the other European countries. In England, for instance, remark was made of 'the unaccountable Fondness which English ladies have for whatsoever is of French Fabrick' in 1713, and in 1747 it was said that 'nothing that is mere English goes down with our modern ladies . . . they must be equipped from dear Paris'.[1] It would not be difficult to fill a whole page with quotations of this kind.

Others viewed the matter more soberly. An English silk-designer who wrote an essay on the design of figured silks, published in 1756, pointed out that 'the French designers of ornaments have been and are at present esteemed the most happy in their inventions. . . . No wonder that all the rest of the European nations take the French patterns of ornaments for their rule and pattern to imitate.' This was particularly the case with silk-patterns, he continued.[2]

Thus the weavers of figured silks in the various other European countries all followed the French lead, and there is a remarkable similarity between the silks produced at any given stage in the different countries concerned. The silk shown in Plate 96A, for instance, was woven in Stockholm, but almost identical patterns were being produced at the same time in Valencia, and both the Swedish and the Spanish designs were based on French originals.[3] An actual example of such direct imitation is to be found in a collection of designs for Italian silks, one of which, as it happens, is for a pattern rather like that of the Swedish example.[4] On it is written *Coppiato da un campione di Francia* — copied

---

[1] Quoted respectively from a pamphlet entitled '*A Letter to Sir R . . . H . . .*', 1713, and from Campbell's *The London Tradesman*, 1747, p. 197, both in the Library of the British Museum.

[2] Smith, *Laboratory . . .* , (see Note 1, p. 19, above), p. 36.

[3] See Santiago Rodriguez Garcia, *El arte de las Sedas valencianas en el siglo XVIII*, Valencia, 1959, e.g. the silks shown in Plates II, XII, XIII, which the author believes to be Spanish.

[4] Musée des Arts Décoratifs, Paris, Vol. DD98. Designs from Venice and Vicenza.

from a French pattern (Plate 96B). In England, too, the silk-designers were imitating French patterns. Among the Spitalfields designs already mentioned there is one that was 'taken from a French brocaded damask' in 1707 and another 'taken from a French stuff all silk' in 1719.[1] Moreover, among the English designs are several French drawings; many of them are stated to be 'French patterns', while the French origin of the remainder can in most cases be demonstrated. These may be examples of a certain deceitful practice of which the Lyons weavers were complaining in the report of 1725 already referred to.[2] As we noted, this explained how the silk-weavers sent their designers to Paris each year in order to discover what was new and what would sell well during the coming season. The designers would then compose their fresh patterns and send them back to Lyons where they were woven and put on the market — thereby launching the next fashion, the one that everyone then had perforce to follow. Unfortunately, a few of the designers sold copies of their latest compositions to the spies of foreign silk-weavers who thus obtained a first-hand idea of the very newest French fashion, and who could then hope to steal a march on the French and their agents, by turning out imitations of the latest patterns in their own country before the French 'originals' arrived in the foreign shops.[3] Otherwise the French weavers always had the advantage over their foreign competitors in that, as an English writer put it in 1713, 'they are generally thought in England to design better and accordingly set the Fashion for us; by which means they usually stock the Beginning of the Market with great Quantitys [of silks], which are sold off before our Weavers are able to follow the Patterns.'[4]

Mounting a draw-loom to weave a new pattern was a long and expensive business and a weaver endeavoured to produce as many lengths of silk as possible (they were known as 'pieces') before he had to change the set-up of his loom. The French could usually hope to weave a sufficiently large number of pieces of a particular pattern to fully cover the costs and make a decent profit as well, but their foreign competitors, forced to dance to a French tune, could normally only hope to weave a few pieces of a pattern before the arrival of new French silks forced them to change the set-up of their looms again.[5]

---

[1] Respectively Vanners & Fennell No. 42, dated 12th July 1707, and the Victoria and Albert Museum's E.4449–1909, dated December 1718 — both by James Leman.

[2] See Note 2, p. 18.

[3] The report says that the culprits *envoient aux fabricants étrangers les desseins les plus nouveaux, ils portent même la fraude jusqu'à leur fournir les mesmes desseins qu'ils ont faits pour des fabriques du Royaume, d'où il arrive que ces fabricans après avoir payé chèrement ces desseins et employé des sommes considerables à faire fabriquer des assortiments d'étoffes riches, sont privez du proffits qu'ils attendroient de leur nouveauté . . . .'* (The spelling is theirs.)

[4] *The Consequences of a Law for reducing the Dutys upon French wines, brandy, silk and linen,* a pamphlet written in 1713, p. 14 (British Museum Library).

[5] House of Commons Journal, Report on the silk-industry (see Note 1, p. 20, above), 1765, p. 210. It was stated in evidence that, of rich brocades, only four pieces were made of each pattern 'which is a very heavy expense, for the charge to the Master [weaver] on every loom is £20 and when the figure [i.e. the pattern] is changed the whole is changed, whereas one set of harness would make 18–20 pieces, if he might be permitted to make that quantity instead

Another great advantage possessed by the French silk-manufacturers as a result of this state of affairs was that they could afford — indeed it paid them — to encourage their designers.[1] Great attention was paid to this question, and it was no accident that the French silk-designers excelled in their very specialized art, to the admiration of all and the envy of their competitors. In the first place, many of their designers were co-directors of silk-weaving houses and thus were more intimately concerned with the success of the patterns they composed than, for example, their English counterparts, most of whom were free-lance artists who sold their designs to many different customers.[2] Not all the designers at Lyons were partners in weaving firms but, whatever their status, it is clear that the best of them were paid extremely well and that they occupied, as a body, a place of honour in the industry.[3]

Importance of the silk-designer

Many Frenchmen were quick to realize not only the importance of the designer but that he needed to be well trained. Already in 1676 a certain Thomas Blanchet had received permission to found a school of design at Lyons but he died before his intention could be carried out.[4] The question was raised from time to time during the next decades,

---

of four, the expense of £20 for the loom would fall upon the greater instead of the lesser number'. The exact length of 'a piece' is not stated and may have varied according to the class of material concerned, but was about 50 yards, perhaps rather less, and was probably enough for about three dress-lengths.

[1] Smith, *Laboratory . . .*, op. cit., p. 37: 'A good designer or pattern-drawer meets with more encouragement and constant employ in France, than he would find here; for there he sells or disposes of his designs not by measure, or so much per inch, but by his merit. Here the most ingenious artist is put upon a level with the meerest bungler. . . .'

[2] Smith, *Laboratory . . .*, op. cit., p. 37: 'Every fabricant, or manufacturer at Lyons, in the flower'd way . . . is a pattern-drawer himself, and qualified as such by his judgment, he has the whole management under his own care and direction. On the contrary here in England, take London and Canterbury together, I know of no more than one manufacturer thus qualified. . . .' That many designers were partners in silk-weaving businesses at Lyons in the eighteenth century is confirmed by M. Audin and E. Vial in the introduction to their useful *Dictionnaire des Artistes et Ouvriers d'Art du Lyonnais*, Paris, 1918, p. xli.

[3] '*N'oublie jamais, ô Lyon, que c'est à tes dessinateurs que tu dois en grande partie la prospérité des tes manufactures . . . !*', so wrote the Abbé Bertolon in his *Étude sur le Commerce et les Manufactures de la Ville de Lyon*, published at Montpellier in 1787. The same sentiment is expressed in the Regulations '*pour les nouveaux desseins*' issued in the same year to all centres of silk-weaving in France. In the preamble it says that '*Sa Majesté auroit reconnu que la supériorité qu'ont acquise les Manufactures de son Royaume est principalement due à l'invention, la correction & le bon goût des desseins . . .*' (Archives Départementales, Tours; C.106). A striking instance of the importance with which this question was regarded at Lyons is provided by the case of Jacques-Charles Dutillieu. He was a Parisian artist who had moved to Lyons and become, after many years, a successful silk-designer. In recognition of his distinguished services the Corporation of Silk-weavers at Lyons took the most unusual step of electing him a Maître-Fabricant although he had never served an apprenticeship of any kind at Lyons. (See F. Breghot du Lut, *Le Livre de Raison de J. C. Dutillieu*, Lyons, 1886.) Casanova, *loc. cit.*, noted that '*Les Lyonnois payent chèr les dessinateurs qui ont du goût; c'est le secret*'. The whole situation was summed up in the evidence given before the Select Committee of the House of Commons in 1765 (see Note 1, p. 20, above; the following quotation is to be found on pp. 211–12) when it was stated that the French weavers 'look upon a pattern Drawer at Lyons of such consequence and give him such high wages . . .', and that 'the best Pattern Drawers at Lyons are always taken into partnership with the weavers, and . . . the salaries of the others are very large', sometimes 6,000–7,000 *livres* a year.

[4] E. Leroudier, *Les Dessinateurs de la Fabrique Lyonnaise au XVIII siècle*, Lyons, 1908, p. 19.

but it was not until 1756 that a proper school was opened, under the direction of the painter Donat Nonotte. The chief objection to its establishment came, strangely enough, it now seems, from some of the Lyonnais master-weavers who claimed that anyone, including foreign competitors, would be able to send young designers and students to the school where they would be able to learn the secrets of the business.[1] This was hardly an enlightened view but it effectively hindered the establishment of the school for some time. Of course it was in fact not so much the technical secrets of the business that the competitors lacked as the carefully nurtured talents of the French designers.

The training of a French silk-designer normally took a long time, and therefore tended to be expensive. According to Leroudier, it was only the sons of the comparatively well-to-do who could afford to learn the trade.[2] In England, on the other hand, we are told by the author of *A General Description of All Trades*, published in 1747, that 'It is an easy, clean, ingenious business . . .', and that it cost only about £100 to establish oneself as a silk-designer. A more informed picture is given in an essay on 'the designing and drawing of ornaments, models and patterns . . . for the use of the flowered-silk manufactory . . .' which appeared in 1756.[3] It is obvious from the text that the author was a silk-designer, so the views expressed carry some weight. He urges those who wish their sons to become silk-designers to start teaching them drawing at an early age, to send them to a drawing school when they are a little older, and later to consider placing them with a flower-painter 'where they may be instructed in designing, colouring and shadowing of natural flowers and ornaments'. After serving his apprenticeship, a silk-designer 'ought to be well versed in drawing of all kinds of things, have a true notion of symmetry and proportion, and above all, excel in drawing of ornaments, and natural as well as ornamental flowers. . . . His imagination must be strong and lively . . . yet so as not to exceed the conceived possibilities or beauties of nature'. He then goes on to say that 'a good designer or pattern-drawer ought to be well acquainted, not only with the implements belonging to a draught-loom, but also with the nature and management of mounting the same . . .'. Later he explains very briefly and none too clearly how this was done.

One gets a far more detailed impression of the work of a silk-designer from an informative book, entitled *Le Dessinateur pour les Fabriques d'étoffes d'or, d'argent et de soie*, by Joubert de l'Hiberderie which was first published in 1764. Joubert, who was himself a designer at Lyons, recommends the student-designer to work for at least a year as a weaver at the loom before even starting to think of designing a pattern.[4] Another French designer, Paulet, who worked at Nîmes and published a very lengthy treatise on the subject in the 1770's, stated that '*chaque Dessinateur a son genre d'étoffe favori, c'est à*

[1] Leroudier, *op. cit.*, p. 21. [2] Leroudier, *op. cit.*, p. 20 [3] Smith, *Laboratory* . . . , pp. 38–39.
[4] Joubert de l'Hiberderie, *Le Dessinateur pour les Fabriques d'étoffes d'or, d'argent et de soie*, Paris, 1764, p. xvij.

dire, dans lequel il excelle.[1] This implies that the designer's task was no easy one and that ideally he should specialize in designing patterns for only a few classes of silk. Even a cursory glance at Paulet's work will convince one that this was so, for there was obviously a great deal to learn — Paulet's work appeared in seven fat volumes! Of course, such intense specialization was probably only possible in the French silk industry where there was a large number of designers. In England all the designs required by the silk-industry had to be produced by a mere handful of designers.

First and foremost, of course, a designer had to have talent; he had to be able to compose beautiful patterns. But this was far from being sufficient. Weaving is a mechanical process in which patterns are produced again and again along the length of the material. It requires considerable skill on the part of the designer to disguise these repeats of the pattern. It requires even greater skill to take advantage of this repetition. Moreover, if there are two or more repeats *across* the width of a silk, these too ought to blend happily with each other. And again, if there is only a single repeat in a width, consideration must be given to the treatment of the flanks of the pattern so that when a costume or a curtain has been made up of several widths of the material, the pattern will be carried across the joins and blend neatly in that direction as well.

There are two basic types of repeat, the Point Repeat and the Comber Repeat. The difference between the two is perhaps most clearly demonstrated by the diagrams on pages 86–87 where some sixteenth- and early seventeenth-century patterns have been drawn schematically. The patterns in Diagram A, C and D, are Point Repeats; that is, they are symmetrical about their vertical axes. Those in Diagram B, on the other hand, are patterns with Comber Repeats. These, it will be seen, have asymmetrical motifs which are reversed in alternate line. This is done to balance the pattern visually and in order to equalize the tensions in the weave.[2] There are several variations that can be played on these two kinds of repeats, as will be revealed if one studies the plates at the end of this book, and the designer must fully understand the potentialities of them all.

A designer must also know exactly what kind of pattern will suit a particular type of weave. In a damask, for instance, where the pattern is produced entirely by the contrast of two different kinds of weave, it is important that the pattern should not be too fussy,

---

[1] Paulet, *Le Fabricant des Étoffes de Soie*, 1779, Vol. III, Pt. II, p. 885. This work appeared in seven tomes. Only Tome VII, which is in two parts, concerns figured silks. This is now very rare. There is a set in the École de Tissage at Lyons and a photocopy in the Library of the Victoria and Albert Museum, London.

[2] As is explained in Chapter I, great pains were taken during the early decades of the seventeenth century to get away from the too obvious basic repetition of such patterns, so that, as in the example shown in Diagram Biii, the repeat only occurs in every fourth line up the length of the material, although the general effect of a pattern swinging first to the left and then to the right remains the same. It should be added that very occasionally asymmetrical motifs are found arranged all leaning in the same direction. This only seems to occur in fifteenth- and sixteenth-century patterns with comber repeats but never, to my knowledge, in seventeenth- or eighteenth-century patterns.

since delicate details will not be apparent even if they are present (cf. Plates 83B and 108B).[1] In silks which were embellished with silver or silver-gilt thread, care had to be taken not to waste it, because the thread was expensive. This could to some extent be avoided by concentrating the areas of metal thread (which incidentally tended to make a more effective show, as well) so as not to waste it at the back of the material, where it could not be seen, when carrying the thread from one area to the next (cf. Plates 21B and 83A). Among the several other types of silk for which a designer might have to compose patterns were lustrings and watered silks. A lustring was a taffeta which had been stretched and, while under tension, smeared with a syrupy gum. This dressing was dried with the aid of a small brazier and gave the material a glossy sheen. Lustrings were mostly plain, striped, or decorated with *chiné* patterns, but they could have large patterns similar to those on other rich silks. In that case, the patterns had to be light and airy so that the attractive glossy ground was not obscured unduly by the decoration (cf. Plates 84B and 86A).[2] The wavy pattern which gives the name to watered silks (known in French as *moiré* silks) was produced by crushing a rather heavily ribbed taffeta, folded lengthways down the middle of the piece, under a wooden roller pressed down by a heavy weight. The ridges of the ribbed material were distorted irregularly by the crushing, sufficiently to reflect light in different directions, and thus produce the 'watered' effect.[3] Any pattern there was on such a silk, would be pressed into the opposite half of the folded material, so it was important that watered silks were decorated with point repeats — that their decoration was symmetrical. These, and many similar things, a good silk-designer had to know. It is to be noted, however, that the *general style* of the patterns used on all the various types of figured silks at any one period — be it a damask, a brocaded lustring, a figured taffeta, or a very richly brocaded silk — was the same, in spite of the technical differences involved, and which, of course, the designer had to understand completely. It is for this reason that little attention is paid in the present study to the technical characteristics of the various silks described and discussed. It is the general similarity between their decorative patterns, phase by phase, that is our chief concern; and it is my aim in the chapters that follow to try and identify the features which are common to the majority of patterns at each stage.

[1] Most plain silk damasks are of a single colour. In the eighteenth century, however, furnishing damasks were sometimes woven with two and even three colours but these were rather exceptional materials.

[2] See Savary des Bruslons, *Dictionnaire de Commerce*, Paris, 1723, under *Taffetas* (Vol. II, p. 1647) where the process of 'lustrating' a taffeta is explained. *Chiné* patterns were produced by dyeing the warp threads with appropriate colours before the actual weaving took place. Most *chiné* decoration was of a quite simple nature but, around the middle of the eighteenth century, more ambitious patterns were executed in this cumbersome technique (see p. 133).

[3] Modern watered materials have patterns produced with great precision with the aid of steel rollers, which tends to make the watered decoration absolutely regular in its repetition, and very different from the pleasing irregularity of seventeenth- and eighteenth-century watered patterns. The patterns of the latter were of course symmetrical either side of the central fold, when the material was later spread out.

Apart from appreciating intimately the possibilities of the various weaves and their decoration, the silk-designer had to understand exactly how his design was translated from a pretty coloured drawing on paper (e.g. Plates 88A and 94B) into a pattern woven in silk on the loom. This involved drafting out the pattern onto squared paper (cf. Plates 69A and 97B) on which each square represents the point where a warp thread — that is, one of the threads that run the length of the material — intersects a weft thread, the wefts being the threads which run at right-angles to the warps, *across* the material. Great care had to be taken over this process or else what may have been a good design could easily become distorted or even badly misrepresented when woven. Guided by the draft, the weaver would then set up the complicated harness of his draw-loom so that the draw-boy, by pulling a series of cords in the correct order, could lift (or draw up) the appropriate warp threads for each step in the weaving of that particular pattern.[1]

Even such a brief survey as this will have made it clear that the designer had to know precisely how the draw-loom worked, what were its limitations, and how to obtain the best results from this somewhat clumsy but remarkably effective piece of machinery. The silk-designer had to be an artist imbued with a high degree of specialized knowledge in order to do his job properly.

The copying of silk-designs

Small wonder, then, that after the application of so much talent and expertise to the question of design, strict regulations were frequently issued throughout the eighteenth century to prevent the copying of designs '*dont le secret ne sçauroit être trop protégé . . .*' as one French official put it.[2] The weavers were concerned not only with foreign competition but also with unfair competition among themselves. With good silk-designers commanding higher and higher fees or salaries, it is hardly surprising that the master-weavers or merchants who had laid out such large sums expected to reap substantial benefits before their competitors could imitate their designs.[3]

[1] I do not propose to explain the process of weaving here. Readers who want to study the workings of the draw-loom should read the following: J. Loir, *Théorie de Tissage des Étoffes de Soie*, Lyons, 1923–28, 3 vols.; F. Guicherd, *Cours de Théorie de Tissage*, Lyons, 1946; Diderot, *Encyclopédie, ou Dictionnaire raisonné des Sciences, des Arts et des Métiers*, Paris, 1751–57, and Neuchâtel, 1765, Tome XV, pp. 268–306 and Plates (Tome XI). See also Paulet, *op. cit.*

[2] Quoted from an *Ordonnance* issued by the Lieutenant General of Police at Tours in 1750 (Archives Departementales, Tours, C.104). A list of the regulations concerning the stealing of designs is given by Godart, *op cit.*, pp. 483.

[3] When new Regulations were provided for the Lyons silk industry in 1737, it was laid down that each piece of silk should be inspected and stamped with the maker's seal. However, when it concerned a silk with a pattern on it, the inspection had to take place in a special room and the material had to be viewed from the back only. Moreover, the inspectors, who were elected annually from among the weavers, were not to be silk-designers (Articles CXI–CXIV). Similar fears must have been in mind when, in 1764, the London Weavers' Company arranged for its members to view the silks in a book of French patterns that had been seized by English Custom officials. Since these were samples of the latest French silks, the English silk-weavers badly wanted to see them. But, again, care was taken that no one should obtain any undue advantage from this scoop, so, once the book had been released by the Customs, it was locked in the Company's strong-box. Thereafter the master-weavers were allowed, but only six at a time and in order of seniority, to study the book under the supervision of one of the Company's officers.

Already in 1688, the weavers at Tours were complaining about unauthorized journey-men-weavers getting to see new patterns.[1] Later on, we find the Lyons weavers deploring the way their competitors were sending children to work in the weaving establishments at Lyons in order to learn the secrets of the trade. However, it was not so much from learners as from other designers and decorative artists that the danger stemmed. A notable case in point was that of the Swede, Jean Eric Rehn, who went to France in 1745 and studied, among other things, the French silk industry, much to the annoyance of the French weavers.[2] Rehn must have picked up a great deal of information on his tour and this, coupled with the fact that he was an exceedingly capable draughtsman, enabled him to compose a number of very satisfactory silk-designs after his return to Sweden (e.g. Plates 116A) The technical business of translating these designs into patterns woven in silk was no doubt largely done by ex-patriate French weavers working in Stockholm, but this instance shows that there was a real danger from professional spying. As it happened, the Swedish silk industry never attained a position of importance in spite of the impressive but limited contribution made by Rehn, but there were other well-established silk industries all over Europe where the weavers were continually watching for opportunities to discover something about the latest patterns and techniques being evolved in France.

Dating the successive general styles

The strict regulations and the severe penalties imposed in those who trafficked in silk-designs failed to prevent up-to-date French patterns getting into the hands of foreign silk-weavers, who thereupon immediately set about imitating the new French compositions. For this reason, it is not much of an exaggeration to say that from the late seventeenth century onwards, if not somewhat before that, *all high-class European silks were either French or virtually French.* (The only important exceptions to this statement are the grand furnishing velvets and damasks of Genoa which set their own style in that particular field and were imitated even in France.) Thus the large collection of precisely dated English silk-designs already mentioned,[3] does in fact tell us not only a great deal about *English* silks of the period but also gives a fairly accurate idea of what the contemporary *French* silks were like. Furthermore, since the designers in other European centres were also following the French lead, this collection of designs even provides a rough yardstick by which to date *all* European figured silks of the period. To the solid framework provided by these drawings can be attached the many varied pieces of infor-

---

[1] Bosseboeuf, *op. cit.*, p. 288.

[2] See Carl Hernmarck, *Svenskt sjuttonhundratal*, National Museum, Stockholm, Skriftserie No. 1., Lund, 1954, pp. 104–10; and G. Malmborg, *Jean Eric Rehn's första verksamhetsår vid Manufakturkontoret*, in *Fataburen*, 1927. See also p. 71, below.

[3] See Note 4, p. 19.

mation that may be gleaned from other sources — like dated portraits, fashionable costume, pattern-books, the occasional dated French silk-design, and the surviving silks themselves. With the exception of two rather special and not very helpful small groups of seventeenth-century designs for woven silks (see Chapter I, p. 93 and Plates 13A and B and 25A) the earliest surviving European silk-designs are to be found among the English drawings. The first of these is dated 1706, while the last of them dates from 1756 — half a century in which almost every year is represented, sometimes by as many as sixty designs and often by at least a dozen. The second half of the eighteenth century, being more recent, has yielded a far greater amount of miscellaneous information, and this, supported by the many designs from this part of the century which are still to be found in various collections, makes it fairly easy to complete the picture and thus obtain a comparatively accurate impression of the general development of silk-design during the whole of the eighteenth century.

Unfortunately we know far less about the seventeenth century, but it has all the same been possible to assemble a considerable amount of data, so that the main phases of the development now seem reasonably clear although one cannot yet pronounce upon the date of a seventeenth-century silk with anything like the precision one can usually bring to bear on an eighteenth-century silk.[1] It is conceivable that one never will be able to do so, because the phenomenon of annual changes of the fashion in silk-patterns had probably not crystallized until some time in the second half of the seventeenth century. The dominance of France in this field was at any rate not completely established until after about 1670, by which time she must have been actively fostering an insistence on new fashions appearing each year. It paid her handsomely to do so.

II. The Centres of Silk-Weaving

Silks such as those illustrated in this book — silks with large and ambitious patterns — could in theory have been made by anybody who had the right kind of loom and who had sufficient experience to operate it properly. In practice, however, such materials were only woven within a complex industrial organization supported by a substantial amount of capital. They were expensive to weave, the raw material was far from cheap, and only comparatively wealthy merchants could therefore afford to tie up their capital in goods of this sort. Moreover, the demand for luxury goods like silks, especially the more expensive classes of silk material, was affected by factors of all kinds — economic recessions, court mournings, war and blockade, the introduction of new tariffs and duties,

---

[1] One ought to be able to date almost all eighteenth-century rich, figured silks to within a very few years — say, five at the outside. One is lucky if one can date a seventeenth-century silk of the same class to within ten years, on the other hand.

changes of fashion, and so on. Such vicissitudes often put a great strain on an industry which only the most resilient and sturdily based could survive for long. At an important centre of silk-weaving, there would be many thousands of people involved in the business. There were the importers of raw silk,[1] there were those who prepared the raw silk for weaving, there were the dyers, the designers, the weavers in their many branches, and there was a large selling organization with, in the case of Lyons, for instance, ramifications all over Europe and stretching out as far as the Americas on the one hand and the shores of the Black Sea on the other.

There were not very many centres of this stature in Europe during the seventeenth and eighteenth centuries, and *the brief histories of the various national silk industries which follow are included here chiefly in order to help us assess the importance of each one and to decide where figured silks could have been made during this period.* Plain silks were made in many places, but figured silks were only produced at the more important centres of silk-weaving. These materials represented the cream of the output of the principal centres of production and, in general, it is fair to say that the finest figured silks were woven at the largest and most important centres of all.

At this point it seems perhaps worth warning the reader that this Section is a long one. By reading the summary on page 77, the main argument of the book can still be followed.

Unfortunately, our knowledge of the history of the different centres varies enormously. We know a great deal about the French, the English and the Swedish silk industries; a good deal less about the German; and hardly anything about the Dutch industry, although this must once have been fairly important. Furthermore, it is extremely difficult to find out from published sources anything very definite about the *general* history of the Italian and Spanish silk industries at this period (the two monographs which recently appeared dealing exhaustively with the histories of the Barcelona and the Valencia silk industries in the eighteenth century keep strictly to the point and hardly touch upon the general position). In order to form a more consistent and balanced view of each of the national industries, one would have to undertake a very considerable programme of original research in the archives of the places concerned. This would undoubtedly take many years to complete and, as I am not in a position to do this, I have had to rely largely on such published material as there is. To this I have been able to add various pieces of incidental information that have come to light during my own researches into the chronology of seventeenth- and eighteenth-century silks. These collections of miscellaneous information provide an unsatisfactory basis on which to form a really valid

---

[1] Theirs was in itself a complex business that involved taking great financial risks, since the raw silk had to come enormous distances, often by perilous routes. For instance, the raw silk consumed by the English silk industry came principally from China, Persia and Italy, but also from Turkey, Bengal and, to a very small extent, from the English colonies in America. The French had the advantage of being rather nearer the sources of their raw material; they used Italian, Levantine, Spanish and locally grown silk.

idea of the general position, but they must suffice for the present. The reader will not, I hope, regard the brief histories that follow in this section as definitive in any way.

Under the appropriate headings below, I have made several comments on the *identification* of the products of the various silk-weaving centres. The central theme of this study, as has been explained, is the *chronology* of seventeenth- and eighteenth-century figured silks and, since all the centres were following the French fashion in this field, these silks may almost all be regarded either as French or nearly so — that is, close imitations of a prevailing French style. For our purpose, one can therefore consider the attribution of silks to a particular centre as a matter of secondary importance. However, certain observations seem worth making, in passing. These chiefly concern the colour schemes; they are to some extent subjective and are not consistent. The present state of our knowledge would not warrant a more thorough treatment of the matter.

France

The French silk industry was by far the most important during the period that concerns us.

Tours

A silk-weaving industry had been established at Tours since the fifteenth century.[1] During the Renaissance period and until the middle of the seventeenth century the majority of the figured silks used in France had come from Italy but the Tours silk industry had already managed to establish a comfortable position for itself in the sixteenth century, owing to the proximity of a considerable body of its potential customers. It will be remembered that many illustrious families had their seats in and around Touraine, and that a number of cities, including Paris and Orleans, lay not so far away. Whenever the French government tried to support the indigenous silk-industries at this period, it was that at Tours which benefited most. Considerable support was given to Tours during the second quarter of the seventeenth century by Cardinal Richelieu, who introduced measures to protect the silk industry and who himself ordered large quantities of Tours silks for the furnishing of his own apartments. This encouragement signalled the beginning of a period of great prosperity for the Tours industry. Even greater prosperity resulted from the far-reaching reorganization of the French silk

---

[1] The most important study of the Tours silk industry was written by the Chanoine L. Bossebœuf and appeared in the *Mémoires de la Société Archéologique de Touraine*, Vol. XLI, 1900, pp. 193–528; it is simply entitled '*La Fabrique de Soieries de Tours*'. Of more limited scope is an unpublished essay by L. Boucheron on '*La Fabrique de Soieries de Tours aux XVIII et XIX siècles*', which was written about 1930 and deposited in the Archives Departementales at Tours. I am very grateful indeed to the Chief Archivist for giving me permission to study and quote from this work, a copy of which has now been made that may be consulted in the Library of the Victoria and Albert Museum, London. The brief history of the Tours industry that follows owes much to Bossebœuf's and Boucheron's studies.

industry in general which was undertaken by Colbert in the 1660's. From about 1640 until about 1680 Tours was clearly the most important centre of silk-weaving in France. Its chief rival was that at Lyons and, although the Lyons industry began to constitute a serious threat to Tours from the middle of the century onwards, it was not until quite late in the seventeenth century that Lyons began to overtake Tours and assume the leading position herself. It is probably no accident that John Evelyn mentions the 'silk manufactures' at Tours in his Diary while failing to say a word about those at Lyons, although he visited both cities during his Continental tour in the 1640's.[1] The Lyons industry was still very much the smaller of the two at that date. A further measure of the relative importance of the two rival centres is provided by another English writer, the author of *England's Interests and Improvements* which was published in 1663. He discusses the products of Lyons and Tours and mentions that silks to the value of £300,000 were imported into England from Tours each year, while only about half that amount was imported from Lyons.[2] The figures are probably exaggerated in both instances, but they suggest that Tours was still predominant in the 1660's. It was almost certainly Tours, at least as much as Lyons, which was responsible for the great leap forward which the French silk industry took at about this time and which resulted in France becoming the principal producer of fine woven silks in Europe. The part Tours played has since been largely forgotten in the light of the later brilliant history of the Lyons silk industry, but there is a good deal of evidence that the Tours industry was still the more important of the two, probably until well into the 1670's.

Then came the decline from which Tours never fully recovered. This was primarily due to the loss of many foreign markets during the calamitous wars in which France was embroiled during the last decades of the seventeenth century. As a result, Tours suffered from a series of depressions which caused much distress amongst the weavers. When the markets were once again opened to French goods, the then more vigorous Lyons industry often took over the areas that Tours had been forced to abandon. Thus the distress at Tours was not fully alleviated after each blow and her favoured position was gradually whittled away. The growing competition from abroad made matters worse. The small English and Dutch silk industries were gaining strength, and Europe was being flooded, or so the weavers claimed, with silks and cottons from China and India: certainly the French, the British and the Dutch East India companies were bringing over Oriental goods of all kinds by the shipload. Furthermore, Lyons had been given a rather unfair advantage, in that all raw silk imported into France had to be brought through the city of Lyons, where a duty was payable. This increased the cost of raw silk for all silk-weavers not working in Lyons and meant that all the raw silk required by the Tours and other

---

[1] *The Diary of John Evelyn*, 8th May 1644.
[2] S. Fortrey, *England's Interests and Improvement . . .*, Cambridge, 1663, p. 22. (In the British Museum Library).

French silk industries had to come to them overland from Lyons — in the case of Tours, no short distance. This unpractical measure had been introduced long before, under François I, but its effect had hardly been felt so long as the consumption of silk by the looms at Tours had been relatively small, and it had been of no great consequence while Tours' prosperity lasted.[1] Now, in the second half of the seventeenth century, with the Scales of Fortune becoming increasingly weighted in favour of Lyons, the additional price of the raw material became a serious burden to the Tours industry and put her at a disadvantage in the competition with Lyons. Lyons naturally benefited greatly from this measure and could as a result produce her silks that much cheaper. What is more, it provided her with a stranglehold with which she could choke, or anyway retard, the supply of the essential raw material to her rivals, the most important of which was Tours. The bitter rivalry that prevailed between these two great industries may seem amazing to us today, and it is curious that the French government allowed it to run its course. It speaks highly of the strength of the Lyons industry that it was able both to fight a powerful rival at home and at the same time win for itself a position as the chief producer of silks in Europe.

Another factor which seriously affected the fortunes of the Tours silk industry was the loss of the Protestant element, which constituted so important a section of the silk-weaving community, due to the persecution of the Protestants which took place in the second half of the seventeenth century. Earlier in the century the position of the Protestants had been difficult, but endurable; their religion was officially tolerated. But in the 1660's a wave of persecution swept through France and it became increasingly hard for a Protestant to live an ordinary life and carry on his trade. For instance, in 1664 it was decreed that no weaver could attain the rank of master-weaver at Tours unless he were a Catholic.[2] Soon the emigrations started and, in spite of this being illegal, many thousands of Protestants left their native country during the last third of the century and took up residence abroad. The actual number of Huguenot weavers who left Tours itself at this stage was probably not very great but the defection of even a comparatively small body of highly-skilled artisans and master-weavers, often with their families, would have been a serious blow to any industry.[3] Because at that time a Protestant could not normally enter the professions in France and had therefore to remain 'in trade', the higher positions in industries in cities where there was a sizeable Protestant minority, as at Tours, were often held by some of the most intelligent and ambitious members of the Protestant community. When they departed, their loss must have been keenly felt. No doubt they

[1] The duty was lifted in 1698 but was reimposed in 1722.

[2] This question is discussed by Bossebœuf, *op. cit.*, p. 281.

[3] A. Dupin Saint-André, in his *Histoire de protestantisme en Touraine*, Paris, 1885, p. 192 *et seq.*, maintains that there were only some 1,500 Huguenots living in the city of Tours in 1685 — the year of the Revocation of the Edict of Nantes — and that, of these, only about a hundred can have been heads of families.

34

left France chiefly for reasons of religion but they cannot have been unaware of the misfortunes that were besetting the Tours silk industry and of the advantages that might be gained from working in freer communities, like those in England and Holland, where one could not only exercise one's trade but could even hope to enter the professions, if one wished and possessed the ability to do so.

The unhappy state of the Tours industry must also have been apparent to Catholics and it is virtually certain that many people who were not Protestants left the city at this period as well.[1] Whatever the causes, the Intendant of Touraine, the Marquis de Nointel, could write in 1688 that, whereas there had been 7,000 looms working in Tours in 1668, there were only 1,600 active there in 1686.[2]

The Lyons industry soon recovered from the economic depression which affected the whole of France at the turn of the century. The industry at Tours, on the other hand, took much longer to regain its strength and it was not until about 1730 that a real measure of prosperity was again achieved there. In 1746, the Inspecteur des Fabriques reported that Tours was still the greatest centre of silk-weaving in France after Lyons. Yet the Tours industry continued to be dogged by troubles of all kinds. An attempt was made to set up an establishment to weave velvets and damasks 'façon de Gênes' (i.e. furnishing damasks and velvets in the Genoese style) but without much success. A spinning establishment was founded, but this too was a failure, and nothing came of a scheme to set up throwing mills on the Loire. More success was achieved with a new calendering machine where watered silks were produced, and with the weaving of silk handkerchiefs. According to a report written in 1744, there had been about 2,000 looms at work in Tours in 1738, while there were now only about 1,600. It is clear from the list given that many of them were engaged in the weaving of figured silks.[3] It was stated that weavers were apt to use raw silk of poor quality, or to weave silks with an insufficient number of threads for the qualities concerned, and that the dyes were poor.

One gets the impression that the long-established craft guilds which governed the activities of the silk industries at Tours and Lyons had, by the middle of the eighteenth

[1] It is sometimes claimed that as many as 30,000 people had left Tours by 1698 although this figure has often been disputed. As has just been explained, the number of Huguenots who left the city cannot have been so very great, which rather suggests that there were many Catholics among those who departed. Anyway, the total figure was probably exaggerated by the authorities in order to help explain away the acute difficulties in which the industry found itself, and they no doubt found it less embarrassing to maintain that all those who defected were Protestants.

[2] The Intendant, Miromenil, writing ten years later (1698), believed that the decline of the Tours industry was due to the following causes: the 'cessation de commerce avec l'étranger', the 'départ de plusieurs ouvriers, particulièrement des religionnaires établis en Angleterre et en Hollande', the 'guerre des tarifs faite aux marchands de Tours par les negocians de Lyon', and 'la vogue des toiles peintes (Indian chintzes, etc.)'. This report is quoted in full by A. Dupin Saint-André, op. cit., p. 215.

[3] Bosseboeuf pp. 324–26. A high proportion of the looms engaged in the production of figured silks were making a type of material called Ras de Sicile, a kind of taffeta with only two colours, the pattern being woven in tabby weave. What is probably a ras de sicile is shown in Plate 78A; this specimen was not necessarily woven at Tours, of course.

century, become far too cumbersome and rigid in their outlook to cope properly with the problems of an age which was becoming increasingly industrialized. This was certainly the view of the progressive minister Turgot, who abolished all the ancient guilds and corporations in 1775, in an attempt to reform French industry. The diagnosis was enlightened but the cure was too radical and merely brought general unrest throughout the industries concerned, with the result that the old trade organizations were hastily reinstated.

The decline of the Tours industry continued and in 1785 a report on the commerce of Tours and Touraine mentioned, apropos the local silk industry, that while it had once been very important, Lyons was now superior to Tours because of its geographical position, because of its wealth and the freedom of action that wealth brings, because of the trade that the annual Fairs at Lyons brought to that city, and because of the duty on imported raw silk which was payable at Lyons. The report goes on to draw attention to the competition that Tours had suffered from silk industries both at home and abroad, and finally it points out that fashions were now changing and that there was a growing preference for muslin over silk.[1] There were no doubt other reasons as well, but this is probably a fair summary of the matter, although one should perhaps add that the Tours industry seems to have had nothing like so efficient and widespread a selling organization as had the merchants at Lyons. Tours always seems to have lacked the commercial vigour of her chief rival in this field.

A few designs for Tours silks have survived but there are not sufficient to give us any clear idea of what Tours silks were like.[2] In the surviving examples, the drawing is on the whole less good than that of undoubted Lyons designs, and this probably reflects an important weakness of the Tours industry, namely, that whereas every encouragement was given to designers at Lyons, less attention seems to have been paid to this important matter at Tours. Apparently no school of design was set up in Tours during the eighteenth century and, although a number of good designers must have worked at Tours, it seems clear that they followed the lead set by Lyons in the field of silk design.

The colours of Tours *designs* dating from the 1730's and 1740's tend to be a little muddy and there seems to have been a preference for a dull mulberry colour instead of the magnificent purples of many contemporary Lyonnais designs. A number of silks with a rather similar dull red colour have survived and these may have been woven at Tours (cf. Plates 39A, 91A and 75A and B). The designs are perhaps not quite so good as

---

[1] *Éclaircissemens sur le commerce de la ville de Tours et la province de Touraine,* a report dated 27th August 1785, p. 27, Bibliothèque de la ville de Tours, HH6. (I am extremely grateful to the City Librarian for the assistance he and his staff gave me when studying this and other documents relating to the Tours industry which are in their care.)

[2] Designs for Tours silks will be found in the Bibliothèque Nationale and in the Library of the Musée des Arts Décoratifs, Paris, and at the Château Plessis-lès-Tours which is an out-station of the Musée des Beaux-Arts at Tours. For details, see Section I of this Introduction, Note 3, p. 19.

those of the best Lyonnais compositions of the period, but such subjective impressions hardly provide a basis for any general attributions of whole groups of silks to Tours. The fact that Tours silks were frequently rather narrower than their Lyons counterparts may help students to distinguish them apart but this too is not in itself an infallible guide because there were exceptions to this rule in force at various times, so that certain classes of silks were woven to the same width at both centres.[1]

Lyons

Of all the silk industries active during the period covered by this book, that at Lyons was the most important of all.[2] It rose to great prosperity during the second half of the seventeenth century and flourished throughout the eighteenth century although it suffered, like the other European centres of silk-weaving, from intermittent depressions which usually brought severe distress in their train. Nevertheless, Lyons kept her lead throughout the period and set the fashions which were followed by all the other centres.

Lyons has long been an important centre of commerce. The city lies at the confluence of two great navigable rivers and was the focal point of major trade-routes from Italy, Switzerland and Germany, which there linked up with the chief route to Paris and northern France. Italian and French merchants trading in Italian silks had long been established there when, in 1466, the French king, Louis XI, decided to start his own industry and chose Lyons as the most suitable site for this royal enterprise. The Lyonnais merchants viewed the infant industry with serious misgivings which soon turned to active hostility. The commerce in Italian silks was after all bringing great prosperity to the city, and the merchants did not particularly want to see their lucrative business spoilt in this way. So great was the opposition that Louis removed the entire industry to Tours where it was welcomed and where, as we have seen, it soon began to flourish — rising to great heights in the first half of the seventeenth century.

The growing prosperity of Tours and the success of its silk industry did not pass unnoticed at Lyons and soon the City Fathers were clamouring for permission to start their own industry. This was granted in 1536 and the city was immediately accorded the same privileges as Tours with regard to the manufacture of silks. A Corporation des

---

[1] The Tours weavers were supposed to weave their silks 48 cm. wide (this was known as 'cinq douze' or eleven-twelfths of a *demi-aune*). This is about 18⅞ inches. Lyons silks were normally 54 cm. or about 21¼ in. wide. Certain Tours silks were however woven at the Lyons width and vice versa.

[2] The history of the Lyons silk industry has been studied in great detail and much has been written about it. The two chief sources of information are E. Pariset's, *Histoire de la Fabrique Lyonnaise*, Lyons, 1901, which deals in a straightforward manner with the industry's history, century by century, and J. Godart's, *L'ouvrier en Soie. Monographie du Tisseur Lyonnais*, Lyons and Paris, 1899, which considers various aspects of the silk-weaving business and traces these separately through the successive periods. The two works naturally overlap but are largely complementary. The chief repository of documents concerning the Lyons silk industry is in the City Library at Lyons. Other relevant collections are among the archives of the Chamber of Commerce and of the City itself. The brief history of the Lyons industry that follows here is to a great extent based on Pariset's and Godart's monographs.

Ouvriers en Drap d'Or, d'Argent, et de Soie was founded at Lyon four years later and the first set of Regulations covering the various activities of the silk industry were presented to the Corporation in 1554. In these, mention is made of velvets, taffetas, and 'rich' materials including damasks, but it is unlikely that Lyons wove anything but plain materials, or silks decorated with the simplest patterns, until the end of the sixteenth century.[1]

Lyons made slow progress until the beginning of the seventeenth century when more effective support was given to the French silk industry, especially by Henri IV and again by Louis XIII. Attempts to prohibit the importation of foreign silks failed at this stage, however, because such prohibition was diametrically opposed to the interests of most of the Lyonnais merchants, even though some of them were by this time actively engaged in the local silk industry as well as the silk import business. The vitality of the industry gradually increased, and the range of its output was slowly enlarged. A list drawn up in 1610 of the figured materials that the Lyons weavers proposed to manufacture sounds impressive, and shows that they were now ambitious and could even hope to compete with the Italian silk-weavers in the realm of figured silks.[2] They were, no doubt, spurred on by the example set them by a weaver of Milanese origin named Claude Dangon who, between 1605 and 1607, had produced at Lyons a number of splendid figured materials that brought him fame, royal patronage, financial support from the Exchequer — and the enmity of his jealous colleagues.[3] He had apparently made various improvements to the draw-loom which enabled him to weave, for instance, a velvet of eight colours with a silver ground and '*pilastres d'or*', and another velvet with a plush surface in four colours on the back, the front having a satin ground enriched with silver and decorated with flowers of silk in eight colours! These were no doubt *tours de force* of weaving (some of Dangon's materials required as many as four draw-boys to operate the figure-harness of the loom), but they may well have inspired the other weavers at Lyons. By 1610 Dangon had nineteen looms at work in his establishment and was weaving, as far as one can judge from the descriptions, silks with rich patterns that were fairly typical of the period.[4]

---

[1] The relevant Article of the 1554 Regulations is discussed by Pariset, *op. cit.*, p. 34. Late in the sixteenth century, *velours façon de Lyons* were listed among the velvets on which a lower duty was to be paid than on the expensive qualities coming from Italy (see F. Michel, *Recherches sur le Commerce, la Fabrication et l'Usage des Étoffes de Soie, d'or et d'argent . . .* , Paris, 1860, Vol. I, p. 212).

[2] Pariset, *op. cit.*, p. 63, quotes the list in full.

[3] See Le Comte d'Hennezel, *Claude Dangon*, Lyons, 1926. The text of this essay on Dangon is excellent and is based on documents of the period, many of which are quoted. Yet the author has for some reason chosen to illustrate this study with a series of photographs showing typical 'lace-pattern' silks (see Chapter IV below). These belong to the *late seventeenth century* and to the first third of the *eighteenth century* and not to the early seventeenth century when Dangon was alive. D'Hennezel's mysterious attribution of these silks to *L'Epoque Louis XIII* has confused much French dating of seventeenth- and eighteenth-century silks although the mistake is now generally recognized by leading French authorities.

[4] D'Hennezel, *op. cit.*, pp. 27–28.

Dangon's contemporaries at Lyons are said to have been less skilled than he. Possibly so, but the industry was daily gaining strength and ability. In 1621 there were 1,698 master-weavers at Lyons, and this number had increased to 3,019 by 1660. By the middle of the seventeenth century Lyonnais weavers were not only producing all kinds of plain and figured silks but had evolved a wide range of half-silks and less expensive materials to cater for the wider, non-luxury market.[1] They also invented new types of rich silk materials, the most notable of which was the lustring (*taffeta lustré*) invented, so it is said, by one Octavio May in 1656.[2] The lustrings of Lyons soon became famous all over Europe and brought great profit to the city. The process and manufacturing of this material long remained a closely guarded secret.

A sumptuary law was introduced in 1644, designed specifically to encourage the consumption of rich silk materials. It was laid down that the dresses and suits of persons of quality were to be of silk adorned with nothing but a narrow border of silk trimming or embroidery not more than one inch wide. Such regulations were never observed for long, but in this case, the measure may well have helped the French silk industry by artificially increasing for a while the demand for rich silks. In 1667 the importation of foreign silks into France was again prohibited, this time with greater firmness than hitherto. By this stage the French silk industry — that is, Tours and Lyons between them — was becoming so strong that it began to equal and even overtake its great rival, that of Italy. The provost of the Lyons merchants wrote to Colbert in 1665, that '*il n'y a point d'ouvrage de soie, d'or et d'argent, de quelque endroit d'Italie qu'il vienne, que nos ouvriers n'égalent (à la réserve du velours noir de Gênes . . .) et que même ils ne surpassent*'. He may have been exaggerating somewhat because, as he himself said, the Parisian silk-merchants still insisted that the Lyonnais weavers should add *foreign* marks and labels to their wares so as not to reveal the French origin of the silks! Presumably the silks were then sold as Italian. For one reason or another the Italian industry slowly began to lose ground at about this time, however, and the French industry began to capture wider and wider markets.

The growth of the French silk industry was not achieved without many set-backs. Wars, like those with England in 1627, with Spain in 1636 and with Savoy in 1639; famine, plague (no silks could be exported to England during the Great Plague of 1665)

---

[1] In the eighteenth century, whole sections of the Lyons industry were occupied in making silks for special markets. Large quantities of silks were produced with an eye on the great annual fairs which were held at various European cities, most notably Leipzig and Frankfurt. A branch of the industry concentrated on weaving silks that were to be shipped in the great convoys of Spanish ships which sailed each year to Central and South America, loaded with European merchandise including special kinds of silk material that were supposed to appeal to the colonists. Savary, in the Supplement to his *Dictionnaire de Commerce* which appeared in 1730 (p. 255), lists the French exports to Canada which included '*taffetas noir lustrin pour le commerce avec les Anglois*' and other goods '*pour la Traitte avec les Sauvages*'.

[2] For a note on the manufacture of 'lustrings', see p. 27 (including Note 2).

and civil disturbances like the Fronde and the Huguenot persecutions, all checked — albeit temporarily — the demand for luxury goods like silks.

We have already mentioned Colbert's far-reaching reorganization of the French silk industry in the mid-1660's which culminated in the issuing of an important new set of regulations for the industry as a whole in 1667. Designed to govern the workings of the industry, these remained the basis of all future sets of regulations for more than a century. The 1667 regulations were not implemented at once but, as they gradually took effect, they seem to have provided a framework around which the Lyons industry could grow. Virtually identical regulations were drawn up for the Tours silk industry, but Tours, as we have seen, was already losing its impetus and so benefited less from the new measures. These and subsequent regulations were later to constrict the activities of the weavers quite unnecessarily, but in the beginning they were probably for the most part beneficial. One weakness of the Lyons industry that the new regulations brought to a head, however, was the division of the master-weavers into two watertight groups — the small master-weavers (*maîtres ouvriers*) who owned, perhaps, a loom or two but possessed no capital, and who were therefore compelled to work for others; and the wealthy merchant-masters (*maîtres fabricants*) who owned capital and could afford to commission work from the *maîtres ouvriers*. The *maîtres fabricants* gave the orders and took the risks, and therefore felt they should also govern the official affairs of the industry. The *maîtres ouvriers*, on the other hand, considered they too should be represented on the governing body — and represented adequately. The long-drawn-out rivalry between these two groups was often intense and must have wasted a great deal of energy; yet, in spite of this, Lyons' prosperity continued to increase and at the same time she gradually replaced Tours as the principal producer of silks in France. Only a basically very healthy industry could have managed to triumph over all her rivals at a time of such virulent internal dissension.

The religious persecutions which so seriously affected the silk industry at Tours during the second half of the seventeenth century seem hardly to have touched Lyons at all, for there were not many Protestants in the Lyons silk industry.[1] On the other hand, the series of economic depressions that hit France at the end of the century and during the eighteenth century *did* cause many weavers to emigrate — for instance, in 1712 a considerable number of Lyonnais silk-weavers went to work in Turin, which they would surely not have done had conditions at home been entirely favourable. The London Weavers' Company recorded the arrival of refugees from France during the whole of the first half of the eighteenth century, and in its Charter of 1707 specifically drew attention to the great increase in the number of foreign weavers then practising the weaving trade in and around London. The financial crises of the 1690's, coupled with the loss of markets due

[1] See Natalis Rondot, *Les Protestants à Lyons*, Lyons, 1891, chapter on '*Les Tisseurs de Soie*'.

to the wars in which France was then engaged, reduced the number of looms operating at Lyons from about 8,000 to something like 3,500 (some said 2,500) and at moments, for instance in 1693 and in 1701, the industry almost came to a standstill. To alleviate the resulting distress among the weavers, the French Government removed all duties otherwise payable on silk materials that were exported from France. At the same time, the English and Dutch silk industries increased greatly, for the most part at the expense of the Lyons industry. Even so, Lyons managed to keep her leading position, partly because the demand for silk materials continued to rise so that, even with the arrival of new and energetic competitors on the scene, there was still room for all; and partly — perhaps chiefly — because of the skill of her designers (this last point has already been discussed above).

The close of the War of the Spanish Succession and the signing of the Treaty of Utrecht in 1713 again opened the foreign markets to the Lyons merchants. The next three decades saw the industry take further strides towards even greater prosperity. New materials were invented, new types of design evolved and new techniques developed. Lyons established herself even more firmly as the leader in the field of silk-design and the new style of decoration evolved by the famous designer Jean Revel and his colleagues in the years around 1730 influenced the whole future course of this art (see Chapter V). With prosperity came content, and the industry was not disturbed by any serious trouble until the mid-1730's when the rivalry between the two classes of master-weaver again came to a head. Regulations designed principally to favour the *maîtres ouvriers* were promulgated by the Government in 1737 but, when the *maîtres fabricants* objected, the new regulations were repealed and yet another set was issued in 1744. These gave rise to serious demonstrations which were savagely suppressed by a Government then pre-occupied with the War of the Austrian Succession. This was not the end of the sorry business, however, which dragged on and was not finally settled until 1770.

In 1739 came another slump and a third of the looms, of which there were then about 8,000, came to a standstill. The squabble amongst the master-weavers further disrupted production. The number of looms operating in Lyons had risen to 9,404 by 1752, but the total then dropped somewhat in the mid-1760's as a result of the restriction of markets during the Seven Years War. But Lyons quickly recovered and, by 1769, there were 11,007 while the figure rose to about 12,000 in the 1770's. By the 1780's, about half the looms weaving silks in France were to be found in the city of Lyons.

It will be remembered that in 1725 the Lyonnais weavers complained about the way their foreign competitors were obtaining copies of the latest Lyons silk-patterns (see page 18). A number of measures were introduced during the eighteenth century to prevent this illegal commerce but the malpractice was never eradicated; the rewards were far too great, because foreign silk-weavers were prepared to pay well for fresh designs from Lyons. Much attention was paid to the problem of design at Lyons, as we have already noted. The Lyonnais weavers' awareness of the importance of this aspect of the silk-weaving business goes back to the seventeenth century and was well established by the early eighteenth century. The great improvements made in this art by several important silk-designers during the first four decades of the century are mentioned by the Lyonnais designer Joubert de l'Hiberderie who published a treatise on the design of silk-patterns in the 1760's.[1] As the size and the prosperity of the industry increased, so did the number of designers. Their number was probably further swelled after the School of Design had been founded in 1756. By 1759 there were about sixty designers in Lyons.[2] Not all of them were necessarily engaged in designing patterns of artistic interest but this number should be compared with the mere handful of designers, perhaps six or seven, working in Spitalfields at the same period.[3]

A matter which worried the Lyons weavers was the defection of weavers to other countries, particularly when business was bad. Sovereigns and governments of other European nations, desiring to establish or bolster up their own silk industries, would frequently invite — entice would probably be a more apt word — French weavers to settle in their countries, where they would usually be given special privileges and considerable financial assistance. Emigration of skilled weavers, often possessing extensive technical knowledge that was useful to competitors, became a serious problem during the middle of the eighteenth century when there was a series of slumps at Lyons, while at the same time the Neapolitan, the Prussian, the Austrian, the Swedish and the Spanish silk industries were expanding, and all required the help of skilled French artisans to supplement and guide the efforts of their native workmen. In 1750 a specially close watch had to be kept on the weavers at Lyons to ensure that none of them packed their bags and left, and severe punishments were imposed on those French weavers who were arrested on their way out of the country.[4]

While the general demand for silk increased during the third quarter of the eighteenth century, the consumption of rich figured silks was frequently reduced by factors quite

[1] Joubert de l'Hiberderie, *Le Dessinateur pour les Fabriques d'étoffes d'or, d'argent et de soie*, Paris, 1764, pp. x–xii, mentions Deschamps, Monlong, Ringuet, Courtois and Revel. (The contributions made by these designers is touched upon in Chapters IV and V below, and examples of their work are illustrated among the Plates.) The very fact that Joubert published this really quite detailed treatise on the designing of silk-patterns shows that there must have been a considerable demand for such a manual in Lyons.

[2] This figure I obtained from checking through the *Rolle de la Capitation de la Grande Fabrique* for the year 1759 (Lyons City Archives, CC178).

[3] House of Commons Journals, Report of the Select Committee investigating the state of the English silk industry in 1766, p. 211, evidence of Mr. Pritchard, silk-mercer, who said that 'there are at present no more than three Pattern Drawers' in London capable of composing designs suitable for figured silks. Correspondence in the *New Daily Advertiser* in May 1765, implies that there were only two or three *good* designers, at any rate.

[4] Godart, *op. cit.*, pp. 232–33, quotes the memoirs of the Comte d'Argenson in this connection, e.g. '*On continue à garder à vue les fabricants de Lyons de crainte qu'ils ne passent à l'étranger . . .*' (11th November 1750).

outside the control of the industry. The year 1765, for instance, was a bad one for Lyons. *'Cette année peut compter parmi les plus mauvaises de la fabrique. Ses faillites devinrent nombreuses et par suite la misère des ouvriers augmenta.'*[1] An important cause of this slump was the coincidence of mourning at several European Courts — the Emperor, the Duke of Cumberland, the King of Denmark, the Queen of Spain, and the Dauphine, all died within a short space of time. On the other hand, the accession of Louis XVI to the French throne in 1774 ushered in a period of brilliant spectacles that brought about a renewed demand, so that the decade prior to the Revolution became the most prosperous that Lyons had ever experienced. Yet even relatively small fluctuations in the demand caused anxiety, and the Lyons silk-weavers found it necessary on several occasions to petition Queen Marie Antoinette to wear only silk. At first she listened to their appeals, but she nevertheless remained the centre of a circle at the French court that set the new fashion for light materials, which of course included light-weight silks and silk voiles, but which also included, and predominantly, cotton materials — muslins, gauzes and the gay printed cottons which were by this time being produced in great quantity in Europe as well as in India.

In 1786 was signed the so-called Eden Treaty with England which had such calamitous results for French commerce in general. Then came the French Revolution and the consequent drop in demand for silk materials on the home market. The riots and commotions in the city of Lyons itself were particularly violent and caused much damage to the silk industry. Yet the Lyons industry was sufficiently robust to survive even this succession of misfortunes and revived in a quite remarkable manner during the Napoleonic period at the turn of the century. This extraordinary resilience was no doubt partly due to the fact that Lyons was still an important centre of commerce as well as the seat of a silk industry, which meant that a substantial number of merchants were rich enough to weather the storm and could still afford to place orders for silks when more favourable conditions returned. It was also partly due to the remarkable adaptability of the industry which was in great contrast to that of its rivals. When the demand for lighter materials came in, the Lyons weavers were quick to develop a wide range of light-weight and simple-patterned silks to satisfy it; and, as the demand for silks with large patterns declined, many of the principal designers switched from the designing of woven patterns to composing patterns suitable for embroidery, which now had a new vogue. At the same time the execution of embroidery on an industrial basis became an important branch of the Lyons industry. The professional skills of the silk-designer were still required in the design of woven panels for vestments (a branch that Lyons had built up during the later decades of the eighteenth century), and in the field of furnishing silks.

The manufacture of furnishing materials had become an increasingly important

---

[1] F. Breghot du Lut, *Le Livre de Raison de J. C. Dutillieu*, Lyons, 1886, p. 38.

branch of the Lyons silk industry during the second half of the eighteenth century. Genoa remained supreme as the producer of fine furnishing velvets, but these came to be less used after the middle of the century and, as the demand for velvet dropped, so the Lyonnais moved in on the market with silk materials that were more in keeping with the tastes of the day. The most spectacular products of this development were the remarkable silks designed by the renowned Philippe de Lasalle (e.g. Plates 117A and B). These astonishing feats of silk-weaving were produced on quite a limited scale, almost exclusively for royal customers, but they earned for Lyons and her designers yet a further measure of fame.

Constant efforts were made at Lyons throughout the eighteenth century to improve the looms on which her silks were made. None of the improvements were as important as the invention of the Jacquard attachment at the very beginning of the nineteenth century but each step forward in technique increased the advantage Lyons possessed over her competitors.[1] New types of weave were also evolved and old ones were adapted to new uses. Perhaps the most notable development in this direction was the increasing use made of patterns produced by the warp threads instead of by the wefts. Striped materials, which were especially in fashion from about 1770 onwards, lent themselves particularly well to this treatment in the cases where small figured effects were required.

Most of the finest silks woven in Europe between about 1670 and 1800 were produced at Lyons but since imitations of them, often very good ones, were made elsewhere throughout the period, it is now far from easy to distinguish the silks made at Lyons from the rest. Quality alone is not sufficient a guide, for excellent silks were made in a number of other places as well. What is more, silks of somewhat inferior quality, both from the technical and the artistic point of view, were also produced at Lyons — with an eye on the wider markets, as we have already noted. The picture is thus blurred, but a certain number of silks and designs can be attributed unhesitatingly to Lyons for one reason or another, while many more can be tentatively attributed to this important centre. Certain colours and colour schemes seem to occur often in silks that I believe to be from Lyons. Particularly striking are the magnificent purples (Burgundy red) that are present in many silks from the 1730's onwards, but perhaps more common are the two shades of pink — the one a brownish pink, the other much lighter — which are so often to be found alongside each other on many splendid silks dating from the first half of the eighteenth century. The leaves of many silks that I take to be Lyons products dating from about 1730 until well into the second half of the century are frequently rendered in a natural light green (very different from the typical dark green of contemporary English silks) which is coupled with a greenish yellow.

[1] See C. Rodon y Font, *L'historique du métier pour la fabrication des étoffes façonnées*, Liege, 1934.

Other French centres

No other city in France had a silk industry during the seventeenth and eighteenth centuries which could match in importance those of Lyons and Tours, and figured silks were made on only a comparatively small scale outside these two major centres.

Avignon had a small silk industry at this period — the last vestige of a much larger manufacture which had first been established in the fourteenth century when the city had for a while been the seat of the Papal Court. Poplin or 'papeline', originally a silk and wool mixture, is said to have first been woven in this city of the Popes. By the seventeenth century, the Avignon silk industry had lost much of its trade to Lyons, while the raw silk she needed for her looms had to pass through Lyons where a duty was levied on it. As with Tours, this imposition became a tiresome burden for the Avignon industry. Defoe, writing in 1722, mentioned only three centres of silk-weaving in France — Tours, Lyons and Avignon[1]. In that very year, Avignon was hit by a plague which much reduced the population and is said to have brought about a further decrease in the size of the industry, but figured silks continued to be woven there until late in the eighteenth century. Samples of Avignon silks from the 1730's are preserved in the Richelieu Collection in the Bibliothèque Nationale, Paris.[2] Most of them are plain but a few have pleasing but relatively simple patterns. Paulet states that Avignon was still producing fine taffetas and damasks in the 1770's.

The other centre of secondary importance was Nîmes.[3] As we have seen, this place was not mentioned by Defoe in 1722 but the city possessed a silk industry of some size in the seventeenth century. In 1679 it was noted that the industry had increased considerably during the previous ten years and, two years later, there were some 1,100 looms there weaving various kinds of taffeta — presumably all plain materials. The industry apparently suffered seriously from the loss of its Protestant element as a result of the persecutions which took place at this time; at any rate the number of looms producing taffetas had fallen to a mere 200 by 1685.[4] Taffetas seem to have remained the city's principal

[1] Daniel Defoe, *A Plan of English Commerce*, 1722, p. 294. Note the order; Tours' reputation was still high, apparently, even though her fortunes were by this time at a low ebb compared with those of Lyons. A brief history of the Avignon industry by Paul Achard appeared, under the title 'Notice sur la Création, les Developpements, et la Décadence des Manufactures de Soie à Avignon', in the *Memoires de la Société Littéraire, Scientifique et Artistique d'Art*, Tome I, No. 2, feuilles 7–10, 1874.

[2] Bibliothèque Nationale, Paris, Cabinet des Estampes. Richelieu Collection of textile samples, Vol. Lh.45d. See P. Rodier, *The Romance of French Weaving*, Paris, 1931, where a page of Avignon samples from the Richelieu Collection is illustrated (opposite p. 282).

[3] H. Algoud, *La Soie*, Paris, 1928, p. 138. See also L. Dutil, 'L'industrie de la soie à Nîmes', *Revue d'histoire moderne*, 1908, Vol. X.

[4] One John Larguier, a weaver from Nîmes, fled to London where he showed the Court of the Weavers' Company an alamode (a kind of lustring; see p. 27) and was as a result elected a Foreign Master on condition that he employed and trained a number of English weavers to make this type of material in London. Court Minutes of the London Weavers' Company, 1684 (see the London Huguenot Society's Publication XXXIII). The making of lustrings and alamodes soon grew into a sizeable and profitable branch of the English silk-weaving industry.

product although damasks were woven there from about 1691 onwards. A list of the materials being made at Nîmes in 1741 seems to indicate, however, that it was still chiefly plain silks like taffetas or silks with small patterns that were then being woven there.[2] There are samples of Nîmes silks in the Richelieu Collection; their simple patterns were presumably not woven on a draw-loom.[1] The city was probably still producing much the same kinds of material in the 1770's when Paulet, who was a designer at Nîmes, wrote his great work on the designing of silks. He said that no *façonné* silks (that is, silks woven on a draw-loom) were made there — only silks produced with the *petit tire*, a much simpler mechanism with which only fairly simple and small patterns could be woven.[2]

Silks were also woven at Marseilles, as a page of samples in the Richelieu Collection proves.[3]

A silk-weaving establishment which created quite a stir when it was set up in the 1670's was that of Mathurin Charlier at St. Maur-les-Fossés, on the outskirts of Paris. Charlier's business was patronized by the King and he apparently wove materials for Versailles. He must have had a number of skilled workmen in his employ, for exceptionally rich materials are stated to have been manufactured by him including '*draps d'or à la façon des Perses . . . d'autres à la manière d'Italie . . .*', etc.[4] There are no samples from this factory in the Richelieu Collection which, it will be recalled, comprises samples collected in the 1730's. This rather suggests that the Charlier enterprise had closed down by that time.[5] A sample of a silk woven at a small factory at Versailles is, on the other hand, included in Richelieu's albums.[6] It is of poor quality. According to Algoud, there was an establishment weaving small-patterned velvets in Paris during the middle of the eighteenth century, and Paulet, the designer from Nîmes, was apparently called to Paris in order to help organize a factory that was to turn out *musulmanes raiés en lamé d'argent* for the marriage of the Dauphin and Marie Antoinette.[7] *Musulmanes* were a speciality of Paulet's.

In Chapter VII (page 145), I have suggested somewhat tentatively that the silk illustrated in Plate 110B may have been woven in Paris, perhaps during the first or second decade of the eighteenth century. This attribution is based on the proposition that

[1] Richelieu Collection, Vol. Lh.45 (illustrated by Rodier, *op. cit.*, p. 283).

[2] Paulet, *Le Fabricant des Étoffes de Soie*, 1779, Tome IX, p. 16.

[3] Richelieu Collection, Vol. Lh.45.

[4] *Mercure Galant*, Paris, 1678. (See J. Nevinson, *L'origine de la Gravure des Modes*, Actes des Ier Congrès International d'Histoire du Costume, Venice, 1952, p. 210.) Most authorities refer to him as Mathurin Charlier but H. Clouzot (*Le Métier de la Soie en France*, Paris, 1914, p. 63) calls him Marcelin.

[5] Although it has been suggested that Charlier's son, Guillaume, who died in 1757, carried on the factory (see Algoud, *op. cit.*, pp. 127 and 137), Savary in his *Dictionnaire de Commerce* of 1723 definitely states that the establishment closed down on the father's death (see under *Commerce*, Vol. I, p. 839).

[6] Richelieu says the factory was started by Noël Desteques in 1731 (Richelieu Collection; illustrated by Rodier, *op. cit.*, p. 255).

[7] Algoud, *op. cit.*, p. 137.

the design appears to fall quite outside the main line of development in the style of fashionable silk-patterns as we now understand it, while it has definite affinities with the kind of ornament that some of the leading decorative artists of the time were composing in the Royal Drawing Offices at Versailles and in a number of Parisian studios. A silk woven in Paris, especially one woven at an establishment under royal patronage (that of Mathurin Charlier springs to mind), might well have been decorated in such a manner — that is, a manner showing close connections with the metropolitan style of decoration evolved under the supervision of Louis XIV and his chief architects. Indeed, it is known that Charlier supplied a quantity of rich furnishing materials for the Palace of Versailles, including a velvet with a pattern by Berain (*Mr. Berin*) who was of course a master of this genre.[1]

Italy

Silks were woven in Italy at an early date. During the Middle Ages Italy gradually became the principal producer of woven silks for the European market — overtaking in this lucrative commerce the combined efforts of the Byzantine and Islamic Empires. Constantinople, Baghdad, Damascus, Alexandria, Almeria and Valencia yielded to Venice, Florence and Genoa. The Golden Age of the Italian silk industry opened in the middle of the fourteenth century and lasted right through the sixteenth century. The superb materials woven in Italy during this long period were famed throughout the Western world and are still the touchstone by which the materials made at a later date may be judged. It is hardly surprising, therefore, that the Italian silk industry of the Middle Ages and Renaissance period has been the subject of a great deal of scholarship and that many learned essays have been devoted to its history and its products. Scant attention has been paid, on the other hand, to the later history of this industry. Obviously the decline of the great Italian silk industry has not proved so attractive a subject as the glorious period which preceded it! This makes the writing of a brief survey, such as this, more difficult than one might expect, for without oneself making a detailed study of the matter — which might take many years to accomplish — one must fall back on the very limited amount of published material, supplementing this with various pieces of information that have come to light in one way or another.

The growing strength of the French silk industry from the late sixteenth century onwards was an increasing cause of alarm for the Italian silk-weavers. The Italian industry steadily lost ground as the French captured first their own home market and then, gradually, an increasingly large slice of the foreign markets as well. After about the middle of the seventeenth century, France assumed the dominant position in the field. However, the demand for silk materials grew as the seventeenth century continued, and

[1] Clouzot, *loc. cit.*

47

it increased very considerably during the eighteenth century, so that there was still sufficient work to keep a fairly large Italian industry active throughout our period.

As we have seen, the strength of the French industry lay chiefly in its ability to dictate the fashion in figured silks. One gets the impression that the Italians slowly retreated from this field and concentrated more and more on plain and simple-patterned silks, leaving the weaving of figured silks increasingly to the French. Most of the references to Italian silks outside Italy during the eighteenth century are either to plain materials or to furnishing silks, and it seems probable that the greater part of the output of figured silks in Italy, with the important exception of the furnishing materials, was intended for home consumption. An English Customs official stated in 1766 that 'there are but few flowered and figured silks imported from Italy' into great Britain.[1] Jean-Jacques Lalande, visiting Venice in 1765–66 when the city must still have been one of the principal producers of woven silks in Italy, noted that only '*damasquettes*' and '*petites étoffes légères*' retained the high quality for which Venice had once been renowned, and that most of the other silks made there were '*mal écrues, dures, sèches, cassantes*'.[2] Figured silks were of course woven in Venice, as we shall see, so the implication of Lalande's statement is that the best weavers in Venice concentrated on silks with small patterns.

During the sixteenth and the first half of the seventeenth century, French silk-weavers tried hard to imitate Italian silks, both the plain qualities and those with patterns.[3] Certain types of Italian plain silks had become famous, and various classes of French silks came to be known by names that remind one of their Italian origin. For instance, in the seventeenth and eighteenth centuries the Tours weavers produced, amongst other things, silks called '*gros de Naples*', '*luquoizes*', '*venitiennes*' and '*ras de Sicile*', while taffetas '*façon de Florence*' were an important branch of the French silk-production. Even in the middle of the eighteenth century, an English silk-designer who had once worked at Lyons could state that 'silks are made there to imitate the Italian'.[4] From the context, it seems that he was referring to certain classes of Italian plain silks — probably '*taffetas de Florence*' and the like. On the other hand, it is probable that, by the early decades of the eighteenth century, the Italian weavers were imitating French designs for *figured* silks — just as their counterparts were doing in England, Holland and elsewhere. Direct evidence for this is not easy to find, but in the library of the Musée des Arts Décoratifs in Paris,

---

[1] House of Commons Journals, Report on the Silk Industry, 1765 and 1766. The Customs official's evidence appears on p. 725 of the 1766 Report. On the same occasion an important weaver named Sabatier talked of 'the slight striped goods, the sort that are now imported from Italy . . .'. In the 1765 Report (p. 211), several weavers stated that 'no draughtsmen are wanted for the species of [silk] goods made in Italy, they being chiefly plain goods'.

[2] Jean-Jacques Lalande, *Voyage en Italie*, Genoa, 1790. The journey was undertaken in 1765–66.

[3] In 1604 the weavers of Tours asked permission to weave '*draps de soie façons de Milan, Gênes . . . Luques, Florence, Venise, Naples, Boulogne* [Bologna], *Reggio* [Regio Emilia], *Modene . . .*' (Bossebœuf, *op. cit.*, p. 251.)

[4] House of Commons Journals, 1765, Report, p. 212, evidence of Mr. Peter Cheveney, a Spitalfields designer who had worked at Lyons.

there is a collection of Italian silk-designs, many of them bearing dates in the 1760's through to 1780, but one of them apparently dating from the 1730's and several more from the 1740's and 1750's.[1] They come from silk-weaving establishments in Venice and Vicenza and they show that, even at these important centres, the Italians were following the French lead. Indeed, one design actually bears an inscription stating that it was 'copiato da un campione di Francia' . . . in 1765 (see Plate 96B here).

While the Italian silk industry was no doubt able to furnish enough figured silks to satisfy the normal requirements of the home market during the eighteenth century, it seems that rich French silks were imported whenever really splendid materials were required — as was the case in England, for instance, and in Vienna (see below). When a lady of the famous Venetian Mocenigo family was married in 1739, rich French silks were obtained for the occasion from Milan. The same was the case when a member of the equally famous Grimani family was married in 1769.[2] In this connection it is perhaps worth recalling that Colbert was still ordering rich silk materials for the French royal household from Florence and Rome in 1660 and that, even in 1662, he received a 'brocat fonds d'argent tiré' and ordered materials from samples supplied to him from Rome. Actual designs were sometimes submitted to him at this period and he would occasionally ask for certain changes to be made before ordering lengths of the pattern, which then had to be woven in Italy. But in 1664 Colbert sent new designs *from France* to be woven in Italy and, after 1666, no more Italian silks were ordered for the French king.[3] This suggests that, by the mid-1660's, France could produce rich silks of as high a quality as those of the chief Italian centres.

Yet even if the French were able to surpass the Italians in the weaving of brocaded silks, they never quite managed to weave velvets as good as those produced at Genoa. The velvets of Genoa were famous all over Europe. They were imitated at Lyons and Tours, and also at Spitalfields; but all agreed that no other centre could equal the genuine Genoese product.[4] Almost as much admired were the silk damasks of Genoa. These, like

[1] Musée des Arts Décoratifs, Vol. DD 98.

[2] P. G. Molmenti, *Venice; The Decadence*, Vol. I, pp. 215–18. The 1739 items were '. . . drappegiato per estate, ombrato, rigato, spolinato con oro di Francia . . .' and '. . . . drappo fondo verde puro spolinato con oro e argento con trama richo de Francia'. The 1769 order included 'stoffa di Francia detta chinee, fatta venir da Milano'. A French *chiné* silk of the period is illustrated here in Plate 91B. See also Beawes, . . . *A Guide to All Men of Business*, Dublin, 1754; while stating that silk was woven in various Italian cities, Beawes bothers to say that French silks were imported into Italy — which rather implies that the amounts imported were considerable.

[3] J. Alazard, *L' Abbé Luigi Strozzi, correspondant artistique de Mazarin, de Colbert, de Louvois et de la Teulière . . .*, Paris, 1924. See especially pp. 22–27, 89, 92, 94, 104 and 111. I am exceedingly grateful to Miss Edith Standen for drawing my attention to this interesting correspondence.

[4] For instance, Diderot noted, in his great Encyclopaedia which began to appear in 1765, that Genoese velvets were of higher quality than other velvets. His view was echoed by Lalande (op. cit.). An important London silk-mercer, Mr. Robert Carr, giving evidence before the Select Committee of the House of Commons which met during 1765 to investigate the state of the English silk industry (House of Commons Journals, 1765, Report, p. 212) maintained that 'Genoa velvet was much superior in Goodness to velvets made in Spital Fields, for that the latter would hardly bear the

the 'Genoa velvets' were also furnishing materials and were used in the decoration of many of the most splendid rooms in Europe during the late seventeenth and throughout the eighteenth century. Velvets with small patterns for men's suits were made with great success in France, and damasks suitable for women's dresses were produced at most of the more important centres of silk-weaving in Europe, but *furnishing* velvets and damasks with large patterns were an Italian speciality and no other country ever succeeded in wresting from Italy the supremacy in this field.

The heyday of the Genoa velvet — the large-patterned, sumptuous furnishing velvet of the kind shown in, for instance, Plates 107A and 112A — lasted from about 1670 until about 1750. Genoa damasks, on the other hand, had a rather longer run, being acceptable for the most fashionable settings right up to the last decades of the eighteenth century. Wallpapers, printed cottons and, to a lesser extent, the kind of grand pictorial furnishing silk of the type for which Philippe de Lasalle was the most famous designer (see Plate 117B) finally drove these superb materials from the walls of Europe's great houses.

One gets the impression that the third quarter of the eighteenth century saw a temporary revival of the fortunes of the Italian silk industry, as the demand for silks rose in a Europe that was becoming increasingly wealthy. At this period, France still regarded Italy as an important competitor, even though the competition was probably, for the most part, confined to plain materials and to the grand furnishing silks. Towards the end of the eighteenth century the consumption of woven silk materials declined due to the change of fashion that favoured cottons and muslins: the Italian industry suffered accordingly. Economic difficulties aggravated by the wars which raged in Italy, especially in the north where most of the important centres lay, further reduced the powers of an already ailing industry as the eighteenth century drew to a close.

Where were the Italian figured silks made? It is not easy to answer this question. We know that Genoa produced her superb velvets and damasks but beyond that the readily accessible sources tell us little. It may therefore be helpful to summarize what a few contemporary writers had to say about the Italian silk industry and its products.

Savary des Bruslons, whose *Dictionnaire de Commerce* appeared in 1723, speaks highly of the '*draps d'or & d'étoffes de soye des fabriques de Venise*' which, he says, are much admired and sold in large quantities in the Levant and Constantinople although they are '*à la vérité moins fins & moins beaux que ceux de France, d'Angleterre et d'Hollande*'. He goes on to say that all kinds of rich silks are made at Genoa, that '*velours à fleurs*' with gold and silver grounds and other fine silks are made at Milan, that Lucca produces large quantities of damasks and satins, but that the number of looms at Bologna weaving silk

---

Needle or Embroidery'. He was probably referring to plain velvets but his strictures would have applied at least as much to figured velvets which were even more difficult to make. Naturally this did not go unchallenged; an English velvet-weaver, who also gave evidence, hotly denied that what Carr said was true.

goods '*sont beaucoup diminuées*'. Through the port of Leghorn are exported the silks of Florence, Pisa, Lucca and 'other Tuscan cities'. Parma and Reggio Emilia are famed for their thrown silk, but no mention is made of their wrought silks.[1] Daniel Defoe, writing about the same time, lists only Milan, Mantua, Genoa, Florence and Naples — in that order — as being centres of silk-weaving in Italy.[2] He says nothing about the Venetian silk industry. Defoe was, of course, nothing like so reliable an authority as Savary, but even so this omission is curious and may indicate that the Venetian industry had already by then declined greatly in importance.

Beawes' *Guide to all Men of Business*, published in 1754, mentions 'the Quantities of gold and silver Tissues and other silks made in Venice'. They are sold 'in all Parts of Europe', he says, and he repeats Savary's statement about their being sold in Constantinople and around the shores of the Black Sea. Beawes very probably obtained a good deal of his information from Savary's great work and, like Savary, he states that all kinds of silk materials, including velvets, were made at Genoa. He adds that silks and velvets were made in Rome and at Ancona, Florence, Milan, Lucca and Turin. The Lyonnais designer, Joubert de l'Hiberderie, writing a decade later, noted that 'the Kingdom of Naples, the Duchy of Tuscany, the Republic of Pisa and Genoa, and other Italian cities' were trying to '*remonter des metiers d'étoffes de soie avec peine infinie & avec peu de success*'.[3] What he says is to some extent confirmed by the evidence given by a certain Mr. Twin Lloyd before a Select Committee of the House of Commons in 1766. He stated that he had only recently returned from Italy and that 'several manufactures for wrought silks are erected at Parma, Pisa and other Parts of Italy, to which all possible Encouragement has been given; and that the troubles at Genoa has greatly contributed to establishing these manufactures, great numbers of Artificers having been driven thence to seek Shelter in other parts of Italy'.[4]

These various statements, particularly those of Joubert and Mr. Lloyd, remind us that Italy was at this time still divided into a number of states. Many of them were far from being on friendly terms with each other, and their respective silk industries were more often than not rivals both in Italian and foreign markets. Strictly, therefore, it is wrong to speak of an *Italian* silk industry at this period, for we are really considering a whole series of geographically separated industries, some of them of little importance, whose total output, however, was very considerable. The fact that Italian was spoken at all these places must have made it easier for discontented weavers to move from one centre to another, but otherwise there does not seem to have been much connection between them. There was almost certainly no common Italian style of silk-decoration and the

[1] Savary, *Dictionnaire de Commerce*, 1723; see section on *Commerce*.
[2] Defoe, *A Plan of English Commerce*, 1722, p. 294.
[3] Joubert, *op. cit.*, p. ix. He calls Tuscany a Duchy, although it was in fact a Grand-Duchy.
[4] House of Commons Journals, 1766, Report, p. 997.

figured silks of, say, Milan were probably no more like those of Naples than those of London.

If we turn to modern sources for enlightenment, we again find very little to help us. Podreider's profusely illustrated book, *I Tessuti d'arte in Italia*, glances only briefly at the later history of the Italian silk industry. More helpful is Luigi Brenni's *La Tessitura Serica attraverso i Secoli*, although this too deals far too briefly with the matter to enable one to obtain more than a very hazy idea of the general position.[1] All the same, it seemed worth trying to summarise what Brenni had to say and the long paragraph which follows is in effect a *résumé* of the relevant chapters in his book. The centres are mentioned in alphabetical order.

Although there was a fair-sized industry at Como, Brenni produces no evidence that figured silks were made there. It is possible that brocaded silks and velvets were woven at Bologna at some stage in the eighteenth century; there was a considerable silk-weaving industry there involving, in 1713, some 20,000 people, it is said. The chief product of Bologna, however, was silk crêpes and gauzes. In the middle of the seventeenth century 1,000 looms were stated to have been at work at Catanzaro weaving silks, including velvets, both plain and figured, and also figured silks, some of them embellished with gold thread.[2] The industry there had declined severely by the 1780's. At Ferrara, where there had been an important industry in the fifteenth and sixteenth centuries, little silk was woven in the seventeenth century, but a Genoese weaver tried to introduce the weaving of velvets there in 1743. Florence was still producing silks in the eighteenth century but the industry had become much reduced in size during the seventeenth century. Genoa had some 4,000 looms at work in the seventeenth century but the number dropped in the eighteenth century. Velvets were woven in neighbouring townships and villages as well, and the hinterland also supported various ancillary industries like spinning, throwing and dyeing. Lucca had suffered from the effects of the Thirty Years' War when it lost its German markets; it never fully recovered from this. There were some 1,600 looms active there in 1619. Damasks and other figured silks were made at Mantua in the late sixteenth century, but thereafter its production consisted almost entirely of plain materials. Late in the eighteenth century figured silks were made there again. Rich silks of all kinds were apparently made at Messina. Milan's industry had declined during the first part of the seventeenth century but revived towards the end of the century. There were 809 looms at work there in 1697. In the eighteenth century the number fluctuated from about 200 to over 1,000; a proportion were always engaged in the weaving of figured silks including damasks and velvets. Silks, including damasks, all

[1] Fanny Podreider, *I Tessuti d'arte in Italia*, Bergamo, 1928; Luigi Brenni, *La Tessitura Serica attraverso i Secoli*, Como, 1925.

[2] Two silk damasks of no great distinction which may have been woven at Catanzaro are illustrated by G. Tescione, *San Leucio e l'arte della Seta nel mezzogiorno d'Italia*, Naples, 1961, pp. 123 and 125.

of rather poor quality it seems, were woven at Naples in the second half of the eighteenth century. Silk materials were also made at Reggio Emilia in the seventeenth and eighteenth centuries, but Brenni gives few details about this centre. In 1656 there were about fifty master-weavers in Rome making taffetas, damasks, cloth of gold and figured velvets. Sienna was still weaving silks in the eighteenth century but on a small scale. An important industry was established at Turin in the late seventeenth century.[1] Regulations governing its productions were promulgated in 1681. In 1702 there were 423 looms in Turin, making damasks for dress and furnishing purposes, brocatelles, and other silks. By 1724 the number of looms had risen to 800 with 23 of them weaving figured velvets. The Turin industry declined in the 1760's but revived to some extent later in the century. Brenni has little to say about the silk industry in Venice apart from stating that 800 looms were active there in 1750. Venice controlled the output of the silk industry at Verona and continually imposed frustrating regulations on the Veronese silk-weavers — from which one may conclude that few figured silks were made there. Black velvets were a speciality of that city. Vicenza was an important centre of silk-weaving. Venice tried to restrict its production but, although the industry in Vicenza had declined in the seventeenth century, there were 2,660 looms at work there by the middle of the eighteenth century.

From this rather tedious string of facts and statements, it will be seen that figured silk were being made at a number of places in Italy during the period that interests us. I imagine that anyone well acquainted with the Italian collections of historic textiles ought to be able to distinguish a number of groups of seventeenth- and eighteenth-century materials that must be Italian. There must be distinctive features that can be recognized by the initiated — certain colours, for instance, that may be associated with, say, Milanese or Neapolitan silks — but no information on this point has so far been published, to my knowledge. No doubt some Italian scholar will one day enlighten us; in the meantime the rest of us may feel consoled in our ignorance by the fact that even in the eighteenth century foreigners experienced the same difficulty. 'It is very difficult', said an English Customs official, in 1765, 'to distinguish French from Italian silks', particularly, he went on, those from Genoa and Lyons of the same class.[2]

England: Spitalfields

Note: This brief history of the principal centre of the English silk-weaving industry is largely based on the findings of my colleague Miss Natalie Rothstein, together with whom I studied for some years the history of seventeenth- and eighteenth-century European silks. Many of the points mentioned below are derived from information that was

---

[1] A velvet in the Genoese style but bearing an in-woven inscription mentioning Turin, is illustrated by Podreider, *op. cit.*, fig. 284. I would have thought the pattern belonged to the period 1665–80.

[2] House of Commons Journal, 1765, Report, evidence of Mr. Trott, p. 209.

discovered by her during our investigations and from conclusions drawn in a thesis she subsequently wrote entitled 'The Silk Industry in London, 1702–1766' (London, M.A. Degree, 1961). I sincerely hope that this well-reasoned and most fully documented thesis will be published in some suitable form in the near future. In the meantime, I am deeply grateful to her for enabling me to make use of her work in this way. P.K.T.

The Worshipful Company of Weavers was founded in London in A.D. 1155 and was granted a Charter by King Henry II.[1] This Charter was confirmed during each subsequent reign until a new one was granted by Charles I (1625–49). It is unlikely that very many members of the London Weavers' Company were concerned with the weaving of silks during the Company's early history. There may have been a small production of broad silks, and items like ribbons and laces were undoubtedly made from quite an early date. Wool and worsted weaving was almost certainly their chief occupation and it is not generally realized that even in the eighteenth century, when the London silk industry was at the height of its prosperity, there were many substantial worsted-weavers at work in and around the city, and that worsted materials woven in the English capital were an important part of the English textile production.

Like several other northern monarchs of his day, James I eyed with envy the very considerable wealth that Italian city-states like Florence and Venice were deriving from their flourishing silk industries and, in the early seventeenth century, he apparently invited a number of French silk-weavers to settle in England in order to help establish an indigenous industry.[2] He also encouraged the planting of mulberry trees in the rather forlorn hope that the silk-worm might thrive in England. Nothing permanent seems to have come from this last project except that a few mulberry trees still survive in different parts of the country and a street in what is now the West London borough of Chelsea still bears the name 'Mulberry Walk'.

A new charter, supplanting that of Charles I, was granted to the London Weavers' Company by James II (1685–88). By that time there seems to have been a silk-weaving industry of some size in London. Already in 1676 the Company could claim that it would be capable of supplying all the silks the nation required if only it were given sufficient support,[3]

---

[1] F. Consitt, *The London Weavers' Company from the 12th to the close of the 16th century*, Oxford, 1933, deals with the early history of the Company. Some additional information will be found in Sir Frank Warner's, *The Silk Industry in the United Kingdom*, London, 1921, which, however, is primarily useful for the study of the industry in the nineteenth century, about which Warner knew a great deal.

[2] State Papers Venetian, 1607–10, p. 153.

[3] See A. Browning, *Thomas Osborne, Earl of Danby and Duke of Leeds, 1632–1712*, Oxford, 1951, Vol. III, pp. 25–27. March 9th 1676: The weavers demanded that 'No persons [was] to wear any silk but what be manufactured in this Kingdom.' March 11th: '... the Weavers call'd in and being asked whether they could furnish all England with silk stuffs, answered "Yes, if they might be incouraged".' They subsequently appeared with patterns to prove their case. The silk shown in Plate 15A may possibly be an English silk of the period.

and it was later stated that the industry had been on the increase, until 1674 when large imports of French silk-goods had caused a slump.[1]

At that stage the weavers were for the most part still living within the walls of the City of London but soon a whole new quarter was to grow up to the east of the City, around Spitalfields market, and was to spread gradually northwards and eastwards to Bethnal Green, Whitechapel and Stepney. In these areas settled a large number of the French Protestant refugees who, during the last third of the seventeenth century were forced or decided to leave France as a result of the religious oppression then rampant in their native land. These Huguenot refugees soon formed a closely knit community, and many of its members came to be involved in the London silk industry. A high proportion of them were skilled artisans and tradesmen, and the talents they brought to the English industry were soon to bear fruit. There was of course opposition to the foreigners, but an enlightened official policy encouraged them and, with the passing of the Act of Settlement which established a line of Protestant monarchs on the English throne, and with the accession of Queen Anne in 1702, the future of the refugees was guaranteed. In 1707 the Weavers' Company received a new charter in which mention was actually made of the great increase in the number of foreigners practising the weaving trade in and around London. Four years earlier the Company had relaxed its regulations somewhat so that foreign weavers could be admitted as Masters of the Company so long as they could prove that they had served the mandatory seven years' apprenticeship somewhere. This did not put the foreign weavers entirely on the same footing as their English colleagues — that was to come — but such toleration was decidedly encouraging for the foreigners.

Although the English must all along have been in the majority, and although English master-weavers usually occupied most of the chief posts in the Company, the Huguenots played an increasingly important part in the affairs of the Weavers' Company until, in the middle decades of the eighteenth century, a very considerable proportion of the master-weavers on the Livery of the Company were Huguenots.[2]

It appears that the prosperity of the English silk industry was finally established during the War of the Spanish Succession which broke out in 1701 and lasted until 1713. During this period French commerce passed through a major depression which seriously affected the French silk industry whose competitors, including the growing English industry, consequently benefited. With the English navy making maritime trade precarious for France, French silks often failed to reach some of her old-established markets overseas, whereupon English silks could be sold there instead. Furthermore, an expanding home market had also perforce to be supplied almost entirely by the English industry:

[1] Report submitted by The London Weavers' Company on *The State of the Silk and Silk and Worsted Manufactures in this Kingdom* in 1719 (Public Record Office, London; C.O.388.21 [137]).

[2] See P. Thornton and N. Rothstein, *The Importance of the Huguenots in the London Silk Industry*, Proceedings of the Huguenot Society of London, Vol. XX, No. 1. A paper read before the Society in 1959.

'And whence is the prodigious increase in our silk manufacture but from the interruption of our commerce with France?'[1] In 1719 silks to the value of some £62,000 were exported from England[2] and it could already be said in 1721 that the English silk industry was 'one of the most considerable manufactures of the Kingdom'.[3] A year later, in his 'Plan of English Commerce', Daniel Defoe maintained that 'the broad silk manufacture . . . is an Encrease of this very age. It is a Surprise to the World as well in its Quantity as in its value, and in the admirable Perfection which our people are arriv'd to in it. . . . It is but a very few Years ago that the making of Broad silks began here in England'.[4] In Plates 51, 53 and 54 can be seen a few examples of the kind of patterns that were being woven in London at this stage. Although they were inspired by French originals, the quality of such silks was of a high order, as far as one can judge by the surviving material. It takes a highly organized industry, backed by considerable capital, and endowed with a substantial measure of technical expertise to weave silks of this class. The surviving designs and silks are themselves most significant evidence that the English silk industry had by this time arrived at an advanced state of evolution. It is also worth recalling that English plain silk materials — most notably her watered taffetas — were greatly admired on the Continent, even in France.[5] It is probable, on the other hand, that English figured silks were still at this time primarily intended for home consumption or export to Ireland and the Colonies.

The Spitalfields silk industry had several advantages over its French rivals at Lyons and Tours. Being situated in the capital, it had its principal market on its doorstep and the cost of transporting the finished goods from the loom to the wearer was thus minimal. There were no internal Customs, as there were in France, to raise the price of silks being sent to distant parts of the kingdom. Silks going abroad often went by sea from the nearby Port of London, which again involved only the shortest of land journeys. Another great advantage to the industry was the support which it usually obtained — and, indeed, expected to obtain — from the Government and city authorities. The Weavers' Company frequently sent petitions to Parliament concerning all kinds of matters affecting the silk industry. These petitions were, for the most part, considered seriously and with reasonable expedition. Numerous Bills were introduced and several Acts were finally passed specifically for the encouragement and benefit of the English silk-industry.[6]

---

[1] C. King, *The British Merchant*, Vol. I, p. 12, 1743 edition.

[2] Miss Rothstein derived this figure from the Customs records.

[3] Statutes at Large, U.260, 1721.

[4] Defoe, *A Plan of English Commerce*, 1722, p. 293.

[5] See Savary, *Dictionnaire de Commerce*, 1723, p. 951. '*Les Manfactures Angloises de soyerie . . . les principales étoffes qui en sortent sont des moires ondées & tabisés* [i.e. watered or moiré silks] *tant noires que de couleurs; des taffetas de diverses qualitez; des toiles de soie; des dentelles aussi de soye. . . .*'

[6] Notably the Act of 1721 by which the making and wearing of printed cottons was prohibited; the Act of 1722, 'for the encouragement of the silk manufactures of the Kingdom' which introduced a system of bounties payable on all

There were, however, two important disadvantages from which the industry suffered — disadvantages which were in the end to prove extremely serious. In the first place, the raw silk on which the whole industry ultimately depended had to be brought by vulnerable routes from distant parts of the world — from Italy by an awkward route under the noses of the French Fleet, from northern Persia through Turkey and the Levant or up the Volga and across to the Baltic, from Spain (until the Spaniards decided in 1749 to prohibit its export and weave it themselves), and from China and Bengal in ships of the East India Company. Attempts were also made to rear silkworms in the American colonies but these failed owing to lack of financial support. The raw silk was thus bound to be expensive and this meant that, in order to compete successfully with French silks in foreign markets, savings had to be made in the costs of production. One of the factors which may have led to the decline of the Spitalfields silk industry later in the century was the apparent failure of its members to evolve or adopt new techniques that could reduce these costs.

The second principal disadvantage from which the industry suffered was that the importance of having first-class designers was never fully appreciated by the English silk-weavers or, at any rate, they were never able to do anything about it, involved as they were in a continual effort to imitate the latest French patterns which their agents were sending back across the Channel (e.g. Plate 79B). Forced to copy French originals, the English designers were rarely able to develop to the full any independent talents of their own.[1] At Lyons, a designer would often be a partner in a silk-weaving business, with the advantage that he not only became personally concerned with all the processes of manufacturing a pattern, but that he also reaped a share of the profits that accrued if the pattern proved successful.[2] In England it seems the designers were mostly free-lance artists who sold their compositions to a variety of customers. They were rarely able to concentrate on the designing of one particular type of silk, and their interest in a silk pattern probably ceased once it had left their drawing-office and their fees had been paid. There were apparently no teachers in London who specialized in instructing young silk-designers, and no school of design was set up in Spitalfields until well into the nineteenth century (the Lyons School of Design was founded in 1756 but several informal schools existed before that)[3] although the Royal Society of Arts did, in 1754, start to offer a series of premiums for the best silk-designs submitted by young English

silks exported from England; the Act of 1749 which sought to prohibit the importation of foreign silks woven with gold and silver thread; and the Act of 1766 which entirely prohibited the importation of all foreign silk materials.

[1] 'The copying of French Patterns cramps the genius and prevents the increase of Pattern Drawers in this country . . .,' said Mr. Peter Cheveney, a Spitalfields designer who had once worked at Lyons, in evidence before the House of Commons Committee investigating the state of the English silk industry in 1765 (House of Commons Journals, 1765, Report, p. 210 et seq.).

[2] See Note 2, p. 24, where is quoted an English designer's comment on this.

[3] See p. 24, where the setting up of the Lyons School of Design is discussed.

artists.[1] This was no doubt encouraging, but it was encouragement from within the industry itself that was required and this was never really forthcoming. The English silk-weavers therefore continued throughout the eighteenth century to rely on French patterns for their inspiration.

The Weavers' Company wielded considerable power during the first half of the century. It ensured that almost all weavers practising their trade in or near London became members of the Company but in return, it offered them a worthwhile measure of protection, and looked after their interests in numerous ways. Apart from enforcing strictly the rules affecting membership the Company allowed its members complete freedom to work how and as they pleased. There were no formal divisions among the Master-weavers as there were among the French corporations of weavers, and once a man had been admitted as a Master, he could either work for another Master or he could set up a business on his own, if he wished and could afford to do so. Nor were there in England regulations governing the manufacture of silks, like those which so hampered the French weaver. An English weaver could in theory make his material any width he chose, although in practice he generally accepted the standard widths,[2] and he was not apparently obliged to furnish it with any particular form of selvedge. The English preferred to place their reliance not so much in safeguards built into cumbersome regulations but rather in their Common Law. If an English weaver were suspected of fraudulent weaving, the remedy was quickly found by bringing him and a piece of the faulty material before a Magistrate. If it was discovered that he had indeed committed a fraud, his reputation would for ever be tarnished and his livelihood would in consequence suffer.[3]

The Spitalfields industry continued to increase steadily during the second quarter of the century. Exports rose and new markets were opened up. The principal consumer of English silks after the Home Country itself was Ireland, but a great quantity was also going to the American Colonies (silks to the value of £233,000 were sent there in 1760). Other important markets were the West Indian Islands, Portugal, Spain and Germany. A leading designer at Lyons, writing in 1765 and describing the beauty of the finest woven silks, mentioned, apart from those of Lyons and Tours, only those made in London. He said nothing about Italian or Dutch or Spanish silks. He added that 'des artistes médiocres se sont formés chez eux [i.e. in England] et depuis 1748 on commence à

---

[1] A collection of prize-winning designs from this period is still preserved in the Library of the Royal Society of Arts, London.

[2] The normal widths woven at Spitalfields were 'half ell', which tended to vary between 19½ and 21 in. (49·5–53·5 cm.); 'three-quarter ell', which was about 27 in. (69 cm.); and 'yard wide' or about 36 or 37 in. (91·5–94 cm.). Most of the rich Spitalfields silks that have survived are of the first variety. The wider types were mostly plain materials used for linings and the like; they have rarely been preserved.

[3] That this was the practice in England was stated in a report on the London silk industry sent to Copenhagen in 1776 by the Danish Consul in London, P. Ancker. I am greatly indebted to Mrs. Ada Polak for drawing my attention to this report, which is in the Royal Library, Copenhagen, and for allowing me to study a photocopy of it.

voir dans les foires d'Allemagne [the great Fairs at Leipzig and elsewhere in Germany provided important channels for the commerce in French silks] *quelques-unes de leurs étoffes assez goutées mais bein inférieures aux nôtres'.*[1] Certainly the English weavers had no cause to feel ashamed of their wares at this stage. French silks may have been better designed but English 'flowered silks' reached a very high standard both in design and execution between about 1745 and 1755 or so (e.g. Plates 84B, 86B, 89B and 92A).

The Seven Years' War saw the fortunes of the Spitalfields industry reach their peak. Once again the British naval blockade helped to reduce French overseas trade and laid open large markets to English commerce. When the war came to an end, however, some of the new markets were lost and English silk weavers began to find themselves with stocks still on their hands. Production was reduced, workmen were laid off, wages were cut — all in an effort to ride out the storm. Mourning at several European courts further reduced the demand for luxury materials (this affected the French weavers as well, but their position at that moment was less precarious). 1763 was a black year in Spitalfields and soon there was unrest among the journeymen, starting with organized demonstrations but ending finally in riots. Much of our information about the English silk industry at this stage comes from the reports of the Select Committees of the House of Commons which investigated the state of the industry in 1765 and 1766. The weavers for the most part believed that their misfortunes were due to the continued legal and illegal importation of foreign, and particularly French, silks into the country. There was perhaps some justification in this complaint although the difficulties in which the industry found itself were probably to a great extent due to more deep-seated causes that were aggravated by the general depression which affected the whole country in the mid-1760's. In any case, the weavers concentrated mainly on persuading Parliament to introduce legislation that would prohibit this importation entirely. Their efforts were finally rewarded in 1766, but the provisions of the new Act proved hard to enforce because it permitted only the sellers and not the wearers of foreign silks to be prosecuted; so the smuggling of silks into England (which was a well-organized and important branch of French commerce) continued virtually unabated.

It is difficult to judge why the Spitalfields silk industry began to decline from the 1760's onwards.[2] The evidence seems to suggest that the inherent weaknesses of the industry now began to become apparent and that many of the principal weavers, including many of the Huguenots, gradually withdrew from the industry, often taking their capital with them. There was a temporary revival in the later 1760's, sufficient to enable the Danish Consul in London to say in 1776 that 'these manufactures have

[1] The designer was J. C. Dutillieu (see Note, 3, p. 24, above).

[2] An assessment of the various factors, supported by a great deal of fresh material and some cogent arguments, has been made by Miss Natalie Rothstein (see the note at the head of the section devoted to the English silk industry, p. 53) and will no doubt be published by her in due course.

increased considerably during the past ten years in England'.[1] In spite of this, it seems that the Spitalfields industry suffered even more than its French competitors from the radical change in fashion that took place during the last decades of the century, a change that brought light materials like printed cottons and muslins into favour and caused a reduction in the demand for rich silks. Plain, striped and sprigged silks were still required, but silks with large patterns were finally only needed for Court dresses. The manufacture of furnishing silks in Spitalfields, which had never been substantial, also suffered a set-back as the use of wall-papers and printed cottons increased from the middle of the eighteenth century onwards.

A number of what are here claimed to be Spitalfields silks are illustrated in this book and it may be asked how these have been identified. The answer is that it is rarely possible to be absolutely certain when making such an attribution except where the original design has been discovered — as has happened in a few cases.[2] All the same, these few examples and the large body of English silk-designs which has survived enable one to be fairly certain of identifying correctly several types of English 'flowered silks'.[3] For instance, a large number of silks with a floral pattern on a white ground, obviously dating from the middle decades of the eighteenth century, have survived and are now mostly to be found in English and American collections. While not all silks with a white ground are English, 'white-ground brocades' were an English speciality at that period, and the English specimens are often quite easy to recognize with practice (e.g. Plates 86 and 90). Certain details in their colouring usually give them away; some of the flowers in a pattern are frequently rendered in a rust-red colour, which is normally used in combination with yellow. It is interesting to note that much the same colour-combination is also found on Chelsea porcelain of the 'Red Anchor' period, produced in the 1750's. A rather strident red tinged with purple is also present in the brocaded patterns of many English silks of this well-known kind, particularly after 1750 or so. It is much more difficult to recognize the same kind of pattern when the ground is not white, as is sometimes the case, but even then the rust-red and the purplish-red often help in their identification (Colour Plate D).

Another well-defined group of English silks is typified by that shown in Plate 65B. They belong to the later 1720's and the 1730's. This group is distinguishable by the dominant dark green of the vegetation. The secondary colours sometimes include slightly bluish pinks and a washed-out mauve or aubergine colour.

[1] Report of the Danish Consul, P. Ancker (see Note 3, p. 58, above).

[2] As this was going to press, Miss Natalie Rothstein was on the point of writing an article about the nine silks which we have so far discovered that correspond exactly with designs in the collections mentioned in Note 3. This is to appear in the *Bulletin* of the Needle and Bobbin Club, New York, during 1965.

[3] The surviving English designs are in the Victoria and Albert Museum and in the possession of Messrs. Vanners & Fennell Bros., Sudbury. (See Note 4, p. 19 for fuller details.)

It is far from easy to distinguish with any certainty English silks woven during the early decades of the eighteenth century from their Continental counterparts. Once again one can identify some of them with the aid of the surviving designs (as in the case of the silk illustrated in Plate 53A which closely resembles a certain group of English designs) but the instances are not many. Several of the silks from this period which are thought to be English have details worked in a red with a purplish tinge, and this is sometimes found, as in the example just mentioned, in conjunction with a dull dark blue.

As a general rule it seems that the English preferred to have their patterns on a light-coloured ground, in contrast to the French, who often used a dark colour. Among the early eighteenth-century silks which are believed to be English, some have light blue grounds, others a mustard colour, and a few are buff. After about 1730, white and shades of off-white become common although yellow, light blue, and a brownish purple are also found. From what has been said, however, it will be seen that, while colour perhaps provides a useful indication of whether a silk is English or not, it is only a guide in certain instances and there are no doubt many unrecognized English silks which have quite different colour characteristics.

It may perhaps be said that on the whole the compositions of English silk-patterns are rather less tightly controlled, are often more open and even straggling, than their French equivalents; but this again is not much help to those who wish to identify English silks. Nor is it much use quoting the opinions of contemporary experts, although they almost invariably agreed that it *was* possible to distinguish English from foreign silks.[1] It has been suggested by various American authorities that English silks usually have flat, taffeta selvedges while the selvedges of French silks are mostly corded.[2] This may occasionally prove a helpful guide although it would, it seems, be rash to lay too much weight on this form of identification because the type of selvedge used depended on the kind of silk being woven — that is, if a silk was a heavy one or had a type of weave which imposed a great deal of transverse tension, a sturdy selvedge (for instance of the corded type) would be required and conversely for a lighter fabric, a taffeta selvedge would suffice. This must surely have been so both in France and England — and, indeed, wherever textiles were made?

[1] For instance, Rouquet, in *L'État des arts en Angleterre*, 1775, wrote that one could recognize English silks '*à leur défaut de goût & la composition & à la distribution des couleurs mal nuancées, sans opposition, sans force, & sans art, quoique tres belles en elles mêmes*'. Their execution was excellent, he said, '*mais, en parlant des desseins, on ne pourra pas . . . leur accorder la même perfection*' as one could French silk-patterns (p. 113). The majority of those who gave evidence before the House of Commons Select Committee, already referred to, would have endorsed this view: several stated that English flowered silks could be distinguished from French, and many felt bound to admit that 'the French excelled in Taste', as one put it (House of Commons Journals, 1765, Report, especially p. 210 *et seq.*).

[2] Notably by the distinguished authority on historic textiles, Miss Gertrude Townsend of the Museum of Fine Arts, Boston, Mass. (see her article in *Antiques*, Vol. XLVIII, No. 5, May 1945, pp. 270–72, especially p. 272).

Other English centres[1]

It seems that silk ribbons were already being made at Coventry quite early in the eighteenth century and that silk handkerchiefs were being woven at Manchester by the middle of the century. These small-wares do not concern us here. Nor need we linger over the history of the great Norwich textile industry although 'half-silks' (i.e. materials composed of mixtures of silk and some other fibre, in this case usually wool) were made there in quantity. Contrary to assertions that are sometimes made, there is no evidence, as far as I am aware, that all-silk materials were woven at Norwich until late in the eighteenth century. Silk-weaving was also started at Macclesfield towards the end of the century. During the greater part of the century, what is more, raw silk was being turned into silk thread in throwing-mills at Derby, Leek and Congleton and then sent to London for the looms at Spitalfields; these centres started to weave silks on their own, late in the century. The products of all these places fall outside the scope of the present study. There was, on the other hand, a silk-industry at Canterbury which is known to have produced 'flowered silks' during the period with which we are concerned.

A book of samples of Canterbury silks was destroyed in a fire at an international exhibition in Brussels early in this century. Illustrations of two pages of the book show silks with fairly simple patterns or stripes. The contents are said to have included samples from the end of the seventeenth century when the Canterbury silk industry was probably at the peak of its activity.[2] Without evidence of the kind provided by this book of samples, we now have little hope of identifying the products of the Canterbury looms although specimens no doubt survive unrecognized in English collections.

Very little is as yet known about the industry at Canterbury; information probably exists and merely awaits a patient scholar. Defoe, writing in 1722, claimed that 'the making of broad silks began in England only a few years ago, but what attempts have been made were chiefly at Canterbury by the Walloons and French refugees and they are so beaten out by the East India silks [i.e. by the importation of silks in ships of the East India Company which was finally prohibited in 1722] that, if I am not misinformed, there were not 20 looms left at work in the whole city of Canterbury, some say, not half as many'.[3] This is probably an exaggeration; the Canterbury weavers themselves stated

[1] A certain amount of information about these other English centres will be found in Warner, *The Silk Industry in the United Kingdom*, London, 1921.

[2] Warner, *op. cit.*, fig. XXXV (p. 316 and p. 658u). Warner states that the book was dated 1685. Luther Hooper ('Silk-weaving in Spitalfields', article in the *Art Journal*, 1909, p. 53; with the same illustration) says 1684. The photograph shows the book open somewhere about the middle. The samples on the two exposed pages are clearly late *eighteenth-century* silks which might well have been woven in 1785 but not in 1685. Possibly the book did contain samples from the late seventeenth century but, since there are late eighteenth-century samples in the *middle* of the book, it seems much more likely that the date on the cover has been misread by historians who knew that the great days of the Canterbury silk industry had been in the late seventeenth century.

[3] Daniel Defoe, *A Plan of English Commerce*, 1722, p. 293.

in 1719 that twenty-five years previously there had been 1,000 looms at work in the city whereas there were now only 334 — the latter being a more plausible figure.[1] In fact, it does seem as if the first silk-weaving industry of any importance in England was situated at Canterbury and that this was either started by refugees from the Continent or that the nucleus of an industry already existed which acted as a magnet and drew refugees to the city. By the 1680's, the industry was probably comparatively well-established because several Huguenots who were to play an important part in the expansion of the Spitalfields industry around the turn of the century are known to have come from Canterbury.[2] From what is known of their careers it is clear they were hardly novices when they arrived in London, presumably attracted there by the more encouraging prospects which the metropolitan industry now offered. It is more than likely that other Canterbury weavers moved to London at about the same time, and it is probable that the Canterbury industry could ill afford to lose people who may well have included some of its most talented members. This, more than the reason given by Defoe, was perhaps the chief reason for the decline of silk-weaving in Canterbury early in the eighteenth century.

In 1765, evidence was given before the Select Committee of the House of Commons that 'there are some men employed in the silk-weaving at Canterbury, but they are ... much reduced'.[3] Indeed, the author of *A Complete Guide to All Men of Business* published in 1754 and listing the textile industries of each country, could only say of Canterbury that 'the sole manufacture ... I believe ... is Thread' by which he presumably means linen thread. Silk is not mentioned.

Ireland: Dublin

There is evidence that silk was woven in Dublin during the eighteenth century.[4] It is not clear what materials were produced there during the earlier decades of the century but, by the late 1720's quite a large amount of raw and thrown silk was being consumed by the industry, and it was claimed that some eight hundred looms were at work in 1730, weaving silk dress materials. The output probably consisted almost entirely of plain silks and of the poplin, a half-silk with a woollen weft, for which Dublin became famous. Figured silks were probably only made on a very small scale, perhaps not long before 1743 when an attempt was made to stimulate this branch of the industry by means of

---

[1] London, Public Record Office, C.O.288:21 195. I am very grateful to Miss Rothstein for calling my attention to this statement, Warner, *op. cit.*, p. 318, states that there were 2,500 weavers in Canterbury in 1676; the total number of looms would thus have been somewhere between 500 and 1,000 at the time.

[2] See the article on Huguenots in the London Silk Industry already mentioned in Note 2, p. 55, above.

[3] House of Commons Journals, 1765, Report, p. 208, evidence of Mr. Triquet.

[4] See J. J. Webb, *Industrial Dublin since 1698 and the Silk Industry in Dublin. Two essays*, Dublin, 1913. (I am indebted to Miss Natalie Rothstein for calling my attention to this book and the reference that follows.)

premiums which were offered by the public-spirited Dublin Society for the best piece of green damask, the best piece of flowered silk, and the best piece of paduasoy — all materials requiring a draw-loom and suggesting that there was by that time a number of skilled weavers in the city capable of executing such work.[1] An Act was passed in 1745 by the Irish Parliament placing duties on the importation of foreign silks. This was primarily intended to give the industry a measure of protection against French competition; English silks were allowed into the country after paying a substantially lower duty. Since it is known that Ireland was one of the chief markets for English 'flowered silks', it is reasonable to suppose that the output of such silks in Dublin was never great.

The Dublin silk industry flourished particularly during the 1770's, when some 1,500 looms were apparently at work there, but in the 1780's its fortunes declined. At the end of the century, only plain silks and silks with simple patterns were made there.

Holland

When studying eighteenth-century records concerning the French and English silk industries, one constantly comes across references to Dutch silks, and one gradually gets the impression that there must have been a fairly substantial silk industry at work in Holland during, anyway, the first half of the century. It is therefore curious that hardly anything has been written about this industry and it is, for the moment, difficult to form more than a very sketchy idea of its history. As I have not had the opportunity of pursuing my researches in Holland, the reader must here be content with the following outline which is based on such information as has so far come to my notice, together with a few conclusions which it seems safe to draw from this most incomplete material.[2]

Several cities in the Low Countries became important centres of the silk trade during the Middle Ages. The commerce was probably entirely in silks coming from the south — from Italy, Spain and the Orient. It is not clear when the weaving of silk was introduced into the Netherlands, but a minor industry seems already to have been established by the beginning of the seventeenth century in Haarlem where, it will be remembered, there was already a flourishing and widely famed linen-damask industry.

Even so, and as happened in England, it was not until after the arrival of large numbers

---

[1] *The Gentleman's Magazine*, 1743.

[2] Dr. G. T. van Ysselsteyn and the Archivist of the City of Haarlem have very kindly told me about the following brief references which all throw some, but unfortunately not very much, light on the history of the Dutch silk industry: S. Kalff, 'Haarlemsche Zijde-Industrie', in the journal *Nederlandsche Fabrikaat*, Sept. 1920; F. Allan, *Geschiedenis en beschrijving van Haarlem*, IV, pp. 569–73; H. J. Koenen, *Geschiedenis van verstiging en invloed der Fransche vluchtingen in Nederland*, pp. 270–71. (I have the impression that a Dutch authority is currently working on the history of the silk industry in Holland. I hope his or her findings will soon be published; they should be of great interest. As this was going to press, Miss Natalie Rothstein kindly showed me an article she had written about the Dutch silk industry which was to appear in *Oud Holland* during 1964. She publishes additional evidence supporting the contention that the Dutch industry was of some consequence during our period.)

of French Protestant refugees during the second half of the century that the Dutch silk industry was properly set on its feet. Apparently the weavers among the refugees settled for the most part in Haarlem. Silks with moderately ambitious patterns were already being woven by 1678, as is proved by a document in the city archives which has attached to it a few samples of what are stated in the document to be Haarlem silk materials.[1] Two of these samples are illustrated in Plates 17A and B. The other samples consist of silks with simpler patterns, and a plain silk velvet. There may well have been Huguenots working in Haarlem by that date although such silks as these could equally well be the product of an industry that was still entirely Dutch.

It seems that the Dutch industry increased rapidly in size at the end of the seventeenth century and during the early eighteenth century, for probably much the same reasons as its rival at Spitalfields. By 1699 the Dutch were in a position to request permission of the French authorities to *'faire entrer en France les étoffes de leurs fabriques'*, much to the consternation of the French silk-weavers who complained that, if such permission were granted, Oriental silks could then be imported into France under pretence of their being Dutch.[2] This suggests that Dutch silks were of a comparatively high standard but were chiefly of a light nature, since the silks then being imported from the East were mostly of this class. It is clear, on the other hand, that rich silks were also being produced: the English Customs in 1712 maintained that 'gold & silver wrought silks of the manufacture of Holland' might legally be imported into England although at the time the importation of French silks was prohibited.[3] Furthermore, among the surviving Spitalfields silk-designs already mentioned is one dated 1711 on which it expressly stated that 'this pattern was taken from a Dutch silk . . .'.[4] It is composed of small, semi-naturalistic flowers arranged around curving trellises and is in a style which shows that the Dutch designers were completely *au fait* with the latest French fashions in their field. Further evidence that this was the case is provided by the small group of patterns suitable for weaving in silk which were composed by the well-known French refugee artist, Daniel Marot, at just about the same date. (One of these compositions is illustrated in Plate 45B, and their close relation to contemporary French silk-patterns is further discussed on pages 99 and 166) Marot's designs were published at Amsterdam.

[1] G. T. van Ysselsteyn, 'Het Haarlemse smalweversgilde', in the *Journal of the Stichting Texteil Geschiedenis*, 1957, pp. 25–46, illustrates. The *'smalwevers'* (narrow-weavers) broke away in 1597 from the *'blauwerkers'* who were chiefly weavers of linen damasks, for which Haarlem was by then already famous. The term 'narrow-weave' was relative and referred to the comparatively narrow width of the silks and half-silks woven by the 'smalwevers' when seen beside the wide cloths made by the linen damask-weavers.

[2] Bossebœuf, *op. cit.,* (see Note 1, p. 32, above), p. 291.

[3] H.M. Customs, Opinions in Council (1701–63), Vol. II, Nov. 12, 1712. (I am extremely grateful to Miss Rothstein for telling me about this judgment.)

[4] Design No. 32 in the collection of Messrs. Vanners & Fennell Bros., Sudbury (see Note 4, p. 19). This design is illustrated by F. Lewis, *James Leman . . .*, Leigh-on-Sea, 1954, fig. 18.

The French silk-weavers were acutely aware of the competition that they suffered from the Dutch industry and there are frequent references to the matter in French documents of the period. In 1727, the silk-merchants of Lyons considered establishing a depot for the sale of their wares in Altona, Hamburg, in order to compete more success-fully with the sale there of Dutch silks.[1] It is probable that a large part of northern Germany and the whole of Scandinavia obtained the silks they needed through Hamburg, so a fairly lucrative market was involved.

Perhaps the most important evidence concerning Dutch silks is that provided by the several pages of *Étoffes d'Hollande*, all of them silks, which are to be found in that fascinating repository of eighteenth-century textiles collected by the Duc de Richelieu between about 1730 and 1737. The collection is now in the Bibliothèque Nationale in Paris.[2] One page is of '*Étoffes d'Hollande dont les Dames font usage à Paris, 1737*'. The samples are excellent; they are mostly from silks with complicated patterns that appear to be indistinguishable from contemporary French productions, even though a long note opposite one of the pages of samples tells us that '*les étoffes d'Hollande se reconnoissent aisement par l'envers de l'étoffe. Les Hollandois se servent d'un aprest comme leuy [?] que l'on met aux Indes. Cet aprest est composé en partie de Ris et autres graines qui viennent des Indes. On ne peut imiter ces aprest en France*'. This seems to imply that the silks received some kind of dressing on the reverse face but, in spite of the above comment, it is now in no way obvious at a glance how these materials differ from contemporary silks made elsewhere.[3] It must have been silks of this kind that in 1739 caused the Tours weavers to demand the death penalty for those caught importing Dutch figured (*façonné*) silks into France.[4]

It is possible that the 1730's saw the Dutch industry at the peak of its prosperity and that thereafter it lost ground to its English and French competitors. It is anyway note-worthy that the officers of the Lyons Corporation of Weavers reported in 1750 that the Dutch Stathouder had urged his people to wear materials made in Holland, which rather suggests that the local industry was in need of encouragement.[5] On the other hand, *A Complete Guide to All Men of Business* could still, in 1754, list silks as an import from Holland into England. This information may either have been out-of-date or perhaps, as is more likely, the materials that were coming from Holland by this time were in reality chiefly French silks (on which a high import-duty was payable) masquerad-ing as Dutch.

---

[1] Godart, *op. cit.*, (see Note 2, p. 37, above), p. 357.

[2] Paris, Bibliothèque Nationale, Cabinet des Estampes, Richelieu Collection, Vols. Lh.45b and 45d.

[3] S. Kalff, *op. cit.*, describes the process by means of which this glaze was imparted to the back of the material. A gum was applied and the material then passed over heated rollers.

[4] Bossebœuf, *op. cit.*, p. 339. They demanded the same severe penalty, be it noted, for the importers of English silks.

[5] Godart, *op. cit.*, p. 219.

No mention is ever made by Dutch scholars of any important centre of silk-weaving in Holland other than that of Haarlem. It is claimed that there were over twenty master-weavers with a total of some 3,000 looms at work in that city in 1750. A certain Pierre Baille from Clermont is said to have started a silk-weaving factory in Amsterdam, late in the seventeenth century, and at one point had 110 looms in operation but the enterprise had declined by the 1720's.[1] Silk was apparently thrown in mills at Utrecht and Amersfoort but does not seem to have been woven there.

Although the Richelieu samples and the design 'taken from a Dutch stuff' in 1711 indicate that the Dutch silk industry was capable of producing silks with large and intricate patterns, the materials that were exported were probably for the most part much simpler. Trade-cards of English silk-mercers often refer to Dutch Mantuas, for instance (mantua was a type of plain silk with a slight rib), and to Dutch velvets which, it is plain from the context, were of silk.[2] The Supplement to Savary's *Dictionnaire de Commerce*, published in 1730 says, under the heading '*Damas*', that three kinds of damask were sold at Amsterdam; that of the Indies, that of Lucca, and that of Holland (lit. *du pays*).[3]

Spain

Magnificent silks were woven in Spain during the Middle Ages, and the Spanish silk industry was in size and importance second only to that of Italy during the fifteenth and sixteenth centuries. It is often thought that Spain continued to hold this leading position in the seventeenth century but this was not the case. A Spanish authority, Professor Niño y Mas, has written that '*en el ultima epoca de la Casa de Austria*', that is, during the period from the middle until the end of the seventeenth century, when the rule of the Hapsburg Dynasty in Spain was weakening (the last Hapsburg king died in 1700) '*nuestra producción textil entra en franca decadencia*'.[4] This decadence was primarily brought about by the

---

[1] See 'The Silk Industry in Amsterdam'. *C.I.B.A. Review*, No. 48, 1944.

[2] There is an eighteenth-century trade-card in the Victoria and Albert Museum advertising 'All sorts of Rich brocaded Silks, Dutch Genoa and English Velvets . . . etc.', from which it is clear that Dutch velvets were classable among silk materials. There is a silk velvet among the samples on the document dated 1678 at Haarlem, mentioned by van Ysselsteyn (see Note 1, p. 65, above), and Miss Rothstein has found a Dutch silk velvet among some records that she intends to publish. She tells me that it is less fine than a sample of Genoa velvet with it but that it is none the less of good quality. This is perhaps the place to remind the student that these Dutch velvets were not woven at Utrecht where, indeed, no velvets of any kind were ever woven in spite of the fact that antique woollen velvets are often called *velours d'Utrecht*. In fact, such woollen velvets were made in many places but principally in north-eastern France at places like Rouen. In conversation, Dr. van Ysselsteyn has suggested that the mistake came from the fact that these woollen velvets that were figured were woven on a draw-loom, and that, in the Low Countries, '*trek*' means to pull or draw. So a velvet woven on a drawloom may have been called a *velours de trek*. From this to *velours d'Utrecht* is an easy stage. Whether this is the correct explanation, I cannot say, but it sounds plausible.

[3] Miss Rothstein, in the article already mentioned, draws attention to a large group of silks in America which she believes may be Dutch. These are distinguished by their narrow width (about 15 in. or 38·2 cm.) and a characteristic colouring which includes an emerald green with a strong bluish tinge, often used for the ground, a greenish yellow, a crimson bordering on mauve, a reddish brown and a Prussian blue.

[4] Felipa Niño y Mas, *Antiguos Tejidos Artisticos Españoles*, Madrid, 1942, p. 31.

economic plight in which the country then found itself, and the resulting decline in orders for luxury goods like silk. Competition from France no doubt also played its part.

The important survey of the Spanish economy compiled by Eugenio Larruga in 1787 tells much the same story.[1] It recalls the fame of the Spanish silk industry in the past and mentions the slump which hit Spain in the late seventeenth century. Toledo, we are told, which had been one of the chief silk-weaving centres, had 622 looms in operation in 1695, 466 in 1701, and only 100 in 1708. Larruga blames the decline not only on external causes but on the way the weavers failed to adhere to the regulations governing their trade. This was possibly a mistaken view, for even a casual study of the history of other silk industries shows that such regulations often served only to hamper an industry if too strictly adhered to, and that they were usually out-of-date within a matter of a few years.

New regulations were issued in 1684 to 'the Weavers of Silks of whatever kind, be it with silver or with gold, within this Realm . . .', and specifically mentioned Toledo, Granada and Seville, presumably because these were the chief centres of production at that time.[2] Of these, Toledo was then probably the most important. Shortly after this, Valencia, which was not mentioned in the 1684 regulations, appeared on the scene as a producer of silks, which by the 1720's she could do in sufficient quantity to threaten the very existence of the Toledo industry.[3] Niño y Mas states that Valencia was the principal centre in Spain from the early eighteenth century onwards.[4] Granada also seems to have been a centre of some importance during the first half of the century, but was probably submerged by the tide of prosperity which lifted Valencia to a position of importance far above that of any of her domestic rivals, during the second half of the century. Seville complained, already in 1726, of the activities of the Valencia weavers, which rather suggests that the Seville industry was in none too flourishing a state either, or else her weavers would have been too busy to bother about the competition offered by a still quite small industry like that at Valencia. One feels that if the silk industries of Toledo and Seville — and probably of Granada too — had been in a really healthy state, and if they had been weaving large quantities of fine silks, they would have been more concerned with the competition from France, if anything. But, in spite of all this, it should be noted that Savary states in his *Dictionnaire de Commerce*, published in 1723, that Spain produced '*étoffes d'or, d'argent de soye & de laine, de toutes qualitez, & de divers prix*'. Much of this output was apparently sent to the Spanish and Portuguese colonies in

---

[1] E. Larruga, *Memorias Politicas y Economicas sobre los frutos, comercio, fabricas y minas de Espana . . .*, Madrid, 1787. See particularly Tom V, p. 191 *et seq.*, and Tom VII, p. 205 *et seq.* Detailed figures are given in many instances.

[2] *Ordenanzas con que se han de labrar en estos Reinos Texidos de Seda de todos generos, y los de Plata, y Oro, en que han convenido los Disputados nombrados por los Ciudades y Fabricas de Toledo, Granada y Sevilla . . .*, 1684.

[3] Santiago Rodrigues Garcia, *El arte de las seda valenciana en el Siglo XVII*, Valencia, 1959, lists in an appendix all the Masters of the Valencia Guild of Silk-weavers. The earliest held his post in 1686.

[4] Niño y Mas, *op. cit.*, p. 32.

America and the West Indies. Great convoys of merchantmen sailed each year loaded with goods for this rich transatlantic market. The Spanish industry could not supply anything like the quantity of silks that were required for this trade, and a whole branch of the Lyons silk industry was therefore most profitably engaged in producing silks for this specialized market. It was a black year for Lyons too, when the Atlantic Convoy was unable to sail! But while Savary says that Spain produced rich silks of all kinds at this time, he also states that France exported the same class of materials to Spain for consumption in that country. This again suggests that the Spanish output was relatively small — incapable even of satisfying the domestic requirements of a nation suffering from severe political and economic difficulties.

Spain was an important producer of raw silk. Most of it was exported[1] until just before the middle of the eighteenth century, when this commerce was stopped by royal decree. This was an important step in the great campaign which the Spanish Government now launched to revive the indigenous silk industry; the raw silk would henceforth be needed at home. In 1749 it was reported to the House of Commons at Westminster that 'the Spaniards are vigorously attempting the increase and improvement of the Manufacture of wrought Silks and Velvets in that Kingdom'.[2] Their efforts proved remarkably fruitful, as two recently published important monographs dealing respectively with the Barcelona and Valencia industries show.[3] Although it was apparently these two cities which principally benefited, other cities were also encouraged by these energetic measures. For instance, Toledo, where there had only been a mere 234 looms at work in 1745, had 589 looms in operation in 1748, and 610 in 1752. Shortly after this, however, the Toledo industry went into a fatal decline and never succeeded in recovering its former glory.

The revival of the Spanish silk industry was achieved largely with the aid of Frenchmen who were induced to come to Spain for this special purpose. In 1750 the Consulate at Lyons passed judgment in a case concerning some French weavers who had helped to organize a silk factory at Talavera and, in the following year, two Frenchmen were sent to the galleys for life because they had assisted the Spaniards with the reorganization of their industry.[4] It is amusing to note that at the time it was alleged that French weavers

---

[1] Larruga, *op. cit.*, Tom V, p. 217, says that, in 1745, Toledo '*no podian surtirse de los sedas necesarias de bueno calidad, porque los Franceses compraban la mayor parte de la cosecha de Valencia*'. Most of the silk cultivated in Spain came from the Valencia region.   [2] House of Commons Journals, 1749, Vol. 25, p. 933.

[3] S. R. Garcia, *op. cit.*, concerning the Valencia industry, and F. Torella Niubo, *El moderno resurgir textil de Barcelona*, Barcelona, 1961. The success of the revival of the Spanish silk industry may be gauged by the fact that the *maîtres gardes* of the Lyons Corporation of Silk-weavers noted, already in 1750, that there were then 8,000 more looms weaving silk in Spain than there had been twenty years earlier, and that Spanish silks were now both good and cheap. High praise indeed from such a source! (Godart, *op. cit.* [see Note 2, p. 37, above], p. 219.)

[4] Godart, *op. cit.*, p. 202. The Capitation Roll of the Lyons Corporation of Silk-weavers for the year 1759 (see Note 2, p. 42, above) mentions a designer named Demontigny who is listed as being '*absent en Espagne*'. S. R. Garcia, *op. cit.*, mentions several French designers and instructors who were active in Valencia during the third quarter of the eighteenth century.

on their way to Spain would pretend to be going on a pilgrimage to Santiago de Compostela. *A Guide to All Men of Business*, which appeared in London in 1754, mentioned that 'in Madrid has been set up a Manufacture of Tissues, Lutestrings and other silks in imitation of those of Lyons in France, whence most of the artificers are drawn'. '*Tout le monde sait que les fabriques d'Allemagne, de Suisse et d'Espagne ne doivent leur origine qu'à des Lyonnais . . .*' says Paulet, writing in the 1770's.[1] He too mentions Talavera as a centre of silk-weaving. Larruga, who, it will be remembered, was writing a decade later, also mentions Valladolid and Burgos. The French, of course, noted the competition which the renascent Spanish industry now provided but they were unable to do much about it. The Spaniards had the raw silk, and labour was cheap. Besides, with the accession of a Bourbon king to the Spanish throne, a measure of stability was again imparted to the Spanish economy and the market became sufficiently large to absorb the products of both the rival industries.

Since the Spanish silk industry of the second half of the eighteenth century was modelled on that at Lyons and was guided by French weavers, designers and instructors, it is hardly surprising that it is virtually impossible to tell Spanish silks of the period from their French counterparts.[2] Nor is sufficient known about Spanish silks of the previous period — the late seventeenth and the early eighteenth century — to enable us to identify any particular groups or styles. There is a cope in Toledo Cathedral, made of a rich silk that was woven there, which bears the in-woven date 1714. It is decorated with large foliate forms in a heavy Baroque style which seems rather old-fashioned but, as this must anyway have been a special commission, it tells us little about Spanish silks in general.[3] It is fairly safe to assume that Spanish silks of the late seventeenth century were mostly rather poor imitations of contemporary French patterns.

Sweden

The Swedish silk industry is well documented.[4] It was never large and it only really flourished during the third quarter of the eighteenth century when it achieved a remark-

---

[1] Paulet, *Le Fabricant des Étoffes de Soie*, 1779, Tome IX, p. 19.

[2] S. R. Garcia illustrates a number of eighteenth-century silks which he claims were woven in Valencia, although it is apparent that only someone who has studied Spanish silks in great numbers could hope to distinguish such materials from contemporary French silks.

[3] Illustrated in P. Artinano, *Catálogo de la Exposicion de Tejidos Españoles*, held under the auspices of the *Sociedad Español de Amigos del Arte* in Madrid, 1917, Pl. XLVII. The cope is inscribed '*Arte e Labore Severin de Medrano Toletani. Toleti anno Dni. 1714. Sede vacante*'.

[4] An excellent résumé appears in Vivi Sylwan and Agnes Geijer's *Siden och Brokader*, Stockholm, 1931. This is unfortunately written in Swedish and so is not readily accessible to most foreign scholars. Some impressive examples of Swedish silks are illustrated there (figs. 142–53). See also Ingegerd Henschen, *Svenska sidenvävnader från sjutton-hundratalet*, in the Journal of the Svensk Slöjdförening, XVII, 1921; and Sigurd Wallin, *Sidendroguet, En notis til 1700-talets svenska sidenfabrikation*, Stockholm, 1920. (This essay is included in *Bohag, Heminredning och Dräkt*, Stockholm, 1946, a book which contains a collection of articles by the same author.)

ably high standard in its products — as witness the fine furnishing-silk shown in Plate 116A. A small but enlightened circle at the Swedish Court, imbued with keen discrimination based on an unusually intimate and up-to-date knowledge of what was fashionable in France, guided Swedish taste during the eighteenth century. They brought in a host of excellent French artists and craftsmen, and ensured that a number of promising young Swedish artists were able to pursue their studies in France. One of the results of this policy was that the Palace at Stockholm can still boast some of the finest French or near-French art outside France, all collected at the time. Superb examples of French craftsmanship were imported throughout the century but a great deal more was produced on the spot in a faithful rendering of the contemporary French taste.

A Dutchman, Jakob van Utenhoven, had been granted the privilege to weave plain and figured silks in Stockholm already in 1649, but nothing seems to have come of this venture. In 1707, a certain Jonas Alströmer was sent on a tour to France, England, Holland and Germany to study foreign industries, and we find him being given permission to set up a workshop to weave silks in the Swedish capital in 1724. Several other silk-weaving enterprises were established there by Swedes during the next three decades or so.

More important was the establishment, in 1739, of a central authority named Manufakturkontoret which was created in order to encourage and supervise Swedish industrial enterprises. Under its aegis, a French silk-weaver called Peyron was invited to set up a silk-weaving business in Stockholm with rather special privileges in 1741. The best silks woven in Sweden during the eighteenth century came from Peyron's factory. It is also recorded that in 1743 a certain Lorenzo Massa, a Genoese damask-weaver, was enticed away from Tours, where only a short while before he had been brought in to help establish a factory for the weaving of damasks and velvets in the style of Genoa, but nothing is known of his activities in Sweden.[1]

The Manufacturkontor also sent a brilliant young Swedish artist named Jean Rehn to France in 1745 (he had already been on a study-tour to Paris in 1740) to study particularly the designing of silks and the processes involved in the making of 'lustrings', and also the calendering machines used for the 'watering' of silks.[2] It is not known exactly where he learnt the art of silk-design but it is clear that he learnt the business most successfully, because the silks designed by Rehn are all decorated with very satisfactory patterns, excellently suited to their medium. Three years later, another Swede, Anders Odel, was sent to France with similar instructions to those given to Rehn. He is said to have studied under the French designer Ringuet, presumably the famous Lyonnais designer Jean Ringuet, who is mentioned by Joubert de l'Hiberderie in his *Dessinateur pour les*

[1] Bossebœuf, *op. cit.* (see Note 2, p. 37, above), p. 367.
[2] See Gösta Malmborg, *J. E. Rehn's Första Verksamhetsår vid Manufakturkontoret*, in *Fataburen*, 1927.

Fabriques d'étoffes . . . de soie,[1] or his son, Jean-Pierre Ringuet, who also became a famous designer (see Plates 58B and 99A).[2] The important part played by Rehn in the early history of the Swedish silk industry is generally recognized but little is known of what Odel's contribution may have been. He was apparently a less competent designer than Rehn and seems to have been later relegated to the technical supervision of the lustring factory which had by then been set up in Stockholm.

Apart from Peyron's comparatively small business — it was chiefly, if not entirely, concerned with commissions for the Court — an important enterprise was that which in 1760 came under the direction of J. A. Meurman and survived, under different management, right into the 1780's. Figured silks of quite high quality were made at this factory which was also situated in Stockholm. There were in all some 900 looms at work in the Swedish capital during the 1750's and early 1760's, when the industry was at its most flourishing. The decline set in with a change in the Government that came about in 1765, in which year only 458 looms were active. This number had fallen to 221 by 1767 and thereafter the Swedish silk industry ceased to be of any importance. For a short while, however, several of the factories — notably Peyron's and Meurman's — had been producing silks of a remarkably high standard, as is shown by surviving examples in the Palace of Stockholm, in the archives of the Kommerciekollegium (Board of Trade), and in the Berch Collection at the Nordiska Museum. The production was never great and all along, Sweden found it necessary to import foreign silks as well. Both French and English silks were sold in Stockholm, and probably mostly reached Sweden through Hamburg (e.g. see Plates 88B and 92A).

Successful attempts were made to cultivate silk-worms in Sweden, unbelievable as this may seem. Queen Louisa Ulrica, a sister of Frederick the Great, was personally interested in this undertaking and silk-worms were raised in the charming group of houses known as Kanton — note the *chinoiserie* of this name — in the grounds of Drottningholm Castle, outside Stockholm. The silk shown in Plate 96A was woven with some of this locally produced silk.

Denmark

In 1619 some Dutchmen were called in to set up a silk-weaving establishment in Copenhagen, under royal patronage. The enterprise was short-lived and of no great consequence. It closed in 1627.[3]

---

[1] See Note 1, p. 42.

[2] Erik Hörnström, *Anders Odel,* Uppsala, 1943, especially Chapter 7. (I am very grateful to my colleague, Robert Charleston, for drawing my attention to this monograph on Odel.) Jean Ringuet was still alive in the 1750's. His son Jean-Pierre Ringuet was born in 1728 and died *c.* 1771.

[3] Sylwan and Geijer, *op. cit.,* give a short survey of the history of the Danish silk industry. Two products of this early factory are illustrated.

A new workshop was set up in the 1680's but this too soon closed down. This was also under royal patronage, and the Court Architect, Lambert van Haven, composed a number of designs for it (see Plate 25 A). These designs are not especially good but they adhere more or less to the prevailing taste in the design of fashionable silks.[1]

Yet another attempt was made to establish silk-weaving in Copenhagen, this time in 1735, and several businesses were at work there, all rather fitfully, by the middle of the eighteenth century. There are said to have been 938 people involved in silk-weaving in the city in 1763. A settee at Rosenborg Castle, Copenhagen, covered with a silk furnishing material that is decorated with the cipher of King Christian VI (1730–46) demonstrates that the Copenhagen weavers were capable of making silks with large patterns during the second quarter of the eighteenth century, but the output of such materials can never have been large.[2] The industry began to decline in the 1770's.

Germany

Narrow-goods, notably silk ribbons and borders with devices and small patterns suitable for trimming vestments, were made at Cologne during the fourteenth and fifteenth centuries and it seems likely that the weaving of silk narrow-goods continued to be practised in the Rhineland during the succeeding centuries. An important new phase in the history of this industry opened in the 1720's with the establishment by members of the von der Leyen family of a factory for the weaving of silk and velvet ribbons at Krefeld.[3] Apparently the von der Leyens also soon began to weave damasks and other figured silks, but probably never on a very large scale. By 1767 they claimed to have 'studied and copied the Dutch silk industry, to the extent that our production by far excels and has nearly ruined theirs'.[4] Four-fifths of their output was exported. The factory was so highly prized by Frederick the Great of Prussia that, in 1763, he exempted the city of Krefeld from paying taxes and having to provide recruits for the Prussian army! Furthermore, Krefeld was declared not subject to the regulations issued in 1766 to the

[1] Lambert van Haven's designs and the Copenhagen silk factory of the 1680's are discussed by Sigrid Flamand Christensen, in *Kongedragterne fra 17 og 18 Aarhundrede*, Copenhagen, 1940, pp. 126–31.

[2] Rosenborg Castle, No. 12–122. Another furnishing silk which must also be Danish and which bears the monogram of Anne Sophie Reventlow, consort of King Frederik IV from 1721 until his death in 1730, is in the Kunstindustri-museum, Copenhagen (No. B. 18/1922). This information was kindly communicated to me by Mrs. Vibeke Woldbye of the same Museum, who has also shown me some very interesting photographs of certain samples of Danish silks from the 1760's which she intends to publish. Most of them were materials with rather simple decoration but several samples must have come from silks with quite large and complex patterns.

[3] The von der Leyens introduced the so-called Dutch loom into Germany. On this could be woven up to forty ribbons at a time with only one operator. Wherever in Europe this loom was introduced, there was always at first a vigorous outcry from the established ribbon-weavers who saw their livelihood threatened by this labour-saving device. Its introduction into Germany came comparatively late.

[4] See *C.I.B.A. Review*, No. 83, 1950, which is devoted almost entirely to the silk industry at Krefeld, now the chief centre of silk-weaving in Germany. The information given here about the Krefeld industry was mostly obtained from that source.

other centres of silk-weaving in Prussia and her dominions, since she had proved eminently capable of working without them.

By the 1790's, all kinds of silks including figured materials, were being made at Krefeld. One gets the impression, however, that only rather modest figured silks were made there earlier in the century, and Krefeld can hardly have been an important centre of production for the kinds of material that concern us here.

If the Krefeld industry may be regarded as an offshoot of the Dutch textile industry, so may that at Hamburg which was active in the seventeenth century. Many Dutch weavers had settled there and were making tapestries, woollen velvets and other woollen and linen materials. Such silks as were woven in Hamburg were probably decorated with rather insignificant patterns, if any. A large part of the production is likely to have been of half-silks, silk-and-linen or silk-and-wool mixtures — which usually had patterns of a somewhat conservative nature. Hamburg was an important entrepôt centre for the silk trade with Northern Europe, as well.

German authorities list a number of places in different parts of their country where, they claim, silks were woven during the eighteenth century — Elberfeld, Göttingen, Hanover, Berlin, Stettin, Eisenach, Kassel, Hanau, Schwabach, Halle, Magdeburg, Munich and Stuttgart.[1] These claims are no doubt correct, but it seems unlikely that figured silks were woven in quantity at any of these places, with the important exception of Berlin. To this list should probably be added, for the record, Mannheim, Leipzig, Maitzschen and Torgau.[2]

Large numbers of the Huguenot refugees who left France during the last third of the seventeenth century settled in the Protestant states of Germany and many of them took up work in the textile industries. All the same, none of the centres of silk-weaving except Krefeld managed to gain a position of any prominence until the middle of the eighteenth century, when the Berlin and Potsdam silk industries suddenly came to the fore, due to the energetic steps taken by Frederick the Great to encourage and increase its output.[3] Already in 1740, proposals had been adopted which established the then quite small Prussian silk industry on a sound footing, but the outbreak of the Silesian

[1] See R. Jaques, *Deutsche Textilkunst*, Krefeld, 1953, p. 268, and H. Schmidt, *Alte Seidenstoffen*, Brunswick, 1958, p. 404 *et seq*. These two books are the most readily accessible works that deal with the history of the German silk industry in general.

[2] Paulet, *Le Fabricant des Étoffes de Soie*, 1779, Tome IX, p. 19, mentions that a Frenchman had set up a silk-weaving establishment at Mannheim 'nine years ago'. Concerning Leipzig, Maitzschen and Torgau, my information comes from Dr. Heiland of the Museum der Bildenden Künste, Leipzig. In that collection is a portrait by Ismael Mengs of Johann Christian Raabe, director of the principal Saxon silk-weaving business which apparently had factories at these three places. The figured silks (damasks?) which can be seen tumbled in the background of the painting seem to be decorated in a style that would have been fashionable in about the 1730's.

[3] It is worth noting that Savary, in the Supplement to his *Dictionnaire de Commerce*, which appeared in 1730, only states that silk ribbons were made in Berlin; he does not mention broad silks. Even Beawes' *Guide to all Men of Business* (1754) does not mention silk as a German manufacture at all.

War prevented these from bearing fruit until about 1750 when peace and prosperity returned.[1]

Weavers were called in from Lyons, Tours, Italy, Austria and Saxony,[2] and regulations governing the qualities and widths of the various classes of material were drawn up. Bounties were offered on exported silks, and a bonus was paid for every loom kept in operation. In 1756 the importation of foreign silks into Prussia was forbidden in order to protect the indigenous industry, and at this juncture it was claimed that all the kinds of silk that had previously been imported could now be made in Berlin. In that year, there were 1,050 looms working in the city. The Berlin industry increased in a remarkable manner during the later decades of the century, and silks became an important item on the list of Prussian exports. In 1766, there were 1,450 looms there, and in 1780, 3,852. Berlin prospered, especially when the French silk industry was to a great extent paralysed by the French Revolution. There were 6,061 looms operating there in 1796.

A number of silk damasks and single-coloured materials like that illustrated in Plate 87A are often attributed to German looms, although evidence to support such attributions is never given. It is very probable, however, that most of the figured silks produced in Germany during the eighteenth century were of this general class. More ambitious designs were woven in the second half of the century at Berlin, on the other hand, as the specimen reproduced on Plate 119B shows. With this example in mind, it is safe to infer that German silk-designers, like their counterparts in other countries, relied principally on French patterns for their inspiration.[3]

Austria

Some French and Italian weavers were invited to Vienna in the 1660's to help establish a silk-weaving factory.[4] From small beginnings the industry very slowly increased in size and by 1710 there were between twenty-five and thirty master-weavers in the city —

[1] Schmidt, *op. cit.*, deals rather fully with the Prussian silk industry. Further information may be obtained from the following articles: G. Schmoller, *Die preussische Seidenindustrie im 18. Jahrhundert*, which was published as a *beilage* to the *Allgemeine Zeitung* in 1892, Nos. 117 and 120; and J. H. Schmidt, *Zwei Seidentapeten von Ph. de Lasalle und die Berliner Seidenmanufaktur*, in *Berliner Museen*, LVI, 1935, pp. 26–32.

[2] Paulet, *op. cit.*, Tome IX, p. 19, says that '*Le Sieur T . . . , un des plus habiles ouvriers de Lyons, a établi & conduit à Berlin, où l'on n'avait pas la moindre connaissance de la soie, plus de mille métiers*'. In the Archives Départementales at Tours is a list (C.103) of weavers who had left Tours about the year 1748. Of some it was said that '*on le croit passé en Prusse*'. Schmoller, *op. cit.*, mentions a number of important firms in Berlin owned by people of French birth or descent.

[3] Germany was an important market for French silks, as is well known, but it is not always realized that large quantities of English silks, including figured materials, were exported to Northern Germany and especially Prussia. The London Weavers' Company (Court Minutes, March, 1750: Guildhall Library) became very alarmed when the Prussian authorities first tried to prohibit the importation — already then considerable — of foreign silks into the Prussian territories; and several important London weavers, giving evidence before the Select Committee of the House of Commons which was investigating the state of the English silk industry in 1766, claimed that they had sent great quantities of silks to Berlin before the prohibition came into force (see House of Commons Journals, 1766, Report, p. 727).

[4] See M. Dreger, *Beginn und Blüte der Wiener Seidenweberei*, in *Kunst und Kunsthandwerk*, 1915.

sufficient to warrant the foundation of a Guild of Silk-Weavers. Towards the middle of the century the Empress Maria Theresa lent considerable support to the little industry, calling in three important Frenchmen who undertook to teach apprentices the art of weaving, issuing regulations concerning qualities and width of materials in 1751 and, in 1758, setting up a school of design — only two years after a similar school had been established at Lyons. At about this time she apparently also set a fashion in Austria for wearing only Viennese silks, which suggests that these were by then of a reasonably high quality. It is not known whether this fashion persisted, but records show that high-class French silks continued to be imported into Austria. This did not prevent the Viennese silk industry from flourishing throughout the second half of the eighteenth century. The revised edition of Savary's *Dictionnaire de Commerce*, which appeared in 1765, stated that silks of all kinds were by that time being made in the Austrian capital, and Paulet, writing in 1779, claimed that 2,500 looms were in operation there, many of them weaving rich silks. He added that thirty years previously there had only been 200 looms in the city. Apparently some of the designers at Vienna came from Lyons.[1] Viennese silks were exported to Poland and Russia.

Switzerland

Silk-weaving was carried on in Switzerland during the eighteenth century but the production consisted almost entirely of ribbons and other narrow goods. The chief centre of this industry was at Zürich.

In 1734 the Lyons Chamber of Commerce considered whether the '*petites étoffes de soie*' of Zürich might present any serious competition to that section of the silk industry at Lyons which was weaving a similar class of goods.[2] Some Huguenot weavers from Tours and Nîmes are said to have settled at Zürich. Figured silks were woven there on a small scale in the second half of the century.[3]

Russia

Silks were certainly woven in Russia during the eighteenth century but there are no indications that figured silks of any pretensions were manufactured there until late in the century.[4] Some samples of mid-eighteenth-century Russian silks may be seen in the Berch Collection, now in the Nordiska Museum, Stockholm. These have small patterns, and include velvets. Some are embellished with silver strip.

---

[1] Paulet, *op. cit.*, Tome IX, p. 19.

[2] This information was kindly supplied by my colleague, Miss Natalie Rothstein. (Archives, Lyons Chamber of Commerce, Letters No. 228, 1743.)

[3] See *C.I.B.A. Review*, No. 119, which is devoted to the Zürich silk industry.

[4] A little information and some illustrations will be found in T. Armand, *Ornamentatsiya tkani...*, Leningrad, 1931.

The Centres of Silk-Weaving

Poland

Silks were woven on a small scale in Poland during the eighteenth century.[1] As far as the richer class of materials is concerned, the Polish production seems to have been confined to the sashes woven by Polish noblemen. These are often finely woven in several colours and with much gold thread, but their patterns are always in a style derived from Persia and have no bearing on our present theme. The most famous factory weaving these sashes was that of Madzarski at Slucz (Slutsk) near Warsaw which was set up in 1758. Sashes were also woven at Cracow later on.

Summary of Section II of the Introduction

From what has been said in the foregoing passages about the various national industries, it will be seen that only a few countries possessed silk industries capable of producing in any quantity the type of large-patterned figured silks in which we are interested and that, of these, only the French and the Italian industries were able to do so throughout the period which concerns us — that is, from about 1640 until about 1770. At first, Italy was the principal producer of such silks, but yielded pride of place to France around the middle of the seventeenth century. Thereafter, France held the dominant position, while Italy came a close second, and only seriously lost ground in the eighteenth century. Spain, although still important during the first half of the seventeenth century, then ceased to be of any consequence until the middle of the eighteenth century when the Spanish silk industry staged a spectacular revival. England and Holland appeared on the scene late in the seventeenth century and the English industry assumed a position of real importance throughout the first half of the eighteenth century. The Dutch industry seems to have dwindled away in the middle of the eighteenth century but the English industry continued to be active right on into the nineteenth century although its health was by then far from perfect. The Spanish, German, Austrian and Swedish silk industries all entered the field during the middle of the eighteenth century. Of these, the Swedish soon fell away, but the others quickly gained strength and importance although the peak of their activities was only reached towards the end of our period, when the Rococo was fast losing its vigour and the renewed interest in Classical ornament was increasingly affecting decoration in every field of the applied arts. The new competitors, like their predecessors, failed to wrest from France her position as the chief manufacturer of fine woven silks in Europe. They too followed the successive fashions created in France, which is why the chief subject for study by those interested in the silks of the Baroque and Rococo periods is bound to be the French silk industry and its products.

[1] See Tadeusz Mankowski, *Polskie Tkaniny i Hafty, XVI–XVIII Wieku*, Wroclaw, 1954.

77

No excuse is therefore offered for the fact that the chief purpose of the present work is to try and establish what were the main stages in the development of French taste in this field, and decide when these stages began and how long they lasted.

III. Figured Silks — Their Sale and Their Use

The Silk-Mercers and their shops

During the seventeenth and eighteenth centuries, woven silk materials mostly reached the consumer through a special class of merchant known in England as silk-mercers. The mercers' shops usually lay in the centre of the larger cities; in London, for instance, they were mostly concentrated around Ludgate Hill, near St. Paul's Cathedral, conveniently accessible both from the City and from the West End and Westminster. Their Parisian counterparts could be found in the area around the Rue Betizi and the Rue de la Limace, which was bounded on the east by the Rue Saint Denis and on the north by the eastern end of the Rue Saint Honoré.

Their shops were often magnificent premises, in keeping with the splendid materials on sale at the counter.[1] Certain English mercers had shops with a rather dark yet imposing entrance hall. Beyond this cave-like approach one came to a well-lit gallery with a glass dome or skylight where the luxurious wares were displayed and where, in this somewhat dramatically staged lighting, they no doubt seemed even more splendid.

The mercers were often rich men. It required a substantial amount of capital to set up in business as a mercer in the first place, and for this reason many of the firms were partnerships. The English mercers would place orders for silks with the silk-weavers — orders often to the value of many thousands of pounds in a year. It was naturally of some concern to a mercer that the silks he ordered should sell well and he therefore took a particular interest, not only in the quality of the silks he bought, but in their designs. And as he often came into personal contact with those who bought his silks, the mercer usually had a shrewd idea of what his customers — both the leaders of fashion and those who merely followed — wanted, and it was on the basis of this knowledge that he placed his orders. Knowing the fashionable taste of the moment more intimately than most, he would often stipulate exactly the kind of patterns he required for the next season, and he would not hesitate to change passages in a design still on the drawing-board — usually to the intense irritation of the designer.[2] The English mercers also saw to it that a goodly

---

[1] The mercers only sold silk materials and the finest qualities of woollen stuffs. Other woollen materials, and printed cottons, etc., were obtained from drapers. No doubt all kinds of materials were sold under one roof in the smaller towns, however.

[2] 'Some weavers [or mercers, it is clear from the context], to shew their taste and judgment, will frequently cause a pattern-drawer to alter a good design, by taking out such and such flowers and leafs as they dislike, putting others in the

supply of fresh patterns were smuggled over regularly from France, so that imitations of the latest French styles could quickly be run off the looms in London.[1] The same thing was certainly being done by mercers elsewhere in Europe. Occasionally some of the wealthier English weavers would themselves produce a batch of silks at their own risk, but even then, it was usually to a silk-mercer that they sold these materials; apparently they rarely had shops of their own. Some of the great Lyons master-weavers (*maîtres fabricants*) on the other hand, did keep shops in their own city but, when they sent their wares to Paris, it was generally through the shops of the Parisian silk-mercers that their silks reached the public.

In France, the silk-designer was generally treated with much greater respect than his English counterpart, and he was in a much stronger position when it came to choosing suitable patterns for each season. As we have already noted, the Lyonnais designers were often directors of a weaving firm. When they went on their annual visit to Paris, they visited the shops of the Parisian mercers to find out what was currently in demand and to try to ascertain what would be wanted during the next year.[2] No doubt they listened carefully to what the mercers had to tell them, but they formed their own opinion as to what should be done and then went off and composed their patterns for the next season as artists in their own right. The best French designers were qualified, and in a position, to have the final word themselves. Unlike their English rivals, they did not have to bow to the whims of a mercer who, while he might appreciate a good pattern, would be unlikely to have more than the sketchiest idea of the intricacies of silk-design.

The people who patronized the shops of the great mercers were almost all members of the upper classes — royalty, members of the aristocracy and the higher clergy, the most prosperous merchants and men of business, and, of course, the members of the fashionable set together with its hangers-on. The mercers' customers had one thing in common — they were all willing to pay a lot of money for their best clothes. On the other hand, not all of them were prepared to lavish money in the same way on the upholstery and hangings in their houses. Many a lady whose wardrobe contained three or four fine silk

room of them, and by that means murder the design, and make it deformed, without any coherence, taste or humour with which the pattern-drawer is obliged to conform, if he values his custom.' (G. Smith, *The Laboratory, or School of Arts*, London, 1756 edition, essay on the designing of flowered silks, p. 38.)

[1] Both designs (drawings) and patterns (samples) were brought over from France (see, for example, the notes on Plates 69A, 73B and 79B). In the middle of the eighteenth century, a 50 per cent duty was payable on French silks imported into England, so it is not surprising that a great deal of smuggling took place. The London mercers strongly opposed the proposed total prohibition on the importation of French silks (introduced in 1766); it was clear to them that this would make it impossible to pretend that smuggled silks had been imported legally. The mercers based their case primarily on the contention that prohibition would in no way help the English silk industry and, moreover, that it was essential to import French patterns in order to provide fresh inspiration for the English designers. One mercer insisted that 'the few French Silks which are now imported, are more for the Sake of Patterns, for the Improvement of our Manufacture, than any Profit arising thereby'; another said that 'Fancy Silks imported are for the Sake of Designs' (House of Commons Journals, Report, 1765, p. 211–12).

[2] See p. 18.

dresses would be quite content to have woollen hangings round her bed and on the walls, even in the best rooms. It was only the very rich who had silk furnishings at home.

The cost of silk materials

That the mercers' customers had to be well-to-do, is clear when we consider the cost of silk materials. Remembering that the raw silk had to come from distant parts of the world and that a weaver could only hope to weave about four yards a day of a plain material and a good deal less of a figured material (the richest and most complicated patterns might only proceed at the rate of a few inches a day) even when the working day was a good deal longer than anything we are used to now, it is not so surprising that the price of these luxury materials was considerable. A plain taffeta might only cost about 8/- a yard but a rich flowered silk brocaded with gold (embellishment with silver or silver-gilt thread increased the price greatly) might cost 70/- a yard and more, although a less richly worked figured silk could be had for under 20/-.[1] These are the prices of the period and in money which was worth very much more than it is today. No really valid scale for comparison of prices like these with their modern equivalents can be obtained, but it is worth remembering that a prosperous merchant's house might be valued at about £500 while a lady's silk dress could cost anything from about £10 to £60 and sometimes more. Among a consignment of smuggled French silks seized by the English Customs in 1765 were 'several dresses worth at least £50 each'. Figures such as these at any rate suffice to show that those who bought materials from the silk-mercers were in the main wealthy people who regarded the clothes they wore as symbols of their social standing. The splendid silk dresses that one sees in museums were therefore the equivalent of today's expensive fur coats, and the richly embroidered suits were more on a par — from the point of view of cost — with a smart car than with a well-tailored suit from Savile Row.

The cost of a dress in the seventeenth and eighteenth centuries lay almost entirely in the material; the charges of the 'mantua-maker' — the maker of *manteaux* — rarely amounted to more than £2 or £3 or so. The workmanship of the seamstresses was usually extremely crude. It was only towards the end of the eighteenth century that dressmakers began to pay greater attention to the finish of the clothes they produced. On the other hand, if a dress were decorated with embroidery by professional needleworkers, the quality and the cost tended to be high, even though the cost of the material on which the embroidery was executed would probably be comparatively low, because a plain, as

---

[1] The figures given here are based on information collected from many different sources. Miss Natalie Rothstein has observed that the prices of silk materials decreased gradually during the seventeenth and first half of the eighteenth century and then began to rise again. The decrease was probably brought about by greater efficiency and improved techniques of production, and by the increasing demand which enabled some of the cost to be spread over the larger number of pieces being produced.

opposed to figured, material was usually chosen for this purpose. The men, too, often wore embroidered suits for great occasions, and the cost of the richest of these was considerable. The Duke of Montague had a suit made for the wedding of the Prince of Wales in 1736, which was reputed to have cost about £400. This must have been decorated with very sumptuous needlework in which lavish use was no doubt made of gold thread, for even the most expensive silk or velvet could never have cost this much on its own.

Such clothes as these constituted a major item in the budget of even a wealthy family; they represent a much greater fraction of the total expenditure than would the purchase of a dress from, say, Balmain, Dior or Givenchy by a person in a similar financial position today. For the fashionable women of the period, the cost of dressing well must have been increased by the fact that it was the *patterns* on the luxury silks of the time that changed regularly and were the keynote of each successive fashion; the *cut* of the dresses altered only relatively slowly until quite late in the eighteenth century. It cannot, therefore, have been possible to alter a dress in order to bring it into line with the latest style, for the pattern on the silk would have given even the cleverest alterations away. To the discerning, a figured silk more than a couple of years old would have stood out as very *démodé* in any fashionable assembly. The men probably had rather an easier time in this respect because the materials of which even their finest clothes were made, were rarely decorated with large and clearly defined patterns. They mostly chose materials with quite small designs (e.g. Plate 98B) which could not so readily be varied in any marked way.

Furnishing silks

Few people could afford to have furnishing materials of silk, and even fewer could afford to change the furnishings of their houses often.[1] Fashion was therefore unable to play so insistent a part in this field as in that of the silk dress-materials, and the patterns on fine furnishing silks and velvets changed much less markedly than those on contemporary dress-materials. Silk furnishing materials were of course being woven all the time and new patterns were continually being brought out, but these tended to differ from their predecessors only in quite insignificant details and it cannot have been easy even for the initiated to tell one year's patterns from those of the year before.

Since they were so expensive, silk furnishing materials were only used in the finest rooms and on the finest furniture. Even in very splendid houses, upholstery was commonly carried out in a humbler material; many very respectable eighteenth century

---

[1] Some idea of the costs involved if one chose silk as a furnishing material can be obtained from the following, admittedly rather extreme, examples. The materials of the State Bed at Houghton, designed by William Kent in the 1730's, cost £1,219 3s. 11d. When George II ordered a bed for Hampton Court in 1725, the 573 yards of broad crimson damask at 28/– a yard, and the 179 yards of crimson taffeta at 11/– a yard came to a total of £934 4s. 3d. It is worth noting that the joiners' charges only amounted to £149 15s. 0d.

chairs were originally covered with a woollen velvet for instance, and very rarely with the kind of silk they now so often sport in the antique dealers' windows. The superb, figured Genoa velvets were the most expensive of all the silk furnishing materials in 'general' use, although small quantities of even more expensive silks were sometimes ordered for special occasions — like the rich gold and blue brocade costing £9 a yard which was used at the Coronation of Queen Anne in 1702. A plain Genoa velvet cost about 32/- a yard in 1719, unless it was crimson, in which case it cost some four shillings more. The next most expensive class was that of the silk damasks. These cost something between 15/- and 21/-, depending on the quality and date; again the crimson shade was rather more expensive. Taffeta was used for hangings round beds and for window curtains; this cost about 8/6 a yard. Less expensive were various half-silks (i.e. materials of silk mixed with wool or linen) many of which were suitable for upholstery. Slightly lower down the scale came the finest grades of woollen cloth and, during the latter part of the eighteenth century, the printed cottons; and finally there came the cheaper grades of woollen, linen and cotton materials.

Silks were used for wall-hangings, bed-hangings and bed-clothes, window-curtains and the covering of chairs. The only place where silk materials were not used was on the floor.

A marked change came over the furnishing of rooms in the great houses of Europe during the seventeenth century. Hitherto, furniture had mostly been of a simple kind and the textile furnishings of even the grandest rooms had been of an entirely temporary nature, although the textiles themselves were often very sumptuous. Hangings were rigged up in the corners of large rooms to form screens; apartments were curtained off with temporary drapes; tapestries and rich hangings were suspended round the walls of a room for some important occasion, only to be removed soon after and hung up somewhere else; splendid cloths and carpets were hung from the balcony to add to the gaiety of some procession in the streets, and material of one kind or another was sometimes hung in the window to exclude draughts or sunlight. Loose cushions were used on chairs and squabs were placed on benches and window-seats. There were few conventions, and nothing was formalized. The mounting and dismantling of all these temporary arrangements was the task of the 'upholder' and his assistants. But gradually the textile furnishings became more permanent, and the upholsterer's work changed character. By the beginning of the seventeenth century wall-hangings had become a fixture and were nailed to a framework or directly on to the walls, and the hangings round beds had increased in complexity. By the middle of the seventeenth century, fine chairs were fairly regularly being provided with padded seats and, soon after, with padded backs and arms as well. Window-curtains, although rare until well into the eighteenth century in England, became fashionable in Paris shortly after the middle of the seventeenth century.

Carpets were no longer used as table-covers but began to be used on the floor in increasing numbers, while carpeting materials of various kinds gradually became available. At the same time — the second half of the seventeenth century — increasing attention was paid to the interior decoration of houses in general, and complete schemes of decoration were conceived by architects (particularly those attached to the French Court) in which every detail in the furnishing of a room was considered and designed in relationship to the whole — a practice that was to become quite common in the eighteenth century. It resulted in the textile hangings of some of the grandest rooms being treated *en suite*, so that the bed-hangings were of the same material as the upholstery of the chairs and stools in the bedroom, for instance, while the window-curtains in the state-rooms were likely to be of the same stuff as that on the walls.

At this point one must resist the temptation to embark on a brief history of textile furnishings, since the subject lies well outside the scope of the present study which is, let it once more be said, to trace the development of fashionable taste in the art of silk-design during the Baroque and Rococo periods. This is the subject of the chapters that follow. How this development affected furnishing silks is discussed in the last chapter of all (p. 135).

CHAPTER I

The Silks of the Baroque Period
(About 1640–1700)

Two main types of pattern were popular during the first decades of the seventeenth century. Typical examples of these are shown in Diagrams A and B below.

It will be seen that the first kind, that shown in Diagram A, consists of a series of compartments that are symmetrical about their vertical axes and which contain a floral device of some sort. Patterns of this kind were evolved from the so-called 'pomegranate pattern' of the Renaissance — a pattern which must be familiar to everyone, for it is represented in innumerable paintings of the period (Diagram C). The 'pomegranate pattern' was fully developed by about 1450 and thereupon quickly assumed pride of place in the silk-designer's repertoire to the virtual exclusion of all other patterns. Its popularity lasted throughout the remainder of the fifteenth century and right through the sixteenth century as well. During this long period numerous variations on the same basic theme were produced. The motifs tended to become increasingly complicated during the sixteenth century (Diagram D) whereas in examples of this kind of pattern woven during the first half of the seventeenth century we find that some of the earlier monumentality has been lost while there has been a corresponding increase in delicacy (Diagram A).

The second kind of pattern in vogue during the first decades of the seventeenth century, the kind shown in Diagram B, consists of rows of closely spaced but isolated motifs, those in each row being made to lean alternately to the left and to the right. The motifs mainly take the form of sprigs and they are usually quite small. Small sprig-patterns of various kinds had of course been woven in earlier centuries but this particular formula only seems to have come into fashion towards the end of the sixteenth century.[1]

---

[1] The size of dress-material patterns at this period must to a large extent have been determined by the requirements of contemporary costume. Clothes during the second half of the sixteenth century were usually decorated with stripes formed by braid, piping or slashing so that the surfaces of bodices, doublets, capes and hose were divided into narrow vertical panels. Any large-scale pattern would have been disrupted by these close-set lines whereas a small pattern could fit between the lines and still be effective.

A (i)   About 1580–1620. Velvet with green and red pile on a cream-coloured ground.

A (ii)   About 1600–1620. Green, orange and white silk tissue.

A (iii)   About 1610–1630. Yellow damask

A (iv)   About 1630–1645. Green, yellow, red, mauve and silver-gilt on a white ground.

Note: These diagrams are intended only to convey the general arrangement of the patterns concerned. They are n

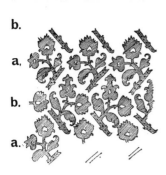

B (i)   About 1580–1610. Velvet with purple pile on a yellow ground enriched with gilt strip.

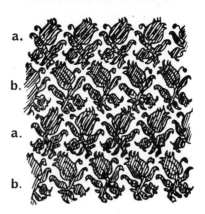

B (ii)   About 1600–1625. Velvet with red pile on a yellow ground enriched with gilt strip.

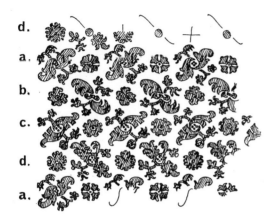

B (iii)   About 1615–1625. Silver thread on a yellow satin ground.

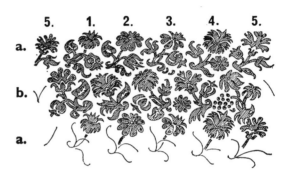

B (iv)   About 1615–1635. Green damask.

C   Mid-15th century velvet.

D   About 1520–1540. Velvet with red pile on a white ground.

urate drawings although the groups of patterns in Diagrams A and B are each drawn approximately to the same scale.

It became extremely common after the turn of the century and its popularity lasted for several decades.

Patterns that are symmetrical tend to look more formal than those which are asymmetrical. This probably explains why the symmetrical formula (Diagrams C, D and A) found especial favour during the Renaissance, when measured, articulate rhythms were so greatly admired, and why, in this field of art, the less stable patterns of the asymmetrical formula (Diagram B) became increasingly popular as the confident spirit of the Renaissance waned. The two very nearly contemporary portraits reproduced in Plate 2A and B serve to illustrate this point. The Bourbon princess wears a velvet with an upright symmetrical pattern. The formality even of this small-scale design will be apparent. By way of contrast the other portrait shows how very informal the small asymmetrical sprig-patterns must have appeared in use. The somewhat rigid arrangement of the motifs in rows that one sees so clearly when these patterns are laid out flat (as in Diagram B) tended to be disguised by the folds in the drapery when such materials were made up as dresses or suits.

The velvet worn by the princess is decorated with just another variant of the symmetrical patterns already described, but in this case it is as if the framing of the compartments has been eliminated leaving the central floral motifs to stand there on their own (compare, for instance, this pattern with that illustrated in Diagram Aiii). Such patterns were common during the first third of the seventeenth century. A later form is to be seen in Plate 3C which shows a cloak worn by the great Gustavus Adolphus who was killed in the year 1632. The feathery outline of the flowers in this design is noteworthy; this same feature, with the petals packed even closer, is found on a silk worn by King Frederick III of Denmark about 1640[1] which in turn helps us to date the two materials illustrated in Plate 4B and C. In all three, the various components of each flower are tightly packed together in a manner that finds an echo in the patterns being produced in lace at the same period (see for instance the collar of the man in the portrait reproduced in Plate 4A).

Two other articles of clothing that belonged to Gustavus Adolphus are shown in Plate 3A and B. They are of silks which are both decorated with the typical sprig-patterns already mentioned (see also Diagram B). By this time, considerable ingenuity was being devoted to making these small patterns seem less regular. Adjacent motifs in a row are no longer identical, and instead of two rows of motifs being repeated alternately up the length of the material, the repeat may sometimes only occur in every fourth row. The third and fourth pattern reproduced in Diagram B already have refinements of this kind but, at first glance, the difference between these two compositions and the first two shown in the same diagram is not very obvious. Even so, such subtleties tended to add variety and liveliness to this kind of pattern.

[1] See S. F. Christensen, *Kongedragterne*, Copenhagen, 1940, Pl. XLVIa.

We noted how patterns with 'tightly-packed flowers' were in fashion around 1640 in symmetrical compositions. They are also found in asymmetrical designs at the same time — for example, in the silk worn by the gentleman whose portrait, dated 1639, is reproduced in Plate 4A. A silk with a later and slightly less compact version of this type of pattern was made up into a suit for the Elector Johann Georg I of Saxony; this still survives.[1] There is a portrait of him wearing this or a very similar suit painted about 1647.

There is quite a different feeling about the two silks shown in Plate 6B and c which seem to be like that to be seen in the portrait reproduced in Plate 6A. The portrait is dated 1642. Here, once again, we have the typical sprig-pattern but the flowers are less formal than anything we have seen hitherto. The leaves and petals seem to be waving about; gone is much of the earlier stiffness.

A somewhat less happy design is that shown in Plate 5B, but here too it seems that an attempt has been made to get away from the repetitiveness and the rigidity of the old sprig-formula. It was perhaps woven during the 1630's; one feels that it must at any rate be earlier than the very pretty pattern illustrated in Plate 7B, which dates from about 1640. This is still basically a sprig-pattern with rows of small flowers leaning first one way and then the other, but much of the regularity of the formula has now at last been largely disguised by the intricate spiralling of the stems. It seems that spiral stems were fairly common in silk-patterns around the middle of the seventeenth century. The King of Denmark, for instance, had a fine suit made for him about 1645 of a richly brocaded silk with a spiral-stemmed pattern, and King Karl X of Sweden, a man who was rather particular about his clothes, selected several similar materials for some of his suits in the 1650's.[2] I have not found any silk-patterns with spiralling of stems that can be dated much before 1640 (perhaps the brocatelle illustrated in Plate 7A is an early example) although such patterns had appeared in embroidery already at the end of the preceding century,[3] and it would be strange if they had not also been adopted by the silk-weavers at about the same time. Perhaps some early examples will one day come to light.

Flowers with tightly packed components remained in favour for some time after the middle of the century. An example from the 1650's is shown in Plate 8A. The curious broken hatching of the motif is a feature commonly met with in silk-patterns from the third quarter of the seventeenth century. The same feature is found, for instance in the

[1] See the *Zeitschrift für Waffen und Kostümkunde*, Berlin, 1935–36, Vol. 5 (new series), fig. 6.
[2] Frederik III's suit is illustrated by S. F. Christensen, *op. cit.*, Pl. XIX, and another spiral pattern of the same period can be seen in Plate XLII of the same work. The suits of Karl X have not yet all been published. They are in the Livrustkammar, Stockholm. (See Gudrun Ekstrand, 1600-talets vita kröningsdräkter . . . , in *Livrustkammaren*, Vol. VIII, No. 10, 1960.)
[3] See, for instance, John Nevinson, *A Catalogue of English Domestic Embroidery of the 16th and 17th century*, Victoria and Albert Museum, London, 1938, Pls. XII, XVI, XVIII, LVI and LVII, all of which show embroideries with spiral patterns there attributed to the period 1590–1630. See also G. Wingfield Digby, *Elizabethan Embroidery*, London, 1963, in which a number of late sixteenth-century spiral-patterned embroideries are illustrated.

pattern of a silk which was found in the tomb of the Landgrave Wilhelm VI of Hesse, who died in 1663.[1] It may also be observed in the patterns illustrated in Plates 9 and 10.

The silk shown in Plate 8A illustrates another point as well. There was apparently a fashion at about this time — the 1660's — for wiry patterns. It will be seen how the scrolls in this design resemble the chased decoration on much contemporary metalwork. Something of the same character may be seen in the patterns illustrated in Plate 11B and C; and in the little striped silk in Plate 11A, which was made into a suit between 1665 and 1669; and also in the silk shown in Plate 15A which is said to have been 'part of King Charles 1st's train', although it is much more likely to have belonged to King Charles II of England who came to the throne in 1666. Stripes, incidentally, seem to have been in vogue at this period; attention has already been drawn to one example — another is illustrated in Plate 12B.

So far, no particular effort had been made to give a sense of depth to the patterns on silks. The patterns have been conceived as flat schemes of decoration, confined to a single plane coinciding with the surface of the material. Admittedly the spiralling stems of the silk illustrated in Plate 7B (which probably dates from about 1640) pass behind each other and give the composition a certain three-dimensional appearance but one gets the impression from the surviving material that it was not until after the middle of the century that more serious attempts were made to impart an appearance of depth to silk-patterns. Two methods came to be used. The first was to provide the pattern with what one may call a 'sub-pattern', which is a subsidiary pattern, of the same colour as the ground, that supports the main pattern. The sub-pattern always appears to be set on a plane that lies parallel to but behind that of the principal pattern, and it seems to thrust the main pattern forwards. A sub-pattern can thus lend depth to a composition. What is more, a skilful designer can, with the aid of a little perspective, make the elements from these two layers of pattern seem to swing backwards and forwards so as to mingle with each other. In this way it became possible to reproduce some of that rolling rhythm which was so characteristic of the Baroque idiom.

The difference made to a pattern by the addition of a sub-pattern may be appreciated if one compares the silk shown in Plate 9A with that shown in Plate 9B. Here we see two very similar compositions but one is set against a plain satin ground while the other has a sub-pattern. The pattern of the second silk (which is not as well designed as the other) has undeniably more depth to it. Another example is furnished by a comparison of the two symmetrical compositions shown in Plates 10B and 15B. The way the main pattern appears to be projected forward by the sub-pattern is particularly clearly demonstrated in this instance.

[1] See the *Zeitschrift für Waffen und Kostümkunde*, 1960, Heft 2, Lore Ritgen and Peter Thornton, *Die Gewänder aus der Gruft der Landgrafen von Hessen-Kassel*, fig. 13.

It has already been said that sub-patterns are always of the same colour as the ground. In fact they are usually produced by using a damask type of weave for the ground so that the two contrasting effects that go to make up a damask produce respectively the actual ground and the sub-pattern on it. To this can then be added the 'main' pattern which, at this period, is always brocaded and is usually executed in silver-gilt thread.[1] Silk damasks with details brocaded in silver-gilt thread had of course been woven for a long time. A fine Renaissance example, woven about 1500, is shown in Plate 1A. At that time it was the damask part of the pattern that played the important part — these were 'brocaded damasks'. Two further and later examples, both probably made during the first half of the seventeenth century, are shown in Plate 1B and C. In all these the damask pattern is still predominant; the gilt thread is merely an embellishment. But the whole idea of the 'sub-pattern' is the reverse of this; it is the embellishment which now becomes the main pattern while the damask assumes the lesser rôle of playing sub-pattern. Technically there is no difference between the old and the new forms of brocaded damask, but a comparison of the Renaissance example (Plate 1A) with the related composition shown in Plate 15B, which dates from about 1670, shows that there is a considerable difference in the way the two patterns have been conceived.

Not all silks with sub-patterns were brocaded damasks, however. A sub-pattern could also be produced by a flush effect — a pattern in the ground formed by short lengths of floating wefts. A silk with a self-coloured flush-effect is shown in Plate 5A. The flush-patterns in silks of this type, which seem to have been in fashion between about 1625 and 1660, were probably intended merely as yet another form of camouflage for the otherwise rather monotonous regularity of the traditional sprig-patterns. The silk-designers of the time must have noted that even these simple self-coloured patterns tended to thrust the main pattern forward, so that the flush-pattern in turn came to serve as a sub-pattern. If so, they must soon have realized that a sub-pattern produced with a damask ground was even more effective than the sort produced with a flush effect which anyway is only applicable to small areas of pattern, whereas a damask pattern is improved by a bold treatment. Flush effects were therefore rarely used in this forward-thrusting rôle after the end of the seventeenth century. They were much used, on the other hand, in the middle of the eighteenth century for creating secondary patterns that could play merrily about the main pattern (see p. 126). Sub-patterns became increasingly common as the seventeenth century came to a close and are an important feature of many silks woven during the eighteenth century.

This explanation of how the sub-patterned designs developed out of the well-

[1] Damask brocaded with silver-gilt thread was the original formula. Later, of course, instead of silver-gilt, the brocading could be in silver thread (e.g. Pl. 22b), or with coloured silks (e.g. Pl. 35b), or with a combination of all these (e.g. Pl. 48b).

established brocaded-damask formula has caused us to digress and we must return to consider the second method whereby the seventeenth century silk-designers produced an impression of depth. This was simply by making use of perspective. They were compelled to do this as soon as they wanted to reproduce the rolling, heaving forms of the Baroque idiom. Leaves were thus made to curl forward and under, flowers began to turn their heads to present a three-quarter view, and vases acquired substance so that they no longer seem flat and as if made of cardboard. Perspective was not used to any great extent in silk design until quite late in the seventeenth century but one begins to notice its limited use in silks already by about the middle of the century. A certain amount of perspective has, for instance, been put into the drawing of the pattern on the brocatelle shown in Plate 7A. The date of this material has not been established but it probably belongs to the years shortly before 1640. A more advanced use of perspective is to be seen in Plate 14B which shows a silk woven about 1670 or so; later examples may be seen in Plates 26A and 30A. Otherwise it is chiefly in furnishing silks that use is made of this technique. The reasons for this may be twofold. In the first place, the larger patterns of furnishing materials naturally offered greater scope for the employment of such artifices. And secondly, the chief producer of fine furnishing silks was Italy and Italy was also the home of the most ebullient form of Baroque. Further study may well show that perspective first makes its appearance in materials that are of Italian origin. Of course, the French also adopted the Baroque idiom, though in a somewhat subdued form, and, while they made furnishing materials after the Italian style, they seem to have been more concerned with dress materials at this stage.

It is no great exaggeration, then, to say that the seventeenth-century silk-patterns were essentially two dimensional, even though a certain amount of depth was given to some patterns by a limited use of perspective or by supporting the main pattern with a sub-pattern. All the same, the undulating rhythms of the Baroque are to be found unmistakably echoed in silk-patterns dating from the second half of the century, for even though the forms do not heave and roll very much, they do wave about and curl over. This wavy quality is to be seen in the little symmetrical damask pattern illustrated in Plate 11D, in the fine silk worn by the lady (is she the Duchesse de Mazarin?) in Plate 12A, and in the striped silk reproduced in Plate 12B. We do not know the date of the first of these examples but it was probably woven at much the same time as the other two, that is, in the 1650's or early 1660's. Two examples from the 1670's are provided by the rich silver material of the pair of breeches shown in Plate 16A, and by the samples from Haarlem (Plate 17A and B). The asymmetrical floral patterns at this stage sway from side to side, almost like waterweeds. But, for all the liveliness imparted to patterns by this date, it will be noticed that the motifs are still arranged in the same way as are those on silks produced during the early part of the century — in distinct rows, leaning first one way and then the other. A sequence of examples typical of each phase in this development may be seen by referring to Plates 2A, 7B, 9A, 10A, 16A and 21B.

Towards the end of the century a new kind of small-scale pattern makes its appearance. This consists of small flowers which are mostly brocaded in silver-gilt thread, often of two kinds. Sometimes a single colour is used sparingly to embellish the motifs. They usually have a sub-pattern. Three examples are shown in Plate 22A to c. They are often extraordinarily pretty. What is probably an early silk of this type — although it has no sub-pattern — is to be seen in Plate 19B, which shows a suit made for Sir Thomas Isham in 1681. There is another more complicated pattern of this sort on a hanging from the Pinkas Synagogue in Prague which bears the date 1687,[1] while two portraits (Plate 23A and B) dated respectively 1684 and 1690 show yet further examples. Two later specimens, both from Sweden, are illustrated in Plates 21A and 24B. Another group of silks, related to these charming little compositions, has rather similar but often slightly bigger floral motifs that are set in panels of various irregular lobed shapes (e.g. Plate 20A). A portrait of a lady wearing a silk of this kind is reproduced in Plate 20B. It is dated 1686.

Several of the patterns from the last decades of the seventeenth century illustrated here have striped grounds. It will be remembered that stripes were in fashion in the 1660's. They seem to have come into vogue again about 1690 and then again during the second decade of the eighteenth century.

The patterns of seventeenth-century figured silks were not as complicated as those of the eighteenth century but they were nevertheless the work of professional silk-designers. No professional silk-designs from the seventeenth century have survived, as far as I know, but there is a group of engravings and a group of water-colour sketches which, while not in themselves proper silk-designs, have some bearing on our subject and perhaps deserve to be mentioned here. The engravings are by a Parisian artist named Paul Androuet Ducerceau and consist of a series of motifs suitable for the decoration of silks (Plate 13A and B). They are not silk-designs in the true sense; but merely suggestions for the guidance of silk-designers. It seems probable that they were published about 1660.[2] The water-colours (Plate 25A), on the other hand, have more claim to be regarded as actual silk-designs although they are not the work of a professional silk-designer. They are the work of a certain Lambert van Haven and were almost certainly intended for the silk manufactory established in Copenhagen under royal patronage in the 1680's. The designs illustrated here are thought to date from about 1690; two of them bear the cipher of King Christian V who reigned from 1670 until 1699. Van Haven was really an architect who worked for the Danish Crown. These designs for silks must just have been one of many commissions executed by him in the service of his

---

[1] Illustrated in *The Jewish Museum, Prague. A Guide . . .* , Prague, 1948, fig. 27.
[2] See p. 103.

royal master. A competent master-weaver would probably have been able to translate the ideas presented in these simple sketches into patterns woven in silk. The sketches are not particularly ambitious and the arrangement of the sprigs would surely have struck a contemporary French silk-designer as somewhat old-fashioned by 1690 although he might have approved of the stripes which would have seemed quite up-to-date.

A number of silks from the 1690's are illustrated in the plates. Some of these are discussed in later chapters[1] but two of them should be mentioned here as they belong to the central seventeenth-century tradition in silk-design. The silk shown in Plate 27A appears to be a late version of the spiral-stemmed group (cf. the silks in Plates 16A and 21B). It has a highly developed sub-pattern and some of the details are perhaps sufficiently imaginative to allow one to regard this specimen as a presage of that taste for the fantastic which is discussed in the next chapter. In this composition there are some feathery leaves that are somewhat similar to those on the splendid silk worn by the effigy of the Duchess of Richmond in Westminster Abbey (Plate 27B). This lady, who is better known as *La Belle Stuart,* died in 1702, and since she was very much a lady of fashion, the dress chosen for her effigy is not likely to have been an old one.

[1] See Chapter II, ref. Pls. 28, 29, 30, 31 and 32; Chapter III, ref. Pl. 35; and Chapter IV, ref. Pls. 26 and 34.

CHAPTER II

The Bizarre Silks
(About 1695–1720)

Just before 1700 a new and extraordinary phase in the history of silk-design begins. It is usually known as the 'Bizarre Phase' because many of the patterns produced at this stage are so fantastic as to be virtually indescribable (e.g. Plates 37A and 42B). The high point of the Bizarre Phase was reached about 1705 and lasted until 1710 or so, although bizarre elements linger on in silk-patterns until as late as 1720.[1]

If one studies the patterns on silks woven during the last years of the seventeenth century, one will often discover motifs that are rather curious but in no way incongruous and which fit harmoniously into the otherwise typical decoration. For example the silk from Eskilstuna in Sweden (Plate 28A) at first sight looks very much like many other late seventeenth-century silks, with a pattern executed in two kinds of silver thread on a damask ground. But among the flowers, which are typical of their period, there are some strange ragged motifs. These are the precursors of true 'bizarre' forms. The wiry pattern of the silk at Oslo (Plate 28B) is also in itself not very strange, but the ground-pattern is full of curious shapes. Both these silks were probably woven around 1695, and certainly not later than 1700.

Plate 29A shows a silk composed in the typical seventeenth-century manner discussed in the previous chapter, with stylized blooms arranged in rows and leaning first one way

---

[1] The term 'Bizarre Silks' derives from the title of a book by Dr. Vilhelm Slomann — *Bizarre Designs in Silks* — published in Copenhagen in 1953. In this superbly illustrated work, Slomann first drew attention to this whole group of curious patterns which he thought, quite correctly, were produced 'about 1700'. In 1958, I wrote an article on 'The Bizarre Silks' in the *Burlington Magazine* (August 1958, pp. 265–70) in which I tried to distinguish between the various stages in the development of these patterns. I then believed they all belonged to the first three decades of the eighteenth century but this was not absolutely correct. In the first place, few silks that can be called 'bizarre', in the sense established by Slomann, can have been woven after 1720. Secondly, I then knew nothing about the earliest stage of the 'Bizarre Phase' which, as is demonstrated in the present chapter, had begun already before 1700. More light was thrown on the early 'bizarre' patterns by Dr. Agnes Geijer in an article entitled *Über die 'bizarren' Stoffe* which was included in the *Festschrift für Erich Meyer*, published in Hamburg in 1959 (pp. 206–11). It is largely due to the help given to me personally by Dr. Geijer that I have been able to carry the investigation several steps further, so that the whole development of these patterns at last seems reasonably clear. The dating of the 'bizarre silks' received attention again in an article by Baron Ludwig Döry-Jobahaza, *Zwei Kässeln der Frankfurter Domschatzes*, which appeared in the *Zeitschrift für Waffen und Kostümkunde*, 1962, Heft 1.

and then the other, with spiralling stems, and with a sub-pattern that echoes the main design. The fact that a silk with an almost identical design was presented to a church in Sweden in 1699 indicates that such patterns cannot have been produced much later than the mid-1690's. Sickle-shaped leaves like those in the sub-pattern of these two silks occur in other designs which probably all belong to the years around 1700. Two examples, both at Lyons, are shown in Plates 29B and 30A.[1] The second of these has quite marked 'bizarre' characteristics. From patterns such as this last example it is no very great step to compositions like that reproduced in Plate 30B which is an unmistakable 'Bizarre Silk' and probably dates from the first few years of the eighteenth century.[2]

Another example of what may be called the proto-bizarre stage is the splendid material from which King Frederik IV of Denmark had a set of night-clothes made in 1699 or 1700 (Plate 31A). Once again the arrangement of the motifs adheres to the seventeenth-century formula with rows of little flowers that lean alternately in one direction and then the other, but in this case the regularity of the formula has been largely obscured by the complexity of the odd serrated forms that cover most of the intervening space. The pattern is entirely worked in silver thread on a ribbed cream-coloured ground. Another all-silver pattern of about the same date is shown in Plate 31B. This is thought to have been worn by a Prussian princess at her wedding in 1700. If so, it shows that quite definitely 'bizarre' patterns were already being produced by the turn of the century. All the same, they are nothing like as strange as the patterns that were to be woven some five years later.

Some further examples of early Bizarre silks are shown in Plates 32 and 33; these were all woven about 1700 or just after. The brown and gold coat in the Castle Museum, Norwich, can be dated by the cut and must belong to the earliest years of the eighteenth century. The silk damask illustrated in Plate 32B probably comes from the furnishings of a house occupied by the Swedish royal family and is unlikely to have been made much after 1700. The odd pattern shown in the composite photograph reproduced in Plate 33A is that of the silk from which were made the cuffs of the waistcoat worn by the effigy of William III in Westminster Abbey. The King died in 1702 and the effigy was displayed at his funeral, so the silk should be of about that date, and indeed, this, like the two preceding examples, fits perfectly well into the picture we are now getting of the development of European silk-design at this period.

---

[1] Another fine silk belonging to the group with sickle-shaped leaves is illustrated by Slomann, *op. cit.*, Pl. XXIII.

[2] Both these silks, incidentally, have designs worked in silver-gilt thread with crimson silk details, on an off-white damask ground. There are many silks with this colour-scheme, all of high quality, in the various great collections of historic textiles. They seem to be related to the even larger group of silks with silver-gilt patterns on a dark grass-green damask ground, that usually have details worked in salmon-pink. Personally, I believe these silks were all woven at Lyons (there are many examples in the Musée Historique des Tissus at Lyons although their provenance is in no case known). As a whole, the silks in these two groups seem to range in date from about 1685 to about 1725. The patterns of course change with the fashion. It should be added that, according to Slomann (*op. cit.*, Pl. XXIV), the silk illustrated in Plate 30B came from a Spanish collection but this does of course not necessarily mean the silk is Spanish.

So far the patterns have been curious, perhaps, but not really fantastic. Now, shortly before 1705, the tempo accelerates and the designs quickly become increasingly abstract and extraordinary. Look at the whipping trails on the silk shown in Plate 33B; look at the incredible forms that appear on the red damask from Kårsta (a small town in Uppland, Sweden), which is dated 1704 (Plate 36A); look at the fine silk that forms the centre of the magnificent curtain presented by the High Rabbi Loeb Rosenberg to the Pinkas Synagogue in Prague in the year 1706 (Plate 36B).[1]

A notable feature of many silks made between about 1705 and 1710 is the way their patterns have a very long repeat; that is, there is a greater distance than usual between a given detail in the design and the point where that detail is repeated again, higher up the material. At this period, vertical repeats of up to three feet occur.[2] In some instances the extraordinary length of these repeats is accentuated by a curving stem or similar motif which is allowed to snake its way up the whole length of the repeat, as for instance in the silks illustrated in Plates 42A and 43B, but more often this feature is cleverly disguised (e.g. Plate 42B).

In Plate 37A we see the second earliest dated silk-design that exists, as far as I know. It was drawn in London in 1706 by James Leman who was then still a young man.[3] At that time he may well have lacked the competence as a designer that he was later to acquire, but there is no doubt that the design shows a typical composition of the period, and it will be seen that the pattern is very bizarre indeed. The silk illustrated in Plate 38B is made up as a dress which belonged to a young German princess who died late in the year 1705. There is some evidence which suggests that the dress was made for the lying-in-state. At any rate, it must have been fairly new when she was buried wearing the dress in January 1706. The dress came to light after the bombing of Kassel during the Second

[1] Many of the Bohemian and Moravian Jews were dealers in fine silks, and when one of them selected a material as a precious gift to his synagogue, one may be sure that he would have chosen the most splendid silk he could afford. It is also probable that he would have chosen one of the latest patterns to arrive from the great silk-weaving centres of the West. It is at any rate a fact that many of the superb materials illustrated by H. Volavkova in her most useful work on the *Synagogue Treasures of Bohemia and Moravia*, Prague, 1949 (several of which are illustrated in the present work), were clearly presented to the respective synagogues when they were quite new. For this reason, some of these silks, bearing, as they so often do, long inscriptions including the date of the gift, are important keys to the dating of eighteenth-century silk-patterns.

[2] There is no technical reason why a weaver should not weave a material with a longer repeat than usual but, in the case of complicated patterns like these, the longer the repeat, the more expensive the material would become. Weaving is a repetitive process and it is one of the textile-designer's tasks to take advantage of this fact. Normally there is no advantage in having an exceptionally long repeat in a dress-material because one does not usually see the full length of the pattern when the dress is made up. Towards the end of the seventeenth century, however, the fashionable woman's dress consisted of a long, slim gown. On such clothes a tall repeat would of course show to advantage. When women's dresses assumed the wider silhouette so typical of the eighteenth century, there was no longer any need for such extensive repeats. It is therefore probably no coincidence that very long repeats are almost all found connected with patterns produced between about 1690 and 1720.

[3] It is only the second earliest by a matter of weeks, in fact the earliest of all the surviving designs is dated August 31st 1706 and is also by James Leman (see p. 163).

World War, when the church containing the princess's tomb was destroyed. This silk, too, displays marked 'bizarre' features, and from now until about 1710 some quite extraordinary patterns were concocted (e.g. Plates 42 and 43).[1]

Judging from Leman's designs, which can be taken as giving a fairly accurate picture of contemporary silk-design, a new idiom makes its appearance in 1707 when small pavilions, archways, diagonal screens and balustrades take the place of the more purely abstract forms (Plate 37B). By 1708, this new style is already well developed (Plate 39B), and the well-known portrait by Ghislandi of Count Valetti (Plate 40B) shows him wearing a waistcoat of just such an 'archway' silk while his gown is of a more strictly 'bizarre' material. The portrait is usually dated about 1710; the silks would allow it to be a year or so earlier but certainly not much later.

Among the fantastic motifs of many Bizarre silks made from 1705 onwards may be seen numerous small, semi-naturalistic flowers (e.g. Plates 38B and 40A). These are discussed at greater length in the next chapter. They hardly ever appear on their own until after about 1715. At first they weave their way in and out of the abstract 'bizarre' forms but the latter begin to lose much of their barbaric vigour after 1710 and finally become mere supports on which the little semi-naturalistic flowers can grow (cf. Plates 47B and 48A). These same small flowers are also found in the 'archway' silks (they are clearly to be seen on Valetti's waistcoat). Plate 40A shows what is probably an English 'archway' silk in which the usual architectural motifs happen to have been replaced by pieces of furniture. All kinds of charming flowers can be seen in this composition, including a rose that has much in common with the rose in Leman's drawing from 1707 illustrated in Plate 37B and which also has affinities with the rather more naturalistic rose set among lush vegetation in the silk shown in Plate 41A. The last is not really a Bizarre silk at all but, for all its naturalism, it has a certain fantastic air about it and there can be little doubt that it belongs to the Bizarre Phase. This and several other silks decorated with similar giant blooms (e.g. the silk shown in Plate 41B), were probably all woven around 1710.

During the second decade of the eighteenth century the floral elements in silk-patterns tend to become more naturalistic than hitherto, and the silks with 'giant blooms' just mentioned are the precursors of the numerous charming silks decorated with semi-naturalistic flowers that are so typical of the period 1712 to 1720. In these, abstract ornamental motifs of a vaguely 'bizarre' nature are often still present (e.g. Plate 48A and B), in which case the bizarre forms will be executed in silver or gilt thread while the flowers are worked in coloured silks. At the same time a much richer class of material was being woven, chiefly for men's waistcoats but also occasionally for women's dresses and

---

[1] Further examples of 'ultra-bizarre' patterns are illustrated by Slomann, *op. cit.;* note especially Pls. IV, XI, XXXI and XXXII.

A. About 1712–14. Probably French

for vestments (e.g. Plates 49B and 51B) which are virtually entirely covered with brocaded silver and gilt thread and which have comparatively little brocading in coloured silks at all. The decoration of these rich silks is always of a more 'bizarre' form than is that of their lighter counterparts in which the brocading is chiefly executed with coloured silks. (If one compares, for instance, the two silks shown in Colour Plate B and Plate 51B, the difference between the two contemporary forms will be apparent.) One may liken the patterns of some of these rich late-Bizarre silks to a peep into some luxuriant tropical undergrowth (e.g. Plate 51A), and it would seem apt to label the whole group 'the luxuriant silks'.

An early version of the semi-naturalistic floral composition with 'bizarre' elements, which we have just discussed, is illustrated in Plate 45B. This shows an engraved design published about 1711 or 1712 by the well-known French architect and ornamentalist Daniel Marot.[1] Marot was not himself a silk-designer but he must have known all about the latest fashion in this field when he composed this design, for it is typical of the new formula that was only just then beginning to make its appearance. It is interesting to compare this with one of James Leman's designs of the same date (Plate 45A) in which the older, more abstract and less naturalistic idiom is still being employed. The green and gold silk of the magnificent wedding dress in the National Museum, Copenhagen, (Plate 46B) may at the same time be regarded as an early 'luxuriant' pattern, later versions of which are exemplified by the little Marquis of Normanby's coat (Plate 49A) and by the striking design shown in Plate 51A. These date respectively from 1714, 1715 and 1718. 'Luxuriant' patterns are well represented among the Leman's designs from the last years of the decade.

The 'luxuriant' silks, with their opulent decoration, represent the last manifestation of Baroque taste in the field of silk-design. They belong to an age in which splendour often counted for more than beauty. Henceforth the new trend was towards lighter patterns — and, indeed, towards lighter materials, as well, in which the aim was to charm, not to dazzle.

What made the silk-weavers of Europe turn out such extraordinary patterns as those of the Bizarre silks? The answer must, I think, be 'Fashion'. We saw how the Bizarre Phase started, not abruptly but developing out of what had gone before. We found rudimentary 'bizarre' features in certain silks woven late in the seventeenth century, and we noted how the movement quickly gathered momentum so that there is no mistaking the 'bizarre' character of many silks from the earliest years of the eighteenth century. And then we followed the development through to about 1710, when the patterns start to lose

---

[1] The design was published in Holland. Being a Protestant, Marot was forced to leave his native country and entered the service of the Prince of Orange who later became William III of England. He came to England several times but most of his work was done in Holland.

their vigour and their abstract quality until finally, about 1720, the 'bizarre' forms have become so tame that they no longer deserve the name. All this indicates that the Bizarre Phase was merely another stage in the development of silk-design in Europe, a phase in the history of European taste.[1]

All the same there is a very definite exotic element in the 'bizarre' patterns. In James Leman's designs from 1706 to 1712, for instance, one can find numerous motifs that are quite obviously inspired by Oriental forms of decoration. There are small Chinese pavilions and Chinese figures, there are what appear to be Japanese chrysanthemum patterns with fancy diapering, there are little temples, and there are decorative elements that seem to owe something to India, or Persia, or perhaps to Turkey. None of these is an exact reproduction of the original but there can be no doubt that Leman and his contemporaries borrowed from the, to them, still strange and exciting repertoire of Eastern art. It will be remembered that Oriental goods of all kinds had been pouring into Europe during the last third of the seventeenth century, so that there was, by 1700, no lack of examples of exotic art to inspire the silk-designers.

Among the piece-goods that were brought back in such quantity from the Orient by the several East India Companies[2] were many textiles; chiefly plain silks and damasks from China, light silks and cotton materials from India, and of course the much-admired Indian *chints* — painted and printed cottons decorated with bright and fanciful patterns. These *chints* captivated the, at that time, extremely receptive European imagination, with the result that it soon became fashionable to have these gay Indian cottons as furnishings about the house and to wear them as dressing-gowns and informal dresses.

---

[1] Slomann, *op. cit.*, claimed that the Bizarre Silks were made in India to the requirements of the East India Company. John Irwin, in a review of Slomann's book (*Burlington Magazine*, May 1955, pp. 153–54 and correspondence in the issue of the following October) pointed out that 'the silk piece-goods shipped to Europe in the late 17th century were of certain distinct and clearly defined types unrelated to the "bizarre" silks of his [Slomann's] thesis'. In my own article on these silks (see Note 1, p. 95), I produced further reasons for thinking the Bizarre Silks must be European. The best evidence of all, however, seems to be the sheer quantity of the surviving material which is technically indistinguishable from (and often stylistically linked with) the other classes of indubitably European silks being produced during the period covered by the Bizarre Phase. A large number of English silk-designs from the period have survived (many are reproduced here and in the article just referred to), many of which display quite distinct 'bizarre' characteristics. Although they are all English, there is every reason to believe that they reflect fairly accurately the contemporary fashion in French silk-design as well — indeed, one design is stated to be a copy of a French pattern (see Introduction, especially p. 23) and I firmly believe that many of the finest Bizarre Silks are in fact French. It is possible, however, that some of the most extreme examples were made elsewhere, perhaps in Italy where the designers were probably less inhibited than their French counterparts by the kind of classicizing tradition that pervaded French art and taste in general at this time. The fact that Daniel Marot's designs, two of which can be classed with the Bizarre Silks, were published in Holland, suggests that such patterns were also woven in Holland. Few if any 'Bizarre' patterns are likely to have been woven in Spain, for, as has been shown (p. 68), the Spanish silk industry was hardly in a position to weave silks of such high quality at this period (the Bizarre Silks are mostly of very high quality). Even so, 'bizarre' silks are often stated to be Spanish by writers on historic textiles.

[2] Operating in the seventeenth century were the Honourable East India Company, founded in 1600; the Dutch East India Company, founded in 1602; the French Compagnie des Indes, founded in 1604 (refounded in 1664); and the Danish East India Company, founded in 1614.

The European silk-weavers soon noted the way these exotic materials were sought by fashionable people and it is hardly surprising that the weavers quickly began to try and satisfy this craving for the strange and fantastic by producing equally strange and fantastic patterns themselves.[1] And once they had started, they must have found that such patterns sold well, whereupon they went further and ordered their designers to draw even more fantastic patterns. This, I think, is how the Bizarre silks came to be made. And, conversely, when people became more familiar with Oriental wares, the craving for the exotic diminished, and the demand for 'bizarre' patterns became correspondingly smaller until it finally dwindled right away. It should be noted, however, that a taste for 'chinoiseries', that is, for more strictly accurate imitations of Chinese decoration and Chinese subjects, recurs from time to time in the history of European silk-design, as we shall see.

The Bizarre silks may also reflect a more deep-seated need than a mere craving for the exotic. During the last years of the seventeenth century, at the very time when 'bizarre' elements were first beginning to appear on silks, there was a certain restlessness in French artistic circles, particularly in Paris and at Versailles. Reacting against the somewhat oppressive grandeur of the Baroque, a handful of artists with men like Claude Audran, Lassurance, Pierre Lepautre and Jean Berain in the forefront, started to search for a new and lighter form of expression. What finally emerged was *Le Style Régence* which, given a slight twist to send it whirling on its way, was in turn to become the Rococo. The atmosphere of restlessness and experiment which saw the genesis of the new style may easily have been inhaled by French silk-designers as well, for it will be remembered that these paid regular visits to Paris to discover what was new and they may have sensed that the rigid canon of taste which governed French Baroque art was beginning to weaken. They may then have returned home with the feeling that they could now allow themselves a measure of artistic licence. Is it not possible that the early Bizarre silks are not only an echo of a yearning for the exotic but are a reflection of that spirit of experimentation which is so fascinating a characteristic of early eighteenth-century art-history? Of course, once the Bizarre taste had become fashionable, such flights of fancy no longer required any licence and the silk-designers could then allow their imaginations free rein.

[1] It is pertinent here to note that many of the *chints* that were coming to Europe during the second half of the seventeenth century were decorated with patterns of a pseudo-Oriental nature composed in England specially for the East India Company and sent out to the Company's factories in India where they were manufactured and shipped to London (see John Irwin, 'Origins of the "Oriental Style" in English Decorative Art', *Burlington Magazine*, April, 1955, pp. 106–116). The finished materials were of course accepted as being completely Oriental by most Europeans. If this was the practice with regard to Indian cottons, it may be asked, could it not also have been the case with silks? In fact, could not the Bizarre Silks be Indian after all? This was Slomann's theory, as has been pointed out, but, in my own view, the reasons given in Note 1, p. 100, above and in the article there referred to (*Burlington Magazine*, August 1958) clearly rule out this possibility.

CHAPTER III

The Early Stages of Naturalism
(Up to about 1720)

We noticed how small flowers could often be found among the fantastic forms of the Bizarre patterns (e.g. Plates 38B and 46A). For lack of a better term, we called these flowers 'semi-naturalistic' — in contrast to the full-blown naturalism of the flowers that are introduced about 1730 (e.g. Plates 64A, 70A and Colour Plate C). It is these semi-naturalistic flowers and their predecessors that concern us now.

Flowers have been the mainstay of textile ornament since very early times. However, the flowers on Mediaeval and Renaissance silks were completely stylized, and it is not until towards the middle of the seventeenth century that a certain amount of naturalism begins to make its appearance. The pace quickens very considerably after 1700 and, from then on, the European silk-designer was to become increasingly preoccupied with the problem of making the flowers on his silks look natural.

In studying the early stages of naturalism in silk-design, one difficulty immediately presents itself, namely that there is a shortage of surviving examples because the greatest naturalism is found on silks where the flowers are rendered in colours — coloured silks, that is. It will not be found on the richer silks whose flowers are worked in silver or gilt thread, it being of course virtually impossible to make a silver or gold flower look really natural.[1] Unfortunately for our purpose it is usually the richer materials that have come down to us; they looked expensive so they were more often preserved. Not so their less splendid contemporaries, the silks decorated with patterns executed with coloured silks only. These did not look so expensive and they were usually less robust materials so that they easily suffered damage and became ragged. Furthermore, the Baroque, with its love of splendid effects, favoured the richer materials and one of the reasons that naturalism failed to make much headway until after 1700 is that the fashion was for materials sumptuously decorated with silver and gold. Pretty flowers were all very well but

[1] As the Lyonnais silk-designer, Joubert de l'Hiberderie, said, 'There are no subjects in Nature which may properly be interpreted in gold thread.' The actual phrase he used was *'présente aucun sujet à rendre en dorure'* (J. de l'Hiberderie, *Le Dessinateur pour les Fabriques d'etoffes d'or, d'argent et de soie*, Paris, 1764, p. 42).

splendour was what was called for! So the output of lighter silks decorated with gay and more or less natural flowers was probably comparatively limited until the Baroque taste began to wane. All the same, they *were* made, and in order to find out about the early phases of naturalism, we have to seek them out.

Whether such silks as those shown in Plate 6B and C are Italian or French we do not know but they represent early attempts to make the regimented flowers typical of the first half of the seventeenth century look less stiff and more natural. The outlines are supple and the colours are something like those of real flowers. The date of this kind of pattern can be established approximately by the portrait shown in Plate 6A, in which the lady wears what would seem to be a similar polychrome silk. The portrait is dated 1642. The charming silk with a black ground illustrated in Plate 7B is of about the same date. The flowers and the spiralling stalks are given a limited amount of modelling by clever juxtaposing of the colours; the stalks, for example, are rendered by parallel bands of green and white. All the same, the pattern adheres to the usual formula for small floral patterns at that period and even the involved spiralling of the stems cannot quite hide this.

It is difficult to give a date to the next example, the silk shown in Plate 13C. Once again the formula is the familiar one just mentioned but the greater complexity of the colour-scheme suggests a date after the middle of the century. There is a resemblance between the rose on this silk and that in the lower left-hand corner of the sheet of engraved flowers by Paul Androuet Ducerceau which is inscribed '*Bouquets propres pour les Estoffes de Tours*', that is, 'Flowers suitable for silks woven at Tours' (Plate 13A). Unfortunately we do not know when this engraving was published. Paul Androuet Ducerceau was an artist-decorator active in Paris from about 1660 until his death in 1710. He was not a silk-designer and this engraving, with its companion pieces (two of which are illustrated here) are not silk-designs but are merely suggestions for the floral decoration of silks that were to be woven at Tours — which was the leading French silk-weaving centre until quite late in the seventeenth century. Presumably Ducerceau was commissioned to execute these engravings; the question is, 'When?' My own feeling is that they belong to the 1660's. In the first place the way the stalks of each motif are curled up is typical of the stylized flowers on silks from the first half of the century and is not a feature one expects to find in silk patterns much after 1650 or so. Secondly, the '*fleurs arabesques*' on the other engraving by Ducerceau illustrated here are very like those stylized flowers we have seen on silks which apparently date from the 1660's (e.g. Plate 8B). Thirdly, the unmistakable naturalism of some of the flowers is of a kind that begins to appear about the middle of the century in various branches of the decorative arts. This naturalism owes much to Holland where a great deal of attention was being paid to flower-painting at this time. By the middle of the seventeenth century, all stiffness in the drawing of flowers — all traces of a botanical approach — had been overcome and one glorious compilation after another came from the easels of a host of brilliant painters.[1] The Dutch 'flower-piece' came to be admired throughout Europe and the influence of this naturalistic style was immense. In France, flowers in the Dutch manner were incorporated in what may be called the Court Style of decoration which was evolved by Charles Lebrun and his teams of assistants during the 1660's for the embellishment of the royal palaces. The same flowers appeared on the magnificent tapestries that were coming off the looms at the Gobelins workshops — an establishment that was also under Lebrun's direction. Is it possible that someone at Court, perhaps it was Colbert himself, commissioned the Parisian artist Ducerceau to produce some ideas for the silk-designers of Tours and that he was requested to draw not only a series of stylized flowers, *fleurs arabesques*, but also some of the new, more natural-looking flowers that were already to be seen on the walls and ceilings at Versailles, on the grand Gobelins tapestries, and on the superb carpets being made at the Savonnerie?[2]

Since this kind of naturalism must have been new to the silk-weavers and their designers, it may well have been difficult for them to interpret Ducerceau's naturalistic flowers in terms of what could be produced on a loom. They must almost certainly have modified his suggestions, because it is unlikely that they were by that time sufficiently mature artistically to imitate the model he had provided — the art of silk-design had not yet been placed upon such a high pedestal as it came to be in the eighteenth century — and because technical and commercial considerations must have set practical limits on what they were able to do. The result of their modifications of Ducerceau's proposals may have been silks like the one in question (Plate 13C).

In Plate 14B we see what seems to be a later stage in the development of this 'Tours' style. The colour-schemes of the two silks are identical and there can be little doubt that they have the same provenance. An attempt has been made in this second pattern to relax the motifs by twisting the flower's head round to a three-quarter view and by bringing down one of the leaves to help disguise the repeat. Unfortunately the result is not a happy one. This silk was probably being woven in the 1670's.

A Dutch linen-damask tablecloth dated 1658 provides our next example (Plate 14A). This is unusual in that the field is entirely decorated with flowers which are fairly

[1] The various stages in the history of the art of flower-painting are most admirably set out by Mr. Wilfred Blunt in his useful work on *The Art of Botanical Illustration*, London, 1950. A working knowledge of this subject is of considerable use to the student of textiles and particularly to the student of seventeenth- and eighteenth-century silks.

[2] Colbert, it will be remembered, was re-organizing the French silk industry in the 1660's (see p. 21). Great efforts were being made to raise the status of the industry, to improve the quality of its products, and to increase its output. It may well have been thought in the French capital that the silk-weavers were in need of a little assistance in the field of design. Perhaps they were thought to be somewhat lacking in imagination, in inventiveness. Why not get one of the promising young Parisian artists to compose a few specimen designs for them — something rather better than they could manage on their own, something in the new style?

naturalistic. Although the traditions of the linen-damask weavers were not identical to those of the silk-weavers, both used the draw-loom and the techniques involved were much the same. So this cloth perhaps gives some idea of the degree of naturalism one can expect to find on European silks of the same period.

We lack firm evidence from the next twenty years and then once again a clue is provided by Holland. This takes the form of some quite small samples of silks woven at Haarlem which are attached to a legal document drawn up in 1678 in connection with some dispute between the weavers and sellers of such silks (Plate 17A and B). The weaving of these is not outstanding, nor is the drawing very remarkable, but we can see how a more natural flow has been given to the compositions and that the floral motifs are no longer isolated from each other. The new trend, which becomes more obvious after 1700, was towards more closely integrated motifs forming much more complex patterns. No longer does one find the motifs kept quite separate from one another as they had been during the first half of the seventeenth century (see Diagram B and Plates 2 and 3). The new formula provided a much better basis for the growth of naturalistic flowers.

Unfortunately the next example (Plate 19A) is not a good one, for the silk is of poor design, but we can none the less see the way the pattern flows more freely and how it is made to fill the ground. The coat which is made of this silk dates from about 1680 or 1681.

A very flimsy silk of the sort that one rarely finds in collections of historic materials is shown in Plate 35A. If such materials were made in any quantity, their frailty has ensured that few have survived. From the still very regular disposition of the motifs one feels this silk still belongs to the seventeenth century, although the comparative naturalism of the flowers indicates a date somewhere near the end of the century. Well-drawn outlines and skilful use of the colours (tones would be a better word in this case, for the far from natural colours consist of dark brown, white and blue set against a light brown ground) make these flowers the most natural we have seen so far. It is clear from this example and those shown in Plate 22 that the silk-weavers were by this time — the last decade or so of the century — capable of producing extremely delicate outlines, even in cases where the pattern was entirely produced with metal thread.

The evidence presented so far in this Chapter has been rather unsatisfactory because we still know too little about the silks of the seventeenth century. Further research would undoubtedly provide more and perhaps better examples which would enable us to form a clearer picture of the early phases of naturalism in silk-patterns. Luckily we find ourselves on firmer ground from the 1690's onwards and then, after 1706, we have the dated English designs to guide us.

Plate 25B shows an engraving from a book of embroidery patterns published in Venice in 1694. There is nothing unusual about this design which is for a stomacher; numerous embroideries in this general style have survived. But this and similar engraved compositions were available to all — including silk-designers — by the end of the seventeenth century. In these patterns scrollwork and extremely naturalistic flowers are combined. Likewise, in designs for woven silks, it is usually in combination with formal or abstract elements that we find 'naturalistic' flowers.[1] This is especially so in the case of silks produced during the first decade or so of the next century (e.g. Plates 40A and 45B). An exception is illustrated in Plate 37B which shows an early design by James Leman, dated 1707. It consists solely of one elongated plant. Here the designer is obviously trying hard to produce a natural-looking flower. Although Leman was at this time a young man at the beginning of his career, it will be seen that this flower, drawn in 1707, is not very different from those on the magnificent silk robe shown in Plate 38B and that on the curious silk illustrated in Plate 41A, which respectively date from 1705 and (probably) from about 1710. The last example is one of a strange group of patterns decorated with similar giant blooms (another is shown in Plate 41B) which, as was pointed out in the previous chapter, seem to be another expression of the Bizarre taste that was current during the first dozen years of the century. The same silk, with its all-over pattern of semi-naturalistic foliage, may also be regarded as a forerunner of that whole group of charming silks decorated with closely spaced plants covered with small flowers that look like a close-up of a meadow in summer — so much so that we may perhaps be allowed to call them 'meadow silks'. These all belong to the second decade of the eighteenth century and the early years of the 1720's.[2] An English design for a rather simple version of this kind of pattern is shown in Plate 50B; it was almost certainly drawn in 1717. What seems to be very early examples of this kind of pattern are illustrated in Plates 35B and 38A. These precursors were probably woven before 1710.

The flowers on the 'meadow silks' are 'semi-naturalistic', that is, they are much more naturalistic than anything we know from the seventeenth century but there is still a long way to go before the full-blown naturalism of the 1730's is arrived at.

---

[1] It will be appreciated that the embroiderer with his needle is far less inhibited than the weaver at his loom, when it comes to interpreting any motif but more particularly a naturalistic one. It is much easier for the embroider to shade and model the motif, since his needle can move off in any direction, enabling him to produce curves with ease, and since he can change colours at will (providing he has a good range to hand). The weaver, on the other hand, is forced to interpret the motif in terms of what can be produced by threads crossing each other at right angles. Moreover, unless the silk is to be extremely expensive, there is also a severe limit to the number of different colours he can use. It is not surprising, therefore, that the rendering of naturalism in floral patterns — which it was the aim of both the embroiderers and the silk-weavers to achieve by 1680 or so — could be found in embroidery rather earlier than in the patterns on woven silks. The very limitations under which the weavers laboured, on the other hand, made their ultimate achievements in this direction even more remarkable (see Chapter V).

[2] Lady Lansdown, writing a letter from Paris in 1721, told her correspondent that 'there are very pretty silks come into fashion without gold or silver'. (*Correspondence of the Countess of Suffolk*, London, 1824, p. 84, letter of 5th December 1962). In 1721 a pretty silk without silver or silver-gilt thread would almost certainly have been of the 'meadow silk' variety with semi-naturalistic flowers. Most of the fashionable silk-patterns of the 1720's, on the other hand, were of a more formal kind (the so-called 'lace-patterns'; see Chapter IV) which one would be far less likely to call pretty.

B.   1715–20. French

These semi-naturalistic flowers are sometimes found on their own (as in the English design just mentioned) but more often they occur on numerous silks of the period mixed in various proportions with formal or abstract motifs, usually of a vaguely 'bizarre' character (e.g. Plates 48A and 50A). It will be remembered that this was also the period which saw the manufacture of the 'luxuriant' silks with their sumptuous 'late-bizarre', jungle-like foliage.[1] These were discussed in the previous chapter where it was suggested that they should be regarded as a last manifestation of the Baroque taste in the field of silk-design. In the same way, one may see the graceful 'meadow silks' with their little flowers as heralds of the Rococo and as one facet of that revolution in taste which was taking place in European art at this time, centering round the work of artists like Antoine Watteau, François-Antoine Vassé and Giles Oppenord. It is interesting to note how sensitive a barometer the art of silk-design was to the changes of taste in the very mainstream of European art at this stage, for although in the silk-patterns the change is in the spirit rather in the delineation, the change is none the less real for that.[2]

By a coincidence Watteau himself provides us with a good example of the international character of silk-design in the eighteenth century. Plate 52B shows a detail from a well-known painting by the master, and Plate 52A shows an English silk-design from the year 1718. It will be seen that the little girl in the painting wears a silk adorned with a pattern very like that of the design — scallop-edged stripes with small sprays of semi-naturalistic flowers. Stripes, incidentally were apparently quite common during the second decade or so of the eighteenth century. They are to be seen not only in these two examples but in Plates 48A and 54B and in a number of the surviving English designs.

Most of the silk-designs which have come down to us from the 1720's are for symmetrical patterns. These are dealt with in the next chapter. Naturalism does not thrive within such a formal structure but small advances were no doubt made throughout the decade. A design which gives some idea of the kind of naturalism prevailing about 1720 is reproduced in Plate 54A. This is for a symmetrical composition of massed semi-naturalistic flowers (in order to judge its final appearance as a silk, one has to imagine the

[1] Proof that the 'meadow silks' and the 'luxuriant' patterns were being made at the same time is to be found not only in the dated English silk-patterns in the Victoria and Albert Museum (see the Introduction Section I, especially Note 4, p. 19) but also in a superb set of vestments presented by the Emperor Charles VI (1711–42) to a church at Linz in Austria, presumably shortly before 1720. These vestments are made of two different materials, a most sumptuous 'luxuriant' silk and a charming silk covered with the semi-naturalistic flowers so typical of the 'meadow silks'. There is no reason to suppose that the vestments have been altered. (See Dora Heinz, *Der Paramentschatz der Stadtpfarrkirche in Linz*, Vienna, 1962, figs. 24–26.)

[2] If lightness was the keynote of the new patterns, so was it a characteristic of the silks themselves. A silk that has no silver or gilt thread in its make-up need not be very heavy. It is noteworthy that women's dresses began to get much larger — the skirts increased in diameter — during the second decade of the eighteenth century (cf. the dress illustrated in Pl. 46B with that in Pl. 59A) at the very time that fashionable silks were in general getting lighter in weight. Perhaps there was a connection between these two developments.

design repeated mirror-wise about the vertical axis, here represented by the left-hand edge of the drawing). Plate 60B shows much the same kind of pattern woven nine or ten years later. The advance is small but unmistakable. The great change in the naturalistic rendering of flowers on silks, however, took place about 1730. This important development is discussed in Chapter V.

CHAPTER IV

The 'Lace-pattern' Silks
(About 1685–1730)

So far we have followed the early development of naturalism in silk patterns up to about 1720, but before setting out to see what happened after that we must pause for a moment and consider the problem of the so-called 'lace-pattern' silks.

These have a pattern with a point repeat; that is, they are composed symmetrically about a vertical axis. Basically these patterns consist of a central floral motif surrounded by a frame of some diaper-pattern which often resembles lace or net — hence the name which has been given to the whole group.[1] Plates 34A and 57A show typical examples.

It will be seen that they range in date from about 1690 to about 1730, but it seems that this type of design was in particular favour during the 1690's and again in the 1720's.[2] During the two decades that intervened, lace-patterned silks were certainly produced when a formal effect was required but the very severity of these symmetrical compositions ran quite counter to the fashionable taste for fantasy and informality — the taste that produced the 'bizarre' silks and the early naturalistic patterns, for both of which a comber or asymmetrical repeat was more suitable.

The lace patterns were evolved from the typical compartmented patterns of the Renaissance, in a direct line through such designs as those shown in Diagrams C, D and A (in that order, see pp. 86–87) and in Plates 10B and 15B. The framing of the compartments

[1] Falke, in his great survey of silk-patterns, drew attention to this group which he described as being decorated with 'Spitzenornamentik' (O. v. Falke, *Kunstgeschichte der Seidenweberei*, Vol. II, p. 134, figs. 586–88). Students following the admirable lead set by this eminent authority have tended to use the term 'lace-pattern' as a result.

[2] Falke, *op. cit.*, was perfectly correct in assigning these silks to the late Baroque period and most historians and students of historic textiles have rightly accepted his general dating. In France, however, there has been a tendency to label all 'lace-patterns' as being in *Le Style Louis XIII* — that is, to place them in the early part of the seventeenth century when they in fact belong to the last decade or so of that century and the first third of the eighteenth century. It seems that this confusion originated with the publication by the Comte d'Hennezel of a book on *Claude Dangon*, a prominent Lyonnais weaver active early in the seventeenth century, in which he illustrated a number of 'lace-patterns' and claimed they were of that period (See Introduction II, Note 3, p. 38). This myth still persists in certain quarters in France. Let it once and for all be said that the 'lace-patterns' can correctly be labelled 'Style Louis XIV' in many cases but that most of the surviving examples date from the reign of Louis XV although, being late-Baroque in style rather than in the Rococo taste, they hardly qualify for what the French call the 'Style Louis Quinze'. By no reckoning can they be termed 'Style Louis XIII' however.

begins to become more complex after about 1650 (cf. Diagram A iv and Plate 18A) but the scale of the compartments is still sufficiently small to allow two repeats to be fitted in across the width of the material. It is not until quite late in the century that the scale is increased so that only a single repeat can be contained in a width (e.g. Plates 15B and 34A). The term 'lace-pattern' is normally only applied to these large-scale designs and not to their prototypes.

The dating of the true 'lace-pattern' silks is not at all easy because they tend to look rather alike. In general the earlier compositions are treated with greater boldness than those woven during the 1720's, but this is, of course, an over-simplification. Perhaps the surest guide is provided by the small flowers that are usually to be found ranged round the central motif. By applying our knowledge of the early development of naturalism — such as it is — we ought to be able to establish the approximate date of any given 'lace-pattern' silk woven between about 1690 and 1720, while for those produced during the 1720's we can refer to a number of surviving designs.[1] These show that there was a very marked increase in the degree of naturalism in the small flowers towards the end of the 1720's, even though the framing remained formal and lace-like. Thus, with the small flowers for guidance, we can hope to sort out the various stages. We get further help from a handful of datable silks which are useful for comparison.

Plate 26A shows the silk damask lining of a suit worn by King Frederik IV of Denmark for his betrothal in 1695. It was presumably a fashionable material at the time. The formal nature of the pattern shows clearly and this would have made the material very suitable for such a grand occasion. Notable is the tall, trumpet-like vase in the centre; this is a feature which occurs in a number of silks that can probably all be assigned to the late seventeenth century. Another bold design of about the same date is shown in Plate 34A.

Quite different in style is the silk illustrated in Plate 26B although it too should be classed as a 'lace-pattern'. The drawing of the design is rather poor (I believe it may be an English silk), but this does not disguise the delicacy of the pattern and the comparative naturalism of the flowers. Yet this silk ought to belong to the 1690's for it is used as a petticoat panel on the effigy of Queen Mary II in Westminster Abbey, and she died in 1694. Without other evidence one might have placed this silk perhaps a decade or so later, but the effigy can surely not have been given a new petticoat after a space of only a few years, and there seems therefore to be no doubt that the material really does belong to the early 1690's.

[1] The most important cache of designs for 'lace-pattern' silks of the 1720's is in the Bibliothèque Nationale, Paris (especially Vol. Lh.44); several of these are dated (see Pls. 58 and 60). There is a related group of the same kind in the Musée des Arts Décoratifs (Collection Martin and Collection Galais). A few undated French designs for lace-patterns of this same period are in the Museum of Fine Arts, Boston. Among the English silk-designs in the Victoria and Albert Museum are several 'lace-pattern' designs by James Leman (e.g. Pl. 53B), a handful by the important designer Christopher Baudouin (e.g. Pl. 55B), and a few early designs in this tradition by Anna Maria Garthwaite from the late 1720's.

At Ham House there is a magnificent toilet set which is thought to have been made for the wedding of Lionel, Lord Huntingtower, son of the 3rd Earl of Dysart, in 1706. The set comprises among other things a voluminous dressing-gown made of a superb silk with a light blue ground largely covered with silver thread (Plate 34B). Both the design and the weaving are of such high quality that one can be fairly certain this silk is French. Once again there are small flowers flanking the central motif and these display rather more naturalism than the earlier examples we have examined.

The material illustrated in Plate 53A is once again of quite a different character although it must still be grouped with the 'lace-patterns', for the composition adheres to the same general formula. It is a much lighter material than the previous example; it has a damask ground with small brocaded coloured flowers. This silk closely resembles a group of James Leman's designs from about 1719–20 and is certainly English. Plate 53B shows another of his designs from the same period (when a design is symmetrical it is of course only necessary to show half the pattern in the drawing, as in this example). Dated 1721 and obviously for a 'lace-pattern', this composition is very formal in character and makes a strange contrast with the drawing shown in the next plate (Plate 54A) which is also by James Leman and again of the same date. The latter is not a 'lace-pattern' in the strict sense because it lacks the 'lace' but the design is in fact for a symmetrical pattern with a rather formal floral motif in the centre (in the drawing, this occurs on the left) which is framed by branches that still form a kind of compartment round the central group. Yet the formality of the composition is almost completely masked by the wealth of foliage that tumbles from the branches. This design is really just as much an example of the 'luxuriant' style as it is of a lace pattern. Its importance from our point of view is that it heralds the new naturalism which is to become the key-note in the 'lace-patterns' of the 1720's.

What is almost certainly another example of Leman's work shows this growing naturalism in a rather curious and early guise (Plate 54B). This pattern has certain features in common with the three we have just discussed and can therefore probably be dated about 1721. The main component is superimposed on blue and white stripes which really play no part in the design. On either side of the main pattern the designer has placed some fairly natural roses and other small flowers. The result is not a happy one but this silk is one of the first links in the chain between the semi-naturalistic patterns of the second decade of the eighteenth century and the fully naturalistic designs of the fourth decade, that is of the 1730's. For these little flowers are of course related to those on the 'meadow' silks discussed in the preceding chapter.

The greater naturalism of the floral forms in the 'lace-patterns' of the 1720's is clearly to be seen even in silks like that shown in Plate 55A which relies for its effect entirely on silver thread set against a red damask ground. It makes an interesting comparison with the blue and silver silk at Ham House (Plate 34B) since the designer has been faced with much the same technical problems in both cases. It will be seen that the drawing of the natural forms in the red and silver example is much more delicate, one might even say fussy, than in the Ham House silk.

Plate 55B shows an English pattern by the Huguenot silk-designer Christopher Baudouin. It is dated 1725. This is still a formal composition but his sensitive pen has imparted considerable charm to the small flowers and vines that meander about the framing. A silk which looks as if it must have been woven between 1725 and 1730 is shown in Plate 57A. This is probably French and represents approximately the same phase as Baudouin's design. The photograph is interesting because it shows what this kind of pattern looked like when made up into a dress.

Two designs which presumably show the very last word in French fashion for the years 1726 and 1728 are shown in Plate 58A and B. The former is stated to be by '*Mr. Molon*' who is presumably identical with the famous Lyonnais designer Jean Monlong, while the latter is by '*Mr. Ringuet*' who must surely be Monlong's equally famous contemporary Jean Ringuet. Joubert[1] says of Monlong that he '*possedoit parfaitement la*

[1] Joubert de l'Hiberderie, in his *Le Dessinateur pour les Fabriques d'étoffes . . . de soie* (Paris, 1764, pp. x–xi) mentions five important Lyonnais silk-designers, namely Deschamps, Monlong, Ringuet, Courtois and Revel, in that order. As we shall see in the next Chapter, Revel's contribution to the history of silk-design was made early in the 1730's, so the other four designers were presumably active before that. We know nothing about Deschamps at the moment and we shall discuss the work of Courtois and Revel in the next Chapter. A certain amount of information is available in the Archives of the Lyons Silk industry (Municipal Library, Lyons) about both Monlong and Ringuet. In 1714 someone stole a design from Messrs. Louis Bron, Benoist Carre and Jean Monlong, obviously partners in a firm, and described as '*marchands*' which implies that they were important weavers, perhaps with a shop, capable of manufacturing silks for sale at their own risk (see Introduction Section III, p. 79). In 1715 the partners complained about a design by Monlong — specified as such — having been stolen, so we realize that he was both a partner and a designer. He was playing an important part in the affairs of the Lyons Weavers' Corporation by 1719 and, in 1720, we find him among the first signatories of a petition from the Corporation. Another signatory was a certain Philipe Emmanuel Barnier. In 1729 and 1731, the Consulat at Lyons recorded their gratitude to '*MM. Monlong et frères Barnier*' for some work they had done on *velours ciselés*. The surviving designs attributable to Monlong — the ones inscribed '*Mr. Molon*' — bear dates between 1725 and 1729 only (e.g. Pls. 58A and 60A) but he was still active in 1743 when he was appointed to a committee formed to consider the draft of the new Regulation which came to be issued the following year. He signed a supplication to the King in 1744, in this connection. (Archives, HH 130, 132 and 139; also Inventaire Chappe Vol. VII, especially p. 172). Dutillieu records that in 1751 a Monlong was a member of an exclusive club called *Le Zodiac* of which Dutillieu was also a member; so was a certain Barnier (see F. Breghot de Lut, *Le Livre de Raison de Jacques-Charles Dutillieu*, Lyons, 1886). A few designs by Ringuet have survived; these are also from the late 1720's (e.g. Pl. 58B). He should not be confused with his son, Jean Pierre Ringuet, who was born in 1728 and whose baptism was recorded on 30th February of that year when he was described as being the son of Jean Ringuet '*marchand et bourgeois de cette ville*' (Lyons Municipal Library, *Etats Civil*, Vol. 467, Baptisms). Ringuet was awarded premiums in 1726, 1727 and 1728 for work on a special type of velvet. When the second edition of Joubert's treatise on silk-design was published in 1764, Ringuet was still described as the '*ancien et fameux Dessinateur*' who was '*encore vivant*'; included in a letter of commendation from the old man, couched in the most modest terms (*op. cit.*, p. xxxix). By this time his son was also excelling in this field (see Pl. 99A). Joubert's statements and the few designs that have survived (all from the second half of the 1720's) that can safely be attributed to Monlong and Ringuet do not enable us actually to identify their individual styles or to decide for which kind of pattern they were famed. It is clear that Ringuet made his great contribution to the art of silk-design — by being the first to introduce 'natural' flowers into his compositions, as Joubert says — before 1730 when Courtois and Revel were already taking the final steps which led to the

composition de l'Étoffe qu'il traitoit noblement', and of Ringuet that he was an *'homme de beaucoup génie & grand Dessinateur'* who was the first to introduce *'les fleurs naturelles sur l'Étoffe'*. The boldness of Monlong's drawing is partly due to the fact that his design is for a silk which was to be almost entirely executed in two kinds of gilt thread. All the same, the flowers do seem to be somewhat larger and more important than was usual at this time. The lace-like passages of this example are confined to the ground which was to have a diaper pattern, as is indicated by the single little diamond-shaped panel sketched in at the top on the left, and by the phrase written across the drawing, *'la moisayque continuée'*. Ringuet's design is much more delicate.

These and many other dated designs prove that the 'lace-patterns' were still highly fashionable at the end of the 1720's (see the paintings reproduced in Plate 59A and B),[1] but

astonishing revolution in this art described in the next Chapter. It is curious that the design by Ringuet dated 1728 and illustrated in Plate 58B seems to have flowers which are not very naturalistic. Unless this design is in some way exceptional, one must assume that Ringuet made his contribution at the very end of the 1720's. Perhaps the silk shown in Plate 60B, which must be of about that date, is an example of his style at that crucial moment. It has something of the same fussy delineation that may be seen in his 1728 design (Pl. 58B). If Ringuet's contribution was made in the late 1720's, then Monlong's must have been made sometime before 1725, it would seem; and, since he was already a man of some consequence by 1714, it is even possible that the advance with which Joubert credits him may have taken place already in the second decade of the eighteenth century. The two principal types of pattern fashionable during the period in question (say, 1714–25) were the 'luxuriant' patterns and the 'meadow' silks which were discussed respectively in Chapters II and III. The former are magnificent but can hardly be regarded as an innovation, since they were developed in a straightforward manner out of the 'bizarre' patterns of the early eighteenth century. The 'meadow' silks, on the other hand, although they had precursors, *were* unmistakable examples of a new development and represent a definite step forward in the advance towards greater naturalism (and the implication of Joubert's statement about the contributions of the five designers could be that each was responsible for advances in this particular direction). Can it be that Monlong evolved the 'meadow-silk' patterns or, at least, was the designer responsible for the best of these charming materials? Whoever was responsible for their design certainly deserves to be remembered, as they must be classed among the finest products of the eighteenth-century silk-weaver's art. Yet, while it is tempting to link Monlong's name with the 'meadow' silks, it is only fair to recall that Joubert says that he treated his compositions *'noblement'*. Nobility is not a term one would normally use in connection with these charming patterns. It would be more apt if used in reference to the 'lace-patterns' which were in fashion throughout the 1720's. These were not in their essence an innovation, either, but the flowers in these patterns developed a marked degree of naturalism during that decade and it was perhaps in this *genre* that Monlong excelled. Certainly the few designs attributable to him have flowers that show a definite advance on those of the previous decade. Whether this reflects the general advance or in fact is a measure of Monlong's genius, is impossible to say. It should, however, be noted that there survives a sheet of sketches among the silk-designs in the Bibliothèque Nationale in Paris which are inscribed *'Fleurs de M. Molon, 1725'* (Cabinet des Estampes, Vol. Lh.44d). This rather suggests that he too was famed for his flowers (the drawing is a tracing of the kind that was apparently offered for sale in Paris, one imagines, a year or so after the patterns in question had ceased to be fashionable; see Joubert, *op. cit.*, p. 86). The flowers are not very special and mark, as one might expect, a halfway stage between the semi-naturalism and small scale of the flowers on the 'meadow silks' and the large naturalistic blooms of the 1730's. They seem to prove nothing and unfortunately leave the question as to exactly what Monlong's contribution may have been, and when it took place, still open.

[1] The two paintings which show fashionable people in Paris and Berlin in 1728–29. It is clear that 'lace-patterns' were also fashionable in England at the same time, for not only do designs for this kind of composition still survive but we have the word of that fascinating observer of the eighteenth-century fashionable scene, Mrs. Delany, for the fact. In March 1729 she wrote to a friend about a dress she had just had made of a French silk which had 'the ground dark grass green, brocaded with a running pattern like lace with white intermixed with festoons of flowers in faint colours'. The dress cost her £17 in all (Lady Llanover, *The Autobiography and Correspondence of Mary Granville, Mrs. Delany*, London, 1861, Vol. I, p. 198).

around 1730 the flowers assume so much importance there there is hardly any 'lace' left. Plate 60A shows another of Monlong's designs in which the lace-like elements have shrunk to a few narrow meanders while the flowers play a prominent part. This design bears the date 1729. The silk in Plate 60B shows this development carried a stage further. No 'lace' is now visible at all. Much the same stage is represented by the silk illustrated in Plate 62A. These probably both date from around 1730 or 1731. The naturalism of the flowers has now become so marked that one can no longer class such silks as 'lace-patterns — even for convenience — for they really form a transitional group bridging the gap between the formal 'lace-patterns' of the 1720's and the full-blown naturalistic designs of the 1730's. We shall follow this development in the next chapter, but before we do so there are three groups of silks related to the 'lace-patterns' which ought just to be mentioned.

Symmetry is the hall-mark of the true 'lace-pattern' but there exist a few silks which may be called 'asymmetrical lace-patterns'. These have the usual lace-like details but the forms are arranged with a comber repeat. Plate 44A shows an example which obviously belongs to the 'bizarre' phase. A slightly later type is seen in Plate 44B, while a close relation of the 'luxuriant' patterns of around 1718 or so is illustrated in Plate 56A. An even later example is provided by the design shown in Plate 56B which is inscribed 'nouveau de l'année 1725'. Such examples remind us that there are always awkward cases which do not quite fit into any of the neatly labelled groups one may try to make.

One should also, when considering the 'lace-patterns', glance at the furnishing silks which are nearly all symmetrical compositions (e.g. Plates 104B, 109A, 112B and 113A; see Chapter VII). While usually conceived on a rather larger scale and with greater boldness, many furnishing materials have features in common with their contemporaries among the 'lace-patterns'.

Another group of patterns related to the 'lace-patterns' but running a somewhat independent course of their own are here represented by the silks shown in Plates 62B and 77B. These may possibly be French silks made for some less discriminating public, perhaps for export. They are brightly coloured and there is a lack of subtlety about the handling of the colours. Brocading is used sparingly if at all, the colours of the pattern being in most cases produced solely by means of pattern-wefts. As was usual throughout the period, the colour of the pattern-wefts could be changed as the weaving progressed, in order to produce motifs of different colours. In the case of these rather gaudy silks, little trouble has been taken to disguise these changes, and the pattern-wefts tend to produce bands of each successive colour across the width of the material. The earliest example shown here (Plate 62B) has several features in common with the early 'lace-patterns' (cf. Plate 18A and B) while the later example illustrated in Plate 77B echoes a much later phase in the development of the fashionable silks.

One should perhaps add that a few 'lace-patterned' silks were still being woven on a small scale during the first half of the 1730's, probably for formal use. The suit worn by King Christian VI of Denmark at his coronation in 1731, for instance, was made of a silk with this kind of pattern (Plate 61B), and Plate 61C shows a sample in the Richelieu collection under the date 1736 which bears the unmistakable features of this now well-seasoned tradition. Fashion had by this time veered away from such formal compositions, however, as we shall see in the next chapter.

CHAPTER V

Naturalism Achieved
(The 1730's)

By far the most spectacular change that was to take place in silk-design during the whole of the eighteenth century occurred just after 1730 when an entirely new style was evolved consisting of great heavy flowers and fruit depicted in a completely naturalistic manner (e.g. Colour Plate C and Plate 70A). The credit for introducing this new naturalistic style can principally be claimed by Jean Revel, who was in his own time the most famous of all the great designers at Lyons.

We have followed the early budding of naturalism from the late seventeenth century and through to the 'meadow' silks of about 1715 or so, and we have seen how the flowers on the 'lace-pattern' silks of the later 1720's become increasingly naturalistic until they reach the stage typified by the two silks shown in Plates 60B and 61A. A further stage in this development is illustrated by the silk in Plate 62A which was probably woven in about 1731 or 1732.

There is no doubt that the chief preoccupation of the leading Lyonnais silk designers after 1730 was with the problem of how to make the patterns on their silks completely natural and life-like. Greater attention was now paid to the drawing of flowers and considerable thought was also devoted to the question of shading — all in order to give the forms a more natural appearance. A designer who is credited with great innovations in this direction was a certain Courtois about whom we otherwise know very little. Jacque-Charles Dutillieu, another Lyonnais designer, writing in the mid-eighteenth century, states that '*En 1730 un dessinateur de fabrique de Lyon, nommé Courtois voulut rompre avec la tradition qui représentait sur les étoffes les objets d'un seul ton ... [et] on n'avait obtenu que des formes plates dont un contour délicat faisait la seule grâce. Courtois, génie inventif, conçut une dégradation complète, c'est-à-dire qu'il mit le clair, puis une nuance moins claire et ainsi de suite jusqu'à la plus sombre, ce qui commença à donner un certain relief aux images tissées*'.[1] What Dutillieu says is confirmed by Joubert de l'Hiberderie

---

[1] F. Breghot du Lut, *Le Livre de Raison de Jacques-Charles Dutillieu*, published and annotated by F. B. du Lut, Lyons, 1886, p. 23. E. Leroudier, *Les Dessinateurs de la Fabrique Lyonnaise au XVIII siècle*, Lyons, 1908, p. 10, states that Courtois died in 1750.

C.   About 1735. French (Lyons)

whose treatise on the designing of silk-patterns was published in the middle of the century. He gives a list of the five Lyonnais designers who had done most to further the art of silk-design, and says that '*M. Courtois . . . à hazardé le premier de mettre plusieurs couleurs par degradation, & a poussé l'intelligence du clair-obscur & l'art de colorer l'Étoffe à un point étonnant*'.[1] Courtois had in fact developed a system of modelling which involved using not one shade of each colour but several shades placed alongside each other and graded from dark to light. When the three or four main colours in a motif were shaded in this way, the transition between each colour would become less obvious. By this method, three-dimensional forms could be represented with much greater subtlety. Shading of this kind has been used in the design shown in Plate 63A which is dated 1733, and the very similar silk shown in Plate 63B. It will be seen that the shading of the forms has been conceived rather like the contours on a map and for this reason we may as well call this system 'contour-shading'.[2]

The composition of such patterns may at first glance seem very different from that of the typical design from the late 1720's but the change is not really so great as it seems. The motifs themselves are not in fact so dissimilar from those in designs like that shown in Plate 62A — tree-like forms with rather large flowers and leaves. It is chiefly in the way the designs are repeated that the difference lies, for in general the compositions were now no longer symmetrical but asymmetrical. Asymmetrical designs were of course not new; they had been plentiful in the seventeenth century and also in the early eighteenth century, as we have already seen. On the other hand, during the 1720's, symmetry had been the key-note of fashionable silk-patterns. Now, in the 1730's, asymmetry once again came into favour and remained in vogue for the best part of half a century. It is not hard to find the reason for this change. Being bent on producing natural-looking flowers, the designers quickly realized that the asymmetrical formula (or comber repeat) offered a far more suitable framework for their compositions. Flowers after all rarely arrange themselves with rigid symmetry in Nature.

A study of the English silk-designer Anna Maria Garthwaite's designs from the early 1730's enables us to follow this whole transition quite easily. At first the designs are typical 'lace-patterns'. Then the flowers increase in size and importance while the 'lace' withers away. Finally the flowers are left suspended on their own although they still remain in the old symmetrical arrangement. Then, in 1733, Garthwaite switches over to the asymmetrical system; Plate 64B shows an example of her work in this new format.

---

[1] Joubert de l'Hiberderie, *Le Dessinateur pour les Fabriques d'étoffes d'or, d'argent et se soie*, Paris, 1764, p. xij. See p. 112 here, Note 1, where three of the five designers are discussed.

[2] When studying this silk, it should be noted that the small white leaves have been embroidered on the finished silk and are thus not part of the original design. It is possible that this pattern was composed by Courtois himself. It has the kind of shading described by Dutillieu and Joubert, it is of about the right date, and drawing is rather poor. Both Joubert and Dutillieu stated that Courtois, clever as he was, possessed only a limited talent as a draughtsman.

Such disconnected floral forms tended to look awkward as they often seemed to be floating about in the air, so the designers began to provide them with platforms from which to grow. Sometimes the platform resembled a piece of turf (e.g. Plate 65A) or a small island (e.g. Plate 63B). More ingenious versions of this rather crude device are shown in Plates 66B and 74A.

Asymmetry, then, is a notable difference between the typical patterns of the 1730's and those of the previous decade. At first the motifs remain much the same although their size begins to increase about 1730 — no doubt the designers wanted them bigger so that there was more room for the new systems of shading they were trying so hard to evolve.

The scene is now set for the entry of the man who was to revolutionize the whole art of designing silks — Jean Revel. His father was a painter who had worked for the great Lebrun at Versailles and who had moved first to Dijon and then to Lyons early in the century.[1] The son was born in 1684 and aimed also to become a painter. For some reason he seems to have given up painting as a profession and become involved with the Lyons silk industry. How this happened is not recorded, but one possibility is that he began to teach the principles of drawing and composition to prospective silk-designers and thus came in contact with this trade. It was not unusual for painters living, or merely staying for a while, in Lyons to take on pupils from the industry and, as the question of design became increasingly important to the Lyonnais silk-weavers, the demand for such instructors must have grown.[2] At some point, however, Revel must have decided to become a silk-designer himself. Nothing is known about this stage of his career but by about 1730 he had not only become a fully-fledged designer of silks but a man capable of introducing important innovations in this field.

The story is now taken up by a certain Abbé Pernetti who published a collection of brief biographies of famous Lyonnais men in 1757. In the whole of this work in two volumes, Pernetti mentions only one man associated with the great Lyons silk industry, and that is Jean Revel of whom he says, '*Il a porté le dessin de fabrique de cette ville au plus haut degré de perfection. C'est à lui qu'on est redevable des points rentrés pour faire la couleur. Cet art consiste à mêler les soies dont les nuances coupent trop, de façon qu'elles soient moins*

---

[1] The Abbé Bonafons, in his *Dictionnaire des Artistes* of 1776, says that Jean Revel's father, Gabriel Revel, went to Dijon with his family and died there. Natalis Rondot, in his *Peintres de Lyons*, Paris, 1888, says there are references in the Archives at Lyons to Gabriel Revel in 1705 and 1708, and that he is recorded as being a *député des peintres* in that city in 1712 and 1713.

[2] Several exceptionally competent painters are known to have given instruction in drawing to aspiring young silk-designers. The three most famous were Daniel Sarabat, under whom Philippe de Lasalle studied (see Chapter VI), the flower-painter Edmé-Jean-Baptiste Douet who had been a pupil of Jean-Baptiste Monnoyer, the most famous of all French flower-painters, and Donat Nonnotte, who had studied under such well-known Parisian artists as François Boucher and Charles-Joseph Natoire, and had worked together with François Lemoyne. Nonnotte became a Professor of Drawing at the Free School of Design which was established at Lyons in 1756. All three were *agréés* of the Paris Academy of Painting. Another famous artist who occasionally gave lessons in this way was Jean Pillement who visited his native city of Lyons several times (see note to Pl. 95A, however).

sèches et dures l'une à côté de l'autre; en allongeant un point de la couleur brune dans la couleur claire, et un point de la claire dans la brune, l'endroit de cette jonction devient plus doux, en participant des deux teintes, et ôte la dureté de la nuance si contraire à l'effet de la nature. De ce mélange ingénieux, inconnu jusqu'à lui, est venue cette harmonie et ce coup d'œil flatteur dans les étoffes, qui surpasse quelquefois l'éclat de la peinture et qui a mérité à la Fabrique de Lyon l'éclat dont elle jouit. C'est encore lui qui a trouvé le secret de placer les ombres du même côté et de produire de vrais tableaux sur ces étoffes. Personne n'a dessiné en ce genre avec plus de grâce que lui, sa composition était noble et hardie, ses nuances parfaites; il sert encore de modèle aux plus habiles dessinateurs: ils le regardent comme leur Raphaël.'[1] Joubert, writing not long after this, says much the same. After mentioning the contribution made to the art of silk-design by Courtois, he goes on, *'Mais il étoit réservé à la Peinture de briser les entraves qui retenoient encore quelques gens de goût; de porter la lumière dans cette précieuse Manufacture, & de changer, pour ainsi dire, les ronces en fleurs. M. Revel, Peintre, parut, devint Dessinateur, & opéra seul ce changement par la supériorité de ses talens. Il introduisit les points rentrés d'une couleur à une autre, avec lesquels il forma si heureusement ces demi-teintes, qu'il donna ce moelleux, ce tendre qui imite la nature. Beintôt ses belles étoffes (ou plutôt ses tableaux en soie) excitèrent la plus grande émulation; & une fortune rapide fut le prix de ses talens. Il eut la gloire de voir de grands hommes parmi ses imitateurs.'*[2]

Let us for a moment consider these two statements. We are told that Revel was an exceptionally talented man who raised the art of silk-design to a quite new level, a man whose work was not only imitated by many of the leading designers of his day but which earned him both fame and riches in his lifetime. Furthermore both authors credit him with the introduction of a system of shading by using what they call *'points rentrés'*. This system consists of making the threads which form adjacent patches of colour interlock, so that the dividing line between the two colours is no longer hard but blurred. Plate 67B shows a close-up of a silk in which this system has been used. The interlocking *'points rentrés'* are always produced by weft threads; that is, they always run horizontally or across the material.

By means of this system, which, as Pernetti says, was unknown until Revel used it, it was at last possible to produce a convincing naturalism, since the subtle gradations of colour which could now be obtained made the shading and thus the modelling of the forms so very much more life-like.

Pernetti also states that Revel took the trouble to place the shadows in his designs all on one side — perhaps an obvious device but one of which he, as a painter, would have

---

[1] Jacques Pernetti, *Recherches pour servir à l'Histoire de Lyon, ou les Lyonnais dignes de mémoire,* Lyons, 1757, 2 vols. The author (1696–1777) was a canon at Saint-Jean, Lyons. He also wrote a *Tableau de la ville de Lyons* (1760). He can presumably be treated as a reliable authority, especially when he is dealing, as in this instance, with events that occurred during his own lifetime.

[2] Joubert, *op. cit.,* p. xij.

appreciated the full importance. Joubert in fact stresses that it was Revel's early training as a painter that enabled him to 'break the shackles' which had bound the hands of his predecessors in the field of silk-design. His designs, we are told, were veritable pictures in silk.

Luckily it is possible to identify the style of Jean Revel because there still exists a fragment of one of his designs which bears his signature (Plate 69A). A large number of designs, chiefly in the Musée des Arts Décoratifs in Paris, and quite a lot of silks in various collections, can be grouped round this, the only design which can unquestionably be attributed to Revel (e.g. Plate 70A).[1] Assuming that the attribution of the whole group to Jean Revel is correct — and I think there can be very little doubt about this — we can get a fairly good idea of what his style was like and why it made such an impression on his contemporaries. For here was something new; here were forms that seemed rounded and solid. All flatness was banished and an exuberant naturalism pervaded the new style. This was partly brought about by Revel's undoubted talents as a designer and partly by his use of the new technique of *'points rentrés'* shading. His designs are often characterized by the free use he made of black and white to increase the depth of his shadows and the shine of his highlights. He may not have been the first to do this but he certainly produced some striking results by this means — even before he adopted *'points rentrés'* shading (see Plate 64A and the Note on p. 173).

The signed drawing is dated 22nd December 1733. I have suggested elsewhere[2] that it represents Revel's style very soon after he had adopted the new technique of shading (one sees quite clearly on this drawing the horizontal hatchings which indicate that *'points rentrés'* were to be used in the silk). It seems probable that Jean Revel had already evolved his style with its ponderous fruit and flowers a year or two before this but that he then still lacked the technical means wherewith to achieve his aim of producing a really naturalistic design. An example of his style at this earlier stage, that is, just before the change-over to the *'points rentrés'* took place, probably about 1732, is shown in Plate 68A. This design is inscribed *'Revelle à vous seulle'* and although this does not prove that Revel executed the drawing it would seem to indicate that he had something to do with it. In fact I believe the drawing to be by Revel himself, for, if one disregards the method of shading, its style is not unlike that of the signed and dated design (cf. Plates 68A and 69A).[3]

[1] See Peter Thornton, 'Jean Revel, Dessinateur de la Grande Fabrique', *Gazette des Beaux-Arts*, July, 1960, in which the identification of Revel's œuvre is discussed more fully. In a footnote are listed some of the most important designs and silks which the author believes can be attributed to Revel. Several of these are illustrated in the present work. As this was going to press, Miss Natalie Rothstein told me that she had now found an actual silk woven from the design shown in Plate 69A.

[2] P. Thornton, 'Jean Revel . . .', *loc. cit.*

[3] I suppose that the rather cryptic inscription *'Revelle à vous Seulle'* is an instruction to Revel, perhaps from one of the senior partners in his firm, requesting him to carry out personally the next stage in the translation of the design into a pattern woven on the loom, namely the draughting out of the pattern on graph-paper. This process had to be

The advance brought about by the introduction of the '*points rentrés*' system of shading is striking enough if one compares these two designs. It becomes even more striking if one compares the '*Revelle à vous seulle*' design with some of Revel's more developed work, for example the very satisfactory composition shown in Plate 70A which probably dates from about 1734, and the astonishing *tour de force* in this *genre*, the magnificent silk illustrated in the Colour Plate C which was probably woven about 1735 or a little later. In this last example, Revel — for it can surely be the work of no other designer — has made full use of the new technique. This silk represents the high-point of naturalism in the history of silk-design. No one, not even Philippe de Lasalle, whose best work was produced during the 1770's, could improve this.[1]

Among the drawings in the Musée des Arts Décoratifs which can, in my opinion, be with confidence attributed to Jean Revel are several in the *chinoiserie* vein. Related to these is the fine silk shown in Plate 72A which must also be from the hand of this Master and can perhaps be dated to about 1735 or so. This particular silk is of special interest because it shows that the designer was fully aware of the most recent developments in the field of ornamental art in Paris, for it was only some five or six years earlier that a few of the more revolutionary artist-decorators in the capital were beginning to evolve the Rococo idiom with its dashing line, its crisp scrollwork and its fantastic forms. Some of the leading French decorators had taken up the new style by the mid-1730's but it was hardly to become generally accepted until quite late in the decade. If this silk, with its combination of *chinoiseries* and true Rococo scrollwork in fact dates from the 1730's, it demonstrates, once again, how very sensitive were the leading Lyonnais silk-designers to important changes of taste in the French capital. It is worth noting, incidentally, that in spite of the enormous popularity which the Rococo style was to enjoy throughout the middle decades of the eighteenth century, one very rarely finds actual Rococo scrollwork reproduced on silks of the period; indeed, this is a rare example. The spirit of the Rococo, on the other hand — its gaiety, its liveliness, its charm — is present in almost all silks

carried out accurately and with intelligence. In the hands of an incompetent draughtsman, even a good design could become distorted or misinterpreted. Presumably the present design was considered so important that it was thought imperative that Revel should execute the draught himself. That he did undertake this work himself on occasions is proved by the signed drawing illustrated in Plate 69A which is in fact just such a draught on squared paper (*mise-en-carte*).

[1] I have mentioned Lasalle on purpose at this point because he is still famous whereas Revel's fame has almost been forgotten. Yet, brilliant as he was, Lasalle was only following the path pointed out by Revel and it is largely a matter of taste which of the two one regards as the greater artist. However, it may be relevant to cite, at this point, what Pierre-Toussaint Dechazelle, (1732–1833) had to say on the matter. Dechazelle was also a famous Lyonnais silk-designer and a contemporary of Lasalle's. He wrote a short book entitled *Sur l'influence de la Peinture sur les Arts d'Industrie Commercielle* (Paris, 1804). On page 49 he states that no one had ever excelled Revel in the field of silk-design because they did not pay sufficient attention to the art of painting and to art in general. He furthermore said that '*si les talens de quelques-uns jetèrent dans la suite et seulement par intervalle, une assez vive lumière, ces météores brillans ne laissèrent aucune trace de leur passage*'. There can be little doubt that Dechazelle here had Philippe de Lasalle in mind because he refers to Lasalle in a footnote at this very point.

woven after the middle of the 1730's and right through to the last decades of the century. But before we study the Rococo silks, let us first see how Revel's style influenced his contemporaries.

So successful a style was of course soon imitated by other designers both at Lyons and elsewhere. The fragment of silk shown in Plate 75A, for instance, is probably by a designer working at Tours, a certain Louis Durand.[1] Another possible Tours silk is shown in Plate 73A. In both cases the influence of Revel is not hard to discern. Across the Channel, the English silk-weavers were equally quick to adopt the new style. Moreover, the Spitalfields silk-designer, Anna Maria Garthwaite, had a collection of 'French Patterns' among which was a French copy of the signed Revel design we have already discussed (Plate 69A) and two others which are actually from Revel's own hand — or so it would seem.[2] How she obtained these drawings is not known, but she received the copy of Revel's design in 1735 and, as we have seen, Revel only composed the pattern in December 1733, so the design was not so very many months old when it reached London. This was apparently the first French design that came into Garthwaite's hands in which '*points rentrés*' were used, and she must have quickly seen the advantages this new system offered, for already in 1735 she began to use this technique herself. The design also influenced her style so that one can find many details in her work from 1735 and 1736 which have obviously been borrowed from Revel's pattern. An example of her work at this stage is shown in Plate 74A, while in Plate 74B is shown an English silk, also possibly by Garthwaite, in the same general style. These patterns are not compact like Revel's but the large flowers, the heavy leaves, the islands with their little sprig curling down under them (a device frequently used with much skill by Revel himself for masking the repeat), and the whole spirit of the design owe much to the example he set. Very different but still deriving from Revel's style is the curious *chinoiserie* silk illustrated in Plate 76A. This is not English and is probably not French either; it may be Dutch or perhaps Italian (it is very wide). With its white pattern on a chocolate ground, it is striking even if the drawing is rather poor. Yet another pattern echoing, but now only very faintly, the style of Jean Revel is the rather silly composition shown in Plate 77A. Although this is a small pattern, the heavy fruit are there, so is the vase (in this case, shaped like a small boat), and the platform with its depending vegetation disguising the repeat — which it here fails to do. All the same this is not an unsuccessful pattern when woven; it has a certain charm, and the colours are bright. The whole effect is made more

---

[1] The attribution of this composition to Durand is discussed in the note to Plate 75A. He was apparently a distinguished designer but in 1768 he was receiving help of some kind from the administration. Perhaps his luck had failed him; possibly there was insufficient work at Tours by that time for a designer of his calibre.

[2] One of the two drawings apparently by Revel and in Garthwaite's possession is a design for the same pattern as the silk shown in Plate 68B (see note to this Plate). This is obviously related to the design inscribed '*Revelle à vous seulle*' (Pl. 68A). It has 'contour-shading' and is dated 1734 in Garthwaite's handwriting.

striking by the use of a great deal of black which gives the motifs a crisp, engraved look. Quite a few silks of this sort have survived. All have small, static patterns, with motifs arranged in a rather old-fashioned manner, that is, isolated from each other and with none of that flowing rhythm one expects to find in silks of this period. They may have been at one of the smaller French centres like Avignon or Nîmes, but there is no evidence for this.

The silks mentioned so far in this chapter have been rich, complicated to weave, and thus expensive. As at other periods, less costly silk materials were also available, such as silk damasks (mostly monochrome) and various classes of silk with two or three colours only. In their patterns these mostly echo the new style. A striking example of this is shown in Plate 78A. Although this silk is woven in only brown and white, the composition obviously owes much to the style brought in by Revel. The English silk shown in Plate 78B also follows the current fashion. This is almost certainly one of Anna Maria Garthwaite's patterns. It resembles in many respects her work in more complicated weaves of about 1733. A more sober style is represented by the red and white silk shown in Plate 81B. This type of pattern must have satisfied a demand for something a little more restrained, a little less striking than the splendid silks of Revel and his imitators. There were after all many occasions when a plain silk would not have been sufficiently grand but when a silk in the Revel class would have been too magnificent. Such silks as this would then have been suitable, for they were expensive but not too showy. Incidentally, one may well ask how silks decorated with the heavy, three-dimensional compositions of the Revel style looked when made up as a dress. Plate 72B shows a Prussian princess wearing what must be an early Revel silk of about 1733 or so, and it must be admitted that the effect is rather odd. On the other hand the silk illustrated in Plate 73B shows that, once mastered, the Revel style could be most effective on the grand dresses of the time.

While discussing the simpler figured silks of this phase, a word should be said about the damask patterns designed by Anna Maria Garthwaite. Those produced between about 1733 and 1737 resemble her other work of that time except that the damask patterns are bolder.[1] But in the years around 1740 she turned out a series of damask patterns the scale of which was very much larger than anything she had done before (e.g. Plate 81A). It may be a coincidence but the author of the essay on the designing of flowered silks in Smith's *Laboratory* writes (in 1756) that 'I remember that one year an attempt was made to introduce small flowers for the fashion, and a great number of looms were set to work accordingly; the late Mr. Hindshliff, at the great wheatsheef, who then employed me in

---

[1] 'Damask patterns require the boldest stroke of any; the flowers and leaves should always be large, and the small work omitted as much as possible, except it be in the middle of a leaf' (see Smith, *Laboratory, or School of Arts*, London. 1756 edit., p. 42, section on silk-design).

drawing of his patterns, ordered me at the same time to draw his damasks more larger and bolder, than I had done any time before; and he judged right, for his fashion prevailed, and had the preference before the other, which was soon over, and the large designs continued in vogue.'[1] Can these large-scale designs be the actual ones commissioned by Hinchliffe — one of the great London silk-mercers whose shop was at the sign of the Great Wheatsheaf? It is not certain.[2] Nor do we know whether the fashion for such large-scale damasks was merely a local one resulting from Hinchliffe's bold decision, or whether it had its origins in France, like so much else in the field of silk-design. I have made no systematic inspection of French costume collections but I have studied the chief collections of historic textiles in France; it may, therefore, possibly be worth recording that I have never found any examples of such large-scale damasks in France whereas I have seen a number of dresses in England of this type of silk and they are occasionally depicted in English portraits of the period.[3]

[1] Smith's *Laboratory, op. cit.,* p. 42.

[2] This question is discussed by P. Thornton in 'An 18th century Silk Designer's Manual, *Bulletin of the Needle and Bobbin Club*, New York, Vol. 42, Nos. 1 and 2, 1958. It cannot be proved but it seems very likely that Anna Maria Garthwaite was the author of this essay in Smith's *Laboratory* which was only included in the 1756 edition.

[3] Allan Ramsay painted a portrait of his wife wearing a damask of this kind in 1739 (Catalogue of the Exhibition of paintings by Allan Ramsay held at the Iveagh Bequest, Kenwood, 1958, No. 2, illustrated; see also A. Smart, *The Life and Art of Allan Ramsay*, London, 1952, fig. 11A).

CHAPTER VI

The Retreat from Naturalism
(About 1740–1770)

Jean Revel had brought fresh inspiration to the art of silk-design during the early 1730's, and for the rest of that decade the European silk-designers were more than content to churn out imitations of his *œuvre*. Some of these imitations were brilliant but many were not, and it is hardly surprising that people (whether it was the designers themselves or the public, we do not know) ultimately began to tire of this style. Yet, having developed naturalism to its fullest extent — having, as it were, pulled out all the stops — there was nothing left for the designers to do but push them back again, and this is exactly what they proceeded to do, slowly, over the next thirty years or so. After about 1740, the patterns start to grow less natural again and more stylized, while the flowers at the same time become smaller. A new flowing idiom also emerges. The heavily laden compositions of Revel give way to a lighter, dancing style, and the flowers begin to be organized in meandering strings that wander charmingly up the length of the material. A silk in which the flowers — here still ponderous — are beginning to form into a meandering system is shown in Plate 79A. It will be seen that the pattern is already less pictorial and more purely ornamental. It is quite possible that this design is the work of Revel himself; it was probably woven in the second half of the 1730's. In England the new flowing style begins to appear just before 1740 (e.g. Plate 80B) but it was not generally adopted over here until about 1742, judging from the numerous surviving designs from this period.

However, at an early stage there was a small setback to this new trend, during which some of the leading designers indulged in a little fantasy. They suddenly began to draw extraordinary floral compositions with strange, heavy, curling, growths of an incongruity that diminishes inversely in proportion to the skill of the designers. Plate 79B shows a French pattern, probably drawn in 1738 and acquired by Anna Maria Garthwaite at Spitalfields during 1739, which embodies this kind of fantastic vegetation. A silk woven after one of Garthwaite's own designs and typical of her style in this vein around 1741 and 1742 is shown in Plate 82B; and what is probably the work of a Tours

125

designer in much the same style and presumably drawn about the same time is shown in Plate 82A.

The silk by Garthwaite just mentioned should be studied in conjunction with those shown in Plate 83A and B, which there can be little doubt were also designed by her and which belong to the same phase, as does the design shown in Plate 115A. They show how varied may be the work of a designer when composing for different classes of silk.[1] We still possess what must virtually be Garthwaite's complete output of silk-designs during the 1740's, with the exception of the volumes containing her work from the years 1744 and 1746 which are missing. She turned out about sixty designs each year so it will be appreciated that we know a great deal about her style during that decade. How much her work can be taken as a guide to the contemporary French taste in silk-design is on the other hand not certain because very few French designs from that decade seem to have survived, and I have only come across a single example that is actually dated (Plate 85A). So it is a little difficult to be sure, and this is especially so because Garthwaite had by 1740 become so well established — and indeed, so competent — a designer that she probably paid no more than the most superficial attention to the prevailing French fashion. Even so I believe one can quite well plot the general development of silk-designs during the 1740's by studying her work and that one should be able to pick out the French equivalents of her compositions among the surviving silks.

From Garthwaite's designs we learn that at first it was the flowers themselves which fell into meandering strings (e.g. Plate 84A). At the same time (i.e. from about 1742), the sub-patterns are released from their servitude; they are no longer compelled merely to support or echo the main pattern, and are now free to roam merrily about in the background, often wending a meandering course that plays counterpoint to the main pattern. This new-found freedom of the sub-pattern is clearly to be seen in the English silk illustrated in Plate 84A which must have been woven about 1744 and must once again be the work of Anna Maria Garthwaite.

The only surviving French silk-design I have discovered which still bears a date in the 1740's (Plate 85A) shows what is the Tours equivalent of such English designs and the general similarity is unmistakable. Once again we see the meandering strings of fairly small flowers (in this case, not very naturalistic) and the playful sub-pattern.

A rather different kind of pattern is represented by the English silk from the mid-1740's shown in Plate 84B. The silk is a lustring and as such has no sub-pattern, although in this case the material has a tartan-like network of yellow in the ground. It will be seen

[1] What may well be Anna Maria Garthwaite's own comments on the different treatment required for the various classes of silk are to be found in the essay on the designing of flowered silks which is included in the 1756 edition of Smith's *Laboratory, or School of Arts*. The relevant passages with a commentary and examples will be found in P. Thornton, 'An 18th century Silk Designer's Manual', which appeared in the *Bulletin of the Needle and Bobbin Club*, New York, Vol. 42, Nos. 1 and 2, 1958.

that plenty of space has been left between the scattered flowers; this is to allow the shiny 'lustrated' ground to show as much as possible. The same airiness in the pattern may be seen in the silk illustrated in Plate 86A, which is also a lustring.[1]

Such gay patterns as those illustrated in Plates 84 to 86 are the equivalent in silk of the High Rococo phase in general art-history. We saw in the previous chapter (see Plate 72A) how Revel occasionally incorporated *rocailles* — the essential ingredient of all proper Rococo decoration — in a few of his compositions, but noted that few designers chose to follow this lead and, unless one may class the fantastic patterns discussed above as examples of Rococo decoration (see Plates 79B and 82A and B), it is clear that very few silks were ever decorated with actual Rococo ornament although many were imbued with the *spirit* of the Rococo — gaiety, lightness, playfulness and charm.

This spirit begins to evaporate about the middle of the century. In the work of Anna Maria Garthwaite, our only proper guide to the patterns of the 1740's, the change may already be discerned in 1748, which suggests that it was apparent in France a year or two before.[2] The change is first registered by the ground-patterns which become more formal and stiff (e.g. Plate 88A). Then the non-floral elements in the pattern follow suit and congeal into irregular frameworks that provide useful supports for the still very naturalistic flowers (Plate 89A). After about 1750 these formal frameworks, often filled with some diaper-pattern, begin to link up so that it is they and no longer the flowers

[1] The importance of leaving sufficient space between the motifs in the patterns on lustrings at this period is stressed in the essay included in Smith's *Laboratory, op. cit.*, p. 41.

[2] It is possible that this change was in some measure brought about by Jacques-Charles Dutillieu, a competent Parisian flower-painter who had studied the designing of silks at Lyons between 1736 and 1738 and who had then returned to Paris where he worked on various important projects including certain decorations at Versailles in connection with the wedding of the eldest son of Louis XV. In 1742 he returned to Lyons and settled there, first becoming an associate designer and then being elected a '*maître fabricant*' at some time between 1747 and 1754. Some contemporary correspondence makes it clear that a most unusual honour had been bestowed on Dutillieu in this way and one can only suppose that he was considered an outstanding designer by his contemporaries in the silk-weaving business (see letter written about 1754; Municipal Library, Lyons, AA62, p. 105). Whether Dutillieu helped to create a new style is not known, but a man who has worked on important decorative schemes in Paris and at Versailles might easily have brought fresh ideas with him to Lyons. He would also presumably have been used to combining naturalistic flowers with formal decorative elements. It may be no more than a coincidence that such blends begin to appear in silk-patterns shortly before 1750 but, in view of what has been said about Dutillieu, it is rather tempting to attribute the introduction of the new tendency to him. I know of no other silk-designer active at Lyons at this period who could have exerted this kind of influence but there were of course many designers at Lyons and we know very little about most of them. It is only fair to add that two designers, Jean Bock, the son of a Prussian officer, and Edmé-Jean-Baptiste Douet, a flower-painter (see Note 2, p. 118, above), were both recorded in 1751 as being capable of instructing fledgling designers in the art of drawing, but neither of them were designers themselves and there is no indication that Bock and Douet were anything but teachers not directly connected with the silk-industry. (Information about Bock and Douet will be found in M. Audin and E. Vial, *Dictionnaire des Artistes et Ouvriers d'Art du Lyonnais*, Paris, 1918. Dutillieu's career is discussed by F. Breghot du Lut, *Le Livre de Raison de Jacques-Charles Dutillieu*, Lyons, 1886.) It is worth noting that Joubert de l'Hiberderie does not mention Dutillieu although they must have been contemporaries. This could be due to professional jealousy or to the fact that the change in style which took place in the later 1740's — the change under discussion — was nothing like so marked and important as that which occurred around 1730 when the designers Joubert mentions were making their far-reaching contributions to the art of silk-design (these developments are discussed in Note 1, p. 112 and in the first half of Chapter V).

which form the meanders, and, from then on, the flowers are fitted in against this formal meandering framework. An unmistakable rigidity begins to affect the designs as a whole after the middle of the century. This characteristic is at its most marked in such patterns as the zig-zag silk of the dress shown in Plate 89B, but may also be recognized in the stiff meanderings of the silver-gilt fronds in the silk worn by Madame de Pompadour in La Tour's splendid portrait executed in 1755 (Plate 93B). This new feeling may also perhaps be regarded as a reflection of current taste in the higher arts, for it will be remembered that it was just in the very years before 1750 that certain leaders of fashion in Paris began consciously to turn their attention once more to classicism in art, not merely to the classical art then being excavated at Herculaneum and elsewhere, but to the classicizing traditions of the still powerful French Academy which had their roots in the Golden Age of Louis XIV. Art-historians usually claim that the turning-point was marked by the departure in 1749 of Madame de Pompadour's brother, the Marquis de Marigny, on his Grand Tour of Italy with the specific intention of studying classical art. But the very fact that he set out with this intention shows that the climate of thought in fashionable and art-conscious Parisian circles had already begun to veer towards a sterner, more classical taste, and to react against the 'disorder' of the Rococo. However, the reviving classicism was not finally to crush the exuberant Rococo for nearly a quarter of a century although it quickly brought about a certain coolness in the rendering of Rococo forms. As we have already noted, the coolness becomes apparent in silk-design shortly before 1750.

The silks of the 1750's, then, are decorated with somewhat more stylized motifs than their predecessors of the 1740's (compare, for example, the silks in Plates 84A and 94B). The flowers themselves are in most cases still comparatively naturalistic but the meandering motifs from which the flowers spring tend to be stiff while the ground-patterns are formalized and repetitive. Diaper-patterns are common, either in the ground (Plate 90A) or as fillings to some ornamental motif (e.g. Plate 94A). These ornamental motifs — meanders, scrolls, fronds, and so on — sometimes form compartments containing the small naturalistic flowers (Plate 90B). Quite a number of such compartmented Rococo patterns are to be found in Garthwaite's work from the early 1750's.

The last design in the Victoria and Albert Museum's collection of Anna Maria Garthwaite's work is dated 1756. Only a few designs from the previous year or two exist and these have so little merit, when compared with her excellent work during the 1740's, that one is forced to conclude that they represent her last work.[1] After that we have much the same kind of difficulty in dating silks as we had with the seventeenth-century materials since no large body of dated designs has survived to inform us about the

[1] Garthwaite died in 1763. If the essay mentioned in Note 1, p. 126, above, is by her, it would seem to confirm the suggestion that her designs from 1756 were her last, because the author of the essay (written in 1756) complains of the way his (her?) customers have been patronizing other designers whose work is of course severely criticized by the author.

D.　1750–60. English (Spitalfields)

patterns of the second half of the eighteenth century. A few dated French and Italian designs exist (e.g. Plates 96B and 97B), and these are certainly a help, but once again we have to search for datable silks to guide us. Even so the general development of silk design during the second half of the eighteenth century is fairly well understood because far more material has of course survived and the whole subject is so much more accessible than is the case with the silks of the seventeenth century.

The stiffness which we noticed in designs from the 1750's becomes a little less obvious, but is none the less still present, in the patterns from the next decade. The typical formula for grand silks of the 1760's consists of two primary meanders wandering tortuously but parallel to each other up the length of the material, and bunches or posies of naturalistic flowers springing from these meanders (e.g. Plate 95B). The primary meander often takes the form of a ribbon or a streamer of lace, or even a strip of fur (e.g. Plates 96A and 97A).[1] Weaving in or out of these primary meanders one usually finds secondary meanders. In the best compositions these two sets of meandering 'trails' interweave in such a way as to produce a three-dimensional effect. Silks of this genre still frequently come on the market; they are often charming, and most people seem to regard them as typical of the Rococo Age although really they represent a late phase of Rococo art when, as we explained, the cooling breeze of classicism had already begun to blow.

Plate 95A shows a design of the same general kind and probably dating from about 1760. Such umbrella-like flowers are usually recognized as being of a kind popularized by Jean Pillement, whose first engraved designs began to be published in the mid-1750's. Pillement was born at Lyons in 1728. He studied art there and in Paris where he became a draughtsman at the Gobelins factory. He had intended to become a silk-designer but there is no record that he ever practised as such. He travelled extensively, working as a painter and decorator in many European capitals and it seems therefore improbable that he ever had time to settle sufficiently long at Lyons to learn the difficult and very specialized business of designing silks. On the other hand his engraved *œuvre*, consisting of a great variety of fanciful flowers (some like the ones on the silk in question), 'Chinese' scenes and other fantasies, was certainly a source of inspiration to the professional silk-designers and a number of silks have survived decorated in what may be called *'le style Pillement'*.[2]

---

[1] Certain French writers have claimed that the fur found in patterns *of this kind* was intended as a compliment to the French queen, Marie Leszczynska, who was the daughter of the King of Poland — fur being the characteristic attribute of East European rulers and noblemen in the eighteenth century. This claim must be incorrect because Marie Leczinska had by this time long played a retiring role in the background of life at the French Court (indeed, she died in 1768) so it is inconceivable that anyone would have bothered to pay her such compliments at this late date.

[2] Important from the point of view of the history of silk-design was the publication in London of the *Recueil de différentes fleurs dans le goût chinois propres aux manufactures d'étoffes de soie et d'indiennes* in 1760, but these engraved compositions were intended for the guidance and inspiration of silk-designers rather than as finished silk-designs. It

During the 1760's stripes began to appear in some designs, usually unobtrusively and in the background, but towards the end of the decade they became more assertive — a sign that the classical taste was beginning to take the lead. At first the meanders with their flowers ignore the stripes but then they start to grow up them, as if they were so many pea-sticks placed there by a considerate gardener (e.g. the secondary meander in Plate 97A). Later still, about the middle of the 1770's, the stripes gain importance; the meanders are constricted until finally they disappear leaving behind them the flowers they once supported — but now much diminished in size — to remind one of the charms of the Rococo Age (e.g. Plate 102B). This development took about twenty years to complete but, as far as silk design is concerned, the Rococo had lost almost all its vigour by the middle of the 1770's.

The meandering silks of the 1760's were composed asymmetrically but, like their predecessors, they have their symmetrical counterparts. An example of this less common form is shown in Plate 99A. Here again are the lace-like meanders (in this case in the ground-pattern), the stiff stems and the fairly naturalistic flowers. The silk was probably woven at Lyons. An English silk which may represent the same phase but the date of which is none too certain, is shown in Plate 99B. It is made up as a dress that can hardly have been sewn much before 1770, judging from the cut of the back. The wreath-like arrangement of the flowers and the geometric sub-pattern behind it both suggest a time when the classical idiom was definitely in the ascendant, that is, after 1765 or so. But the flowers themselves are so naturalistic that one might even place them back in the 1750's. I confess that I am not sure about the date of this material but it would seem that the English designers kept on decorating their silks, until quite late in the century, with flowers very like those drawn by Anna Maria Garthwaite in the 1740's and I suspect that this silk is an example of such a tardy use of Rococo flowers.

Numerous examples of rather less imposing patterns like that shown in Plate 101B have also survived. These are of course derived from the meandering formula of the 1760's but they have lost the robust quality of their predecessors. They are typical of the Louis XVI form of watered-down Rococo — pretty but entirely frivolous and with none of the gusto of the real thing. They belong to the period between 1775 and 1790.

has become something of a habit among students of historic textiles to label all silks decorated with *chinoiseries* as being in '*le style Pillement*' (even silks like the one illustrated in Plate 72A which must have been woven when Pillement was a boy of about ten). Pillement was merely one of many eighteenth-century ornamentalists who indulged in *chinoiserie* fantasies and he was a late if brilliant exponent of the *genre* at that! Although it seems that Pillement was in Lyons in 1768 when his son was baptized there it is unlikely that he designed silks at that period since he was by then already '*peintre du roi de Pologne*'. About 1770, he went on to Paris where he was commissioned to paint three pictures for the Petit Trianon which later earned him the title of '*peintre de la Reine*'. An artist able to undertake commissions of this kind would hardly have been likely to have bothered to give up his time in order to design silks. Pillement did, however, find time to make some kind of an improvement in the technique of printing patterns on silks and cottons. With printed materials fast coming into general use, this kind of thing was something of a fashionable pastime. Did not Casanova set up a factory in Paris at about this time to produce painted silks?

The silk illustrated in Plate 101A probably dates from the 1770's or thereabouts. Among the wreaths and garlands of typical late-Rococo flowers are medallions and trophies of musical instruments, executed in a dark silk on a white ground, in what is an extraordinarily convincing imitation of engraved ornament. The intention must here have been to imitate a contemporary printed cotton. By the 1760's, English calico-printers had developed the technique of printing cotton with designs engraved on copper plates and it then became possible to print much more precise and delicate patterns than hitherto, when the printing had had to be done by the wood-block technique. Printed cottons, already in favour due to their lightness and gaiety, now began to invade markets which had previously been the preserves of the silk-weavers. Both in England and in France, the new, delicately patterned cottons were sought by fashionable people, often for all but the most formal uses. The result was that the competition from copper-plate printed cottons had become a serious problem for the silk-weavers by the 1770's.[1] The present silk (Plate 101A) was presumably made in the hope of cashing-in on the fashionable demand, and the shopkeeper who sold it no doubt drew his client's attention to the fact that, in buying *this* material, she would not only be demonstrating her awareness of the newest fashion but also her discrimination in seeking out such a pattern on luxurious silk and in not being content to have it merely on cotton! One is compelled to admire the skill of the weaver who produced such little woven pictures as these but his efforts, and those of his colleagues who were trying to compete in the same way with the calico-printers in their own field, were to prove of little avail. The demand for lighter materials, like the printed cottons, grew and the silk-weavers were forced to reduce their output of the richer kinds of material and concentrate more and more on light-weight silks — plain, striped or with only very simple patterns. Paradoxically the weavers also tended to make their rich silks even richer — often to the point of gaudiness — by enriching the ground with transverse lines of silver or gilt strip, for instance, and by using silver and gilt thread lavishly for the brocaded passages and sometimes by using coloured tinsel to increase the brilliancy of their creations. The general effect was usually garish but it was one the calico-printers could not imitate. Silks of this kind were used for court and ball-dresses where etiquette prescribed that a more formal and, by then, old-fashioned form of dress be worn. Everywhere else people tended to wear the lighter silks, the printed cottons and the muslins which were more in keeping with the new spirit.

There remain a few odd groups that have to be mentioned. The velvet suit shown in Plate 98A must serve as a single example of the rich silk materials that were specially

---

[1] The origins of copper-plate printing on textiles were the subject of detailed study a few years ago by the late Peter Floud and by Mrs. Barbara Morris. The main results of their investigations were published in *Antiques*, March 1957–April 1958, and in *The Connoisseur*, October 1957–February 1959.

woven for the most expensive men's suits throughout much of the eighteenth century.[1] The material for the coat was woven in two halves of the correct shape, with places marked for the buttonholes and pockets, so that it only needed to be trimmed and stitched together. Sleeves and flaps for the pockets were woven alongside the coat shapes and only had to be cut out and assembled in the same way. Waistcoats were woven in the same manner, as this instance proves. During the second and third quarters of the eighteenth century, most of the figured silks specially woven for men's suits (not only those woven to shape, that is) were decorated with small patterns usually consisting of stylized sprigs, often within compartments or, as in the single example shown in Plate 98B, among meanders that produce a tightly packed, compartmented effect. These suit-materials differed from each other in detail and in technique but their general appearance was always much the same, so that it is now a hard task to date them even to within ten years or so. In France these materials are now generally referred to as 'droguets de soie' although they are not always technically 'droguets', a term which distinguished a particular kind of weave; but the name serves as a convenient label for the whole group. The patterns of these two materials, incidentally, seem to have much in common with the meandering patterns of the 1760's and I imagine they both belong to about that period.

The two silks shown in Plate 87A and B are rather less splendid than the majority of those illustrated in this book but they must none the less be classed with the grander materials of their day. Like their more ambitious sisters, these also have large and complicated patterns but they are less flamboyant and must have been intended for rather more humble use when silk was called for but a more sober effect was required. Such patterns give fewer clues to their date and normally one can only hope to place them approximately. They are also likely to have been woven in larger quantities than their richer counterparts, so that the production of an individual pattern may well have extended over a rather longer period than usual. The two present examples probably belong to the 1740's but the damask could have been woven slightly before 1740 while the blue and white silk may have been made after the middle of the century. It is the kind of silk which Madame de Pompadour might very well have chosen for informal wear in the 1750's.

The silks discussed in this book are decorated with comparatively large patterns produced by the process of weaving; that is, the patterns have been woven into the fabric during the course of their manufacture. There is, however, a special class of silk which deserves to be mentioned in the present survey although the manufacturing

---

[1] The earliest waistcoats made of specially woven panels like this seem to date from the 1720's. There is a design for such a shape among Anna Maria Garthwaite's drawings from the 1730's and in Paris there are several more designs of this kind, apparently from the 1730's and probably by Jean Revel (e.g. Bibliothèque Nationale, Lh.44d, No. 42).

process involved was entirely different. The silks in question are the so-called *chiné* silks which, during the middle decades of the eighteenth century, were often embellished with large patterns reminiscent of those found on contemporary silks with woven decoration. The patterns of *chiné* silks were produced by dyeing the warp thread with the appropriate colours *before* the actual weaving process took place. The dyeing process was a cumbersome one which made these materials expensive although, since they were technically straightforward taffetas, the weaving of the material afterwards presented no special problems.[1] *Taffetas chinés*, as they were called in France, were usually lustrings and came to be known in England as 'clouded lustrings' which was an apt name since *chiné* silks may easily be distinguished by their hazy, indefinite, and rather pale patterns (Plate 91B). Lustrings were light-weight materials particularly favoured for summer dresses and cloaks. The lustrating process tended to make these materials brittle so that they often cracked and have thus rarely survived the ravages of time.

In the seventeenth century, striped and wavy effects were produced by the *chiné* technique but it was probably not until sometime in the second quarter of the eighteenth century that French silk-weavers began to produce *chiné* silks with large patterns such as that shown in the illustration. Most of the *chiné* silks with large patterns are probably French. They were apparently so expensive to manufacture that no other country found it possible to compete successfully with the French in this special branch of weaving.[2] *Chiné* silks with simpler patterns, on the other hand, were certainly made in England, and no doubt elsewhere, during the last third or so of the eighteenth century. Since so few of these materials have come down to us, it is difficult to study their stylistic development but it is most probable that the patterns on *chiné* silks were very like those on silks with woven patterns at each stage, for the simple reason that *chiné* silks were manufactured at the same places as the other silks. Thus, comparison with the woven patterns of the period suggests that the *chiné* silk illustrated in Plate 91B dates from the 1750's or early 1760's.

This chapter has covered a much greater span than any of the other chapters devoted

---

[1] The dyeing process involved masking all those parts of the warp (that is, all the many threads which were to run the length of the material) which were *not* to receive each successive dye; there might be six or more colours in a pattern of this kind. Tying the protective sheaths round the appropriate sections of groups of warp threads was a tedious business which had to be carried out with considerable precision. The process was a slow one and thus became expensive. It is explained more fully by Joubert de l'Hiberderie, *Le Dessinateur* . . . , pp. 32–37.

[2] Only the French seem to have found it worth producing large-patterned *chiné* silks and this was one class of silk that it always paid to smuggle into the other European countries where, of course, these pretty materials were avidly sought for summer dresses. *Chiné* silks with large patterns were probably not made in France in any quantity much before 1740. As late as 1733, an *Ordonnance* had been issued prohibiting the manufacture of materials with painted warps 'in imitation of the Indian and Levantine wares' because it was feared that their production made it much easier to smuggle the Oriental *chiné* materials into the country. All the same samples of *chiné* silks, presumably of French origin, are included in the Richelieu Collection of samples compiled during the mid-1730's (Paris, Bibliothèque Nationale, Richelieu Collection).

to silks of the eighteenth century. The retreat from the full-blown naturalism of the 1730's began already soon after 1740 but the gay Rococo flowers remained fairly naturalistic to the end and were not completely stifled until well into the 1770's and even later. At the end of the century, all that remained was tiny sprigs — and the stripes of a dominant classicism (e.g. Plate 102B).

CHAPTER VII

Furnishing Silks

With a very few exceptions, the silks discussed so far have been dress materials. Any one of them *could* of course have been used for making, say, a table-cover or a cushion or even a curtain, but they were not primarily made for furnishing purposes. On the other hand there existed during the seventeenth and eighteenth centuries a whole range of silk materials specially designed for use in the furnishing of rooms — for wall-hangings, bed-curtains, and upholstery.

As with the dress materials, it is only those with grand patterns that concern us here, but one should remember that there existed at the same time a wide choice of humbler materials for those whose purse was not so deep.

In the preceding chapters we were able to trace with some precision the various stages in the development of fashionable silk dress-materials during the Baroque and Rococo periods. It is much more difficult to obtain evidence about contemporary furnishing materials. Very few designs for these seem to have survived and they are rarely depicted with any accuracy in paintings (unlike dress materials which are sometimes most carefully reproduced in portraits). Furthermore, comparatively few examples of such materials have survived. This is simply because furnishing materials tend to be used until they are completely worn out, whereupon they are generally thrown away. Once they have begun to rot — as they mostly do after being exposed for years to the ravages of damp, dirt, sunlight and normal wear and tear — they are usually not worth keeping. Sentiment or piety rarely step in and decree their preservation — as may happen to a much-loved ball-dress or a fine set of vestments. With the evidence accumulating so slowly and in such a haphazard way, the picture one gets of the changes in the patterns of furnishing materials is thus still far from clear. From the middle of the seventeenth century onwards, new designs were probably brought out each year, as with the dress-materials, but the changes of pattern were probably less marked.[1] Most furnishing

[1] It is noteworthy that when, in 1787, special regulations were introduced at Lyons concerning a designer's copyright of a pattern, designs for dress-materials were to be protected for only six years whereas furnishing materials were to be covered for twenty-five years (E. Pariset, *Histoire de la Fabrique Lyonnaise*, Lyons, 1901, pp. 216–17). Presumably these periods were judged to be the very longest possible time in which a Lyonnais weaver could hope to make a profit out of a particular pattern; after that it really would be out of fashion. In fact, of course, patterns went out of fashion much sooner than this, as we have noted (see Section I of the Introduction and especially Note 2, p. 19).

materials tend to have rather formal patterns, and symmetrical upright designs have always predominated. This tends to make them all look rather alike at first glance and it takes considerable practice to distinguish even the main phases, let alone to date a particular pattern with any accuracy. All the same our knowledge of the development of fashionable dress-silk patterns does help us to date the furnishing silks, for the pervading style in each phase is the same in both classes, while details from the contemporary dress-materials were sometimes borrowed by the furnishing designers (e.g. the little archway that appears on the furnishing silk shown on Plate 109A must have been borrowed from a pattern rather like that shown in Plate 39B).

In this Chapter, then, an attempt is made to follow the broad outline of the development of furnishing-silk patterns (including silk velvets) but, for lack of firmer evidence, these comments can only be offered as a preliminary and very incomplete survey of the subject. Given time and patience it should one day be possible for someone greatly to improve on this.

During the Renaissance, and even more so before that, there was no particular distinction between silk dress-materials and furnishing silks. Figured silks were mostly decorated with comparatively large, formal patterns that were equally suitable for hanging round a bed or for making into a cape or a gown. The more light-weight materials were for the most part plain or decorated with quite simple patterns. Towards the end of the sixteenth century, however, a new fashion in clothes was introduced which called for materials decorated with small patterns — clothes with slashes and narrow panels that would have disrupted a larger pattern. So new types of pattern were evolved in which the scale was small and specially suited for use with the new fashion. These, the small-scale symmetrical patterns and the asymmetrical sprig patterns (e.g. Plate 2A and B, and Diagrams Aiii and B on pp. 86–87) were discussed in Chapter I. This new trend brought about a definite parting of the ways between the weavers of silk dress-materials and the weavers of the larger-scaled furnishing silks. At first the latter continued much as before and there does not appear to be any great difference between the furnishing silks of, say, 1570 and 1630; they are mostly derivations of the well-known Renaissance 'pomegranate pattern' (see p. 87 Diagrams C and D, and Plate 1A), and their general effect is very formal. Asymmetrical patterns were rare at that period although larger-scaled versions of the diminutive sprig-patterns were produced for such purposes as covering chair-seats and for ecclesiastical vestments.

As we have already seen, the Baroque taste began to make its appearance in silks about 1640. The tightly packed type of formal flower which is a common form on dress-materials at about that time (e.g. Plate 4A, B and C) is also found on furnishing silks that are presumably of approximately the same date (Plate 103A). Early evidence of the

Baroque taste may also be discerned in the grand symmetrical-patterned velvet shown in Plate 103B. In the latter design there is a certain voluptuousness about the forms although the composition, with its crown-linked scrolls, is still basically that of the traditional Renaissance compartmented patterns. We do not know when this material was woven but it was probably made around the middle of the seventeenth century, perhaps at Genoa. Several examples of a more wiry version of this pattern exist in various museum collections: these may perhaps be French imitations of what was probably a successful Genoese line.[1]

If we are uncertain about the date of this kind of pattern, what are we to make of the extraordinary spiralling pattern illustrated in Plate 104A? It seems to have several features that relate it to the crown-linked velvet just mentioned — for instance, the ears of corn, the cornucopia and the 'Tudor' roses — so it may belong to the same period. As we noted in Chapter I, we have the evidence of the silk shown in Plate 7B for the fact that complex spiralling patterns were in fashion around 1640. They probably remained in favour until about 1660, judging from a material in the Livrustkammar in Stockholm.[2] In my view this extraordinary velvet seems to belong to that phase but I may be wrong. What are the alternatives? That it is an example of an early striving for a natural and free type of composition — the kind of thing that was being evolved around 1680 (e.g. Plates 19A and 35A)? Or that it belongs with the 'luxuriant patterns' that were current in the second decade of the eighteenth century (e.g. Plates 46A and 51A)? Neither of these suggestions seems really satisfactory and I still prefer the first proposal, namely, that this velvet was woven about the middle of the seventeenth century or soon after.

Sub-patterns, which we met when studying the contemporary dress-materials, also appear on furnishing silks — on brocaded damasks again — around the middle of the century (Plate 15B). A splendid late seventeenth-century example is shown in Plate 105B. In this instance one feels the design might have been happier without the birds but these belong to a well-established Italian tradition; there are numerous late sixteenth and early seventeenth-century furnishing silks on which small confronted birds play a part in the decoration.

During the seventeenth century the conception of interior decoration, in the sense of a conscious planning of the fittings and furnishings of a room as a whole, began to take shape. Although the Italians had been first in this field, it was the French who developed it into an art governed by rather strict rules. This new conception was greatly encouraged

---

[1] Other specimens of this material are, for instance, illustrated by Falke, *Kunstgeschichte der Seidenweberei*, Vol. II, fig. 582; by Flemming, *Das Textilwerk*, ed. R. Jaques, 1957, p. 108b; and by Volavkova, *Synagogue Treasures*, fig. 24, this being of a piece made up as a curtain and presented to a synagogue in 1673 when, of course, it may have been old-fashioned. There is also a panel of this material in the Victoria and Albert Museum (No. 616–1892).

[2] See Chapter I, p. 89.

by Louis XIV whose ambitious building enterprises, notably of course that of the vast palace at Versailles, provided virtually unlimited scope for his interior decorators.[1] The pattern thus set in Paris and by the French Court was soon followed all over Europe. If the French insisted that the wall-hangings and the bed-curtains should be of the same material as the upholstery of the chairs — so be it. And if window-curtains — still rare at this stage — were to be provided, it was understood that they also should be of the same stuff, if one wanted to follow the best French examples. Such rules for decoration began to crystallize towards the end of the seventeenth century and, although they were modified in detail, they held good throughout the eighteenth century.

An early example of this new attitude towards interior decoration, dating from the 1670's, may still be seen at Ham House, which lies some miles to the west of London, close to the River Thames. There the so-called Queen's Closet, which was one of the State Rooms reserved for grand visitors, still has its original silk wall-hangings (Plate 17C). In the room there are also two large, high-backed 'sleeping chayres', upholstered in the same material. The closet is not large so the pattern on the walls could be a comparatively small one, and in fact the two materials that have been used are more like dress-materials than furnishing silks. One gets the impression here that the conventions were not yet firmly established; it was fashionable to have the walls and upholstery of the same material but there were no particular rules as to what *kind* of material it should be. Any splendid silk would do, as had been the case in the Renaissance period and before. Later on, as a wider range of materials came into being, each created for a specific furnishing purpose, the choice was simpler and the result more stereotyped.

The upholstery of chairs, as we now know it, was of course a relatively new departure at this period. In earlier times, cushions had been used when comfort was called for. Then, during the sixteenth century, ceremonial and certain luxurious chairs were sometimes provided with padded seats and backs, but the padding was simple and the covering of it quite straightforward. In other respects, the chairs were hardly different from those of the fifteenth century. It was only towards the end of the seventeenth century that comfortable chairs and settees, specially designed for upholstering, came into use. Three are illustrated here; they are the sleeping chairs at Ham House (about 1675), the chair from Kimbolton dating from about 1685, and the magnificent settee from Hornby Castle of about 1695 (Plates 17C, 106A and 107A).[2] The last two are covered with Genoa velvets which appear to be contemporary. This kind of material, with its accommodating pile surface, is of course far more suitable for the purpose than silks like that on the sleeping chairs at Ham House, brocaded as this is with silver thread. One can

---

[1] Work on the new Palace at Versailles was started in 1668 and the Court moved there in 1678 although the building was by no means completed and was to undergo numerous alterations for the next century or so.

[2] For further examples, see R. Edwards, *The Dictionary of English Furniture*, London, 1954, sections on 'Chairs' and on 'Settees and Sofas'.

imagine how uncomfortable the rich metal thread must have made these chairs, especially if one were wearing an equally splendid suit or dress embellished in the same way with silver or gold thread — as must often have happened at the time. The rasping of the two materials against each other as one took one's seat can hardly have been pleasant! And the wearing properties of such materials must have been very poor.[1] It is not therefore surprising that after the turn of the century, when the upholstering of chairs became more common, silks decorated with silver and gilt thread were hardly ever used for this purpose.[2] Velvets, like that on the Kimbolton chair and the Hornby Castle settee, and silk damasks like that shown in Plate 105A, took their place as the grand fashionable materials.

The flowing idiom of the Baroque style becomes more obvious from about 1680 onwards. It may be discerned in the velvet on the Kimbolton chair and in the contemporary velvet on the bed at the London Museum which bears the entwined monograms of James II and his queen, Mary of Modena, that places it between 1685 and 1688 (Plate 106B). The still somewhat niggly outlines of such patterns are later smoothed out so that the easy flow of the pattern becomes quite unmistakable by about 1690. The silk damask from the royal palace of Hampton Court (Plate 105A) ordered in 1689, is a good example of the new flowing style. The next stages in the development are exemplified by the velvet on the curtain presented to the synagogue at Lipnik (Plate 109B) in 1711, and the velvets shown in Plates 111B and 113B. The materials mentioned in this paragraph were probably all woven at Genoa where, from the middle of the seventeenth century onwards, great quantities of sumptuous, large-patterned furnishing materials of this kind were being produced. These superb Genoese materials were copied elsewhere, notably at Lyons but also in England, and what is thought to be an English 'Genoa Velvet' is shown in Plate 110A. It is used for the hangings of a bed that was ordered for Queen Anne in 1714. The bed, with its matching furniture, was originally at Windsor Castle but has since been removed to Hampton Court where it can still be seen. The richly brocaded silver and gold material shown in Plate 104B would appear to be related to the Genoese patterns of the 1680's although it may have been woven slightly earlier. The small flowers flanking the central motif are somewhat reminiscent of those on the silk illustrated in Plate 16A.

When studying the dress-materials, we noted how the Baroque phase was followed by

---

[1] That the covering of the Ham House sleeping chairs has survived is indeed remarkable. Specimens of seventeenth-century furniture with their original upholstery are very rare (bed-hangings are more often preserved than chair covers). The more expensive coverings were, however, provided with loose covers, or 'false cases', as they were called; and these helped to preserve some of the most magnificent materials which were of course recognized all along as being rather special and worthy of protection.

[2] Some of the rare exceptions among the surviving furniture are the two magnificent chairs at Glemham, in Norfolk (Edwards, *op. cit.*, Vol. III, p. 79, there dated 'about 1720'), which are covered in a silk richly brocaded with metal thread which has a pattern resembling designs by James Leman drawn in 1718 and 1719.

a taste for bizarre patterns (see Chapter II). Although these also find an echo in the details of certain designs on furnishing materials, it is probable that completely 'bizarre' compositions were rarely used for furnishing purposes where the more formal, symmetrical patterns were always preferred. The yellow silk damask with the somewhat 'bizarre' pattern shown in Plate 108B is supposed to have come from bed-hangings used in 1709. The tradition seems to agree with the evidence provided by the design itself which does in fact suggest a date around 1710. A more formal and traditional pattern is to be seen in Plate 109A. Once again two details help to date it. These are the small fountains and the tasselled parasols, both features that one finds in the 'archway' type of Bizarre silk woven about 1708 (cf. Plate 39B). In other respects this pattern is not unlike the splendid red velvet shown in Plate 111B, which of course has nothing 'bizarre' about it. The well-modelled flower in the centre of this panel shows that it belongs to the 'semi-naturalistic' phase that we noted occurring in the dress-material patterns during the second decade of the eighteenth century. It so happens that there is a chair in the Victoria and Albert Museum covered with a poor but apparently original imitation of this pattern which is datable to about 1717 on account of a coat of arms carved on the chair. 'Semi-naturalistic' flowers can also be seen on the Pagodenburg velvet which is of about the same date (Plate 112A). Closely related to these two velvets is the silk shown in Plate 111A which may, however, be slightly earlier.

The two architectural designs illustrated in Plates 107B and 108A are of uncertain date but are more likely to belong to the early eighteenth century than to any other period. The curious vases with cacti on the rich silk remind one of the 'giant blooms' of certain Bizarre silks woven around 1710 (cf. Plate 41A). The general similarity in the conception of the two designs suggests that the velvet, which is very well-woven and probably comes from Genoa, belongs to the same phase. The style of the architecture, while not much of an aid in this respect, is however perfectly consonant with such a dating.

One might have thought that the 'lace-patterns' of the 1720's (see Chapter IV) would have been eminently suitable for furnishing purposes, but I have not yet come across any instance of their being used in this way except as inserted panels in synagogue curtains. Perhaps the tracery of these patterns was too delicate for the purpose. What in many ways amounts to a bolder and enlarged version of the typical 'lace-pattern', however, is to be seen on a small bed which is supposed to have been used by George II in about 1725.[1] This material links the true 'lace-patterns' with the pattern of the velvet shown in Plate 113A, which is on a settee at Houghton made about 1730. It has a bold pattern arranged in the same symmetrical, compartmented manner as the contemporary 'lace-patterns'. That this 'strapwork' compartmenting was fashionable at the time is confirmed by the

[1] Edwards, *op. cit.*, Vol. I, p. 60, fig. 42.

charming conversation piece illustrated in Plate 59B. On the walls of this smart Parisian room is a material, probably a damask, with a rather similar design. The painting was probably executed in about 1728.

The revolution in design introduced by Jean Revel around 1730 in the field of silk dress-materials (see Chapter V) also affected the patterns of furnishing silks, but much less obviously. The very formality of most furnishing materials scarcely lent itself to the new naturalistic treatment. All the same, greater naturalism *is* found in some furnishing silks that presumably belong to this period (e.g. the velvet illustrated in Pl. 112B).

What is the date of the fine *chinoiserie* silk shown in Plate 114B and C? The repeat of this remarkable design is about 13 feet high so there can be no doubt that this is a furnishing material. *Points rentrés* are used for the shading and used to good effect. The style owes much to Jean Revel although the composition does not seem sufficiently well integrated to be the work of the master himself. *Chinoiseries* were apparently popular in the 1730's (Revel composed several including, I am fairly sure, that illustrated in Plate 72A) and it is probably safe to say that this *tour de force* of silk-weaving belongs to that phase.[1] If so, it marks a new departure in furnishing silks. So far their patterns had been purely ornamental; in this case the pattern is essentially pictorial. The weaving of silk wall-hangings with pictorial subjects was of course a logical outcome of Revel's demonstration to contemporary silk-designers of how to produce virtual pictures in silk, although Revel's own compositions were all, as far as is known, for dress-materials. This tall *chinoiserie* composition must surely be an early adaptation of Revel's new pictorial style for use in wall-hangings of silk that could rival the traditional wall-hangings produced by the tapestry-weavers. If this assumption is correct, one may then regard this silk as a forerunner of the class of silk for which Philippe de Lasalle was to become famous later in the century (e.g. Plate 117B).

In Plate 114A is shown a pattern which was immensely popular throughout the middle decades of the eighteenth century. This example is in the form of a silk damask; a velvet version of the same kind of pattern is shown in the view of the state bedroom at Holkham Hall which was built and furnished in the mid-1730's (Plate 113B). When the Privy Council refurnished their office in Whitehall in about 1735, the walls were covered with a green and yellow flock wallpaper almost exactly imitating the pattern of the damask shown here. Many examples of this kind of pattern have survived to testify to its popularity. It seems to have been evolved around 1730 and to have been popular for several decades: no doubt minor alterations were made all the time to comply with

---

[1] It may be a coincidence that the scampering animals on this silk resemble in many respects the strange beasts painted on porcelain by Adam Friedrich Löwenfinck at Meissen during the second half of the 1730's (see W. B. Honey, *German Porcelain*, London, 1951, Pl. 5A, for example). A search might well reveal a common source of inspiration for these animals. Their resemblance anyway suggests the silk is of about that date as well.

changes in taste.[1] The basic pattern can easily be recognized by the pairs of great downward-curling pointed leaves that are always present.

Very different in taste is the design illustrated in Plate 115A. It was drawn by the Spitalfields silk-designer Anna Maria Garthwaite in 1741 and closely resembles some large damask-patterns of hers produced during the same year (e.g. Plate 83B). We happen to know that such large damasks were fashionable as dress-materials in England about then (see p. 123). The present design, which is obviously not for a damask, was probably also intended for a dress-material. It is mentioned here just in case it proves to have some bearing on the present subject: it is perfectly conceivable that furnishing silks in something like this style were being produced about 1740.

What is apparently the equivalent in velvet, and on a furnishing scale, of the lighter and more graceful kind of patterns which came in after 1740, is illustrated in Plate 115B. The material has been cut down the middle, so that only half the pattern is shown here. Together, the two halves almost certainly produced a symmetrical pattern although the formality of this kind of composition would have been somewhat disguised by its easy rhythm. While asymmetry was the general rule in the patterns of mid-eighteenth-century dress-materials, the contemporary furnishing silks nearly always had symmetrical patterns. The Swedish silk shown in Plate 116A was woven in 1753 and conforms to the general idiom of its day (it has the required diaper-pattern in the ground, for instance) but the motifs are arranged in a symmetrical pattern. The same is true of the magnificent furnishing silk shown in Plate 116B which seems to be related to the typical meandering patterns of the 1760's although, once again, it is composed symmetrically as befitted a furnishing silk. The date of this silk, which is in the form of a throne canopy and is now in the Museum of Applied Arts in Vienna, is not known for certain, but I would suggest that it was woven in the 1760's and that this splendid canopy was perhaps made for the coronation of the Emperor Joseph II who came to the throne in 1765.[2] This silk is an example also of the large-scale, brocaded furnishing silks already mentioned in connection with the *chinoiserie* pattern illustrated in Plate 114B. Silk damasks were still the accepted wall-covering for the grand apartments of those who could afford them, but a few very rich people were now beginning to cover their walls with what almost amounted to a series of woven silk pictures. The Vienna silk is not the most pictorial of these materials but it is technically in the same class as the material shown in Plate 117B which was designed by Philippe de Lasalle. Lasalle was born in 1723 and must therefore have been

---

[1] A damask of this type was bought for furnishing a room in the castle of Strömsholm in Sweden as late as 1769 (see V. Sylwan and A. Geijer, *Siden och Brokader*, Stockholm, 1931, Pl. 133).

[2] A large-scale equivalent of the typical ribbon-meander pattern of the 1760's and early 1770's is to be seen on the walls of the Drawing Room at Syon House (see Edwards, *op. cit.*, Vol. I, p. 12). A somewhat similar material is on the walls of the Van Dyck Gallery in the Palazzo Reale in Genoa (see F. Podreider, *Storia dei Tessuti d'Arte in Italia*, Bergamo, 1928, fig. 299). A rare example of a completely asymmetrical furnishing silk of this period is to be seen on the walls of a room in the Palazzo Calbo-Crotta in Venice (Podreider, *op. cit.*, fig. 298).

active from the 1750's onwards. The height of his career was reached in the 1770's (he was decorated with the Order of St. Michael in 1773) and continued into the 1780's, but his fortunes came to an abrupt end with the eruption of the French Revolution, and he died in poverty in 1805. The heavy composition illustrated in Plate 117A is stated to have been designed by Lasalle for the former King of Poland, Stanislaw Leszczynski, better known as *le roi Stanislas*, whose court was at Nancy. Since Stanislas died in 1766, the silk is not likely to have been commissioned after that; and indeed the design is once again an example of the 'meandering-ribbon' patterns so typical of the 1760's. But the scale of the design is far greater than that of the corresponding dress-materials and the whole conception is in every way much grander. Another composition by Lasalle, more typical of his style, is shown in Plate 117B. The pictorial nature of the work for which he is most famous is well illustrated by this example. The scene with the partridges is really nothing less than a picture woven in silk although there is of course no technical difference between the execution of this scene and that of the more conventional but equally brilliantly drawn wreaths of flowers above and below it. Both passages demanded the same exceptional skill on the part of the designer, who had to be able not only to draw the birds and the flowers in the first place, but to work out the composition and colouring in terms of what could be produced on an eighteenth-century draw-loom. Jean Revel had pointed out the way; Philippe de Lasalle followed it and thereby achieved such astonishing results as this. Lasalle's work was the last brilliant flowering of the naturalistic style evolved by Revel. Not all Lasalle's designs, however, are equally happy, to my mind. His flowers are extremely well drawn but his birds are sometimes awkward.[1] What is more, his later designs — those from the 1780's — display some of that frigidity that so often pervades works of art fashioned in the *Louis Seize* style. This was not Lasalle's fault; he was merely following the prevailing fashion, but one feels he might have been happier working in the age of Louis XIV or even Louis XV than that of Louis XVI.[2]

[1] Particularly I have in mind the birds on the otherwise superb material on the magnificent bed at Fontainebleau which was originally made for Marie Antoinette, and the ducks and swans on the silk known as '*Au Faisan*' (the pheasants are not too bad) made for Catherine the Great (see Belle N. Borland, *Philippe de Lasalle*, Chicago, 1936, Pls. II and III). What a contemporary Lyonnais designer had to say about Lasalle has already been noted (see Note 1, p. 121). It was not particularly flattering but the critic was wrong in assuming that the work of Lasalle would be forgotten by posterity. Quite the reverse has happened and his is the only name of an eighteenth-century silk-designer which is generally remembered today. The result is that his work has been somewhat over-rated, in my opinion, for, while it is technically brilliant, it lacks some of the strength, and the depth one finds in the work of Lasalle's great predecessor, Jean Revel, for instance, and his compositions are surely not superior to the best work of the now unknown designers who produced the charming but beautifully balanced 'meadow-silks' of the first quarter of the century.

[2] Lasalle and his contemporaries may have been spurred on in their endeavours to introduce this large-scale pictorial style into silk-weaving by the success which the calico-printers were having with rather similar compositions printed on cotton with engraved copper-plate designs. These were being produced in England already in the early 1760's and the style had been adopted in France by about 1770. Perhaps Lasalle's pictorial silks were seen as a rich equivalent of these copper-plate printed cottons.

Lasalle's style was imitated by others. A fine 'School of Lasalle' composition is shown in Plate 118A. This silk bedecked the walls of the Stadtschloss at Potsdam and was ordered from Lyons, where the original design is still preserved. It is thought to date from about 1785, although I wonder if it may not be slightly earlier than this. A German silk from the same palace at Potsdam and composed in the same idiom is illustrated in Plate 119B. These designs are typical of the first phase of the Louis XVI style — that is, they are decorated with rather pompous, formalized renderings of standard Rococo ornament. The second phase of the *Style Louis Seize*, when the more rigid forms of a renascent classicism begin to constrict the Rococo forms, is exemplified by the design shown in Plate 119A which is dated 1780 and is stated to be *'pour meuble'*. The design was executed at Tours. A later example of this late *Louis Seize* classicized Rococo is to be seen in Plate 120A which shows a silk upholstery material that must belong to the very last decades of the century.

Frivolous Rococo elements, now quite lacking the exuberant character that had imbued the style when it was fresh, lingered on to the end of the century, long after the Neo-classical taste had become dominant. A particularly magnificent example of an amalgam of the two styles is shown in Plate 120B. This valance is part of a set of bed-hangings thought to have come from Madrid and apparently dating from the 1790's. They could be Spanish although it is more probable that they are French. The acanthus, the torches, the vases and the rectilinear frame are all drawn in the best Neo-classical manner. The flowers and musical trophies, on the other hand, belong to 'Louis XVI Rococo'. But while such compositions were still being turned out, a new kind of pattern was coming into fashion in France. On plain grounds, rosettes or stars or heraldic bees or *fleurs de lys* were disposed in rigid order, bordered by crisp strings of bay-leaves, key-fretting and acanthus scrolls. The new style, nowadays usually labelled *le Style Empire*, was blatant and overbearing but its vigour must have seemed refreshing to a generation brought up in the years of revolution, swept along on the tide of Napoleonic victory, and which had little in common with its elders, the people who had tried to keep the flagging Rococo alive. It was the brassy Empire style which finally stamped out the dying Rococo and it was not until the second quarter of the nineteenth century that the sensuous Rococo idiom was allowed back into favour, and imitations of Rococo patterns were again seen on silks.

So far we have said nothing about the pretty silver and sky-blue fragment shown in Plate 110B. It will be seen that the composition, with its fantastic arches, its delicate trees, its charming goddesses, its trophies and garlands, is based on the kind of orna-mental *'portière'* which was being evolved around 1700 at Versailles and in Paris by people like Audran, Gillot and Watteau.[1] These *portière* compositions, derived from the

---

[1] See, for example, Fiske Kimball, *The Creation of the Rococo*, Philadelphia, 1943, figs. 171–73.

grotesque patterns of Berain and his contemporaries, would no longer have been in fashion in the French capital much after 1725. From what we know about the development of silk-patterns — the development we have attempted to follow in this book — designs with the degree of naturalism to be seen in the trees and the figures on this silk were not woven *at Lyons* until after 1730 or so; and, since Lyons was setting the fashion for silk-weavers all over Europe to follow, one might conclude that the silk could not have been woven much before 1730. One might have accepted this silk as a Lyons production of about 1730 if it were not for the fact that compositions with figures and architectural forms happen not to have been in fashion at Lyons until after the middle of the century, when formal and rather flat designs in a classical vein came into favour. What is more, these classical compositions are not really very like the pattern on this silk, when one comes to compare them.[1] So we are back where we started. What, then, *is* the date of this silk?

From the technical point of view, any high-class European silk-weaver would have been capable of producing this silk from 1700 onwards and, as we have already noted, designs for *portières* very like this were in fashion in Paris and at Versailles between about 1700 and 1720. Could this silk have been woven in Paris at that time? There were, after all, several small silk-weaving establishments in Paris operating during the seventeenth and eighteenth centuries. The most important of these was that of Mathurin Charlier, which achieved a considerable measure of fame for the high quality and richness of its wares late in the seventeenth century, and which was probably still active during the early eighteenth century (see p. 46). The output of these small workshops was probably never large and only a few pieces of each pattern are likely to have been woven. This may account for the fact that no other silks like this seem to have survived.[2] Had it been woven at Lyons or in the Lyons tradition, other specimens of the material or silks with closely related patterns would surely have been preserved in the various collections of historic textiles.

Another point which suggests a Parisian provenance for this beautiful material is the very fact that the pattern is so closely related to the fashionable *portière* compositions favoured by the Parisian decorators about 1700. With this kind of decoration being produced virtually on their doorstep, the Parisian silk-weavers would probably have thought it quite natural to select such a pattern, especially for a furnishing silk. They may well have felt in no way obliged to follow the lead set by Lyons. Indeed, it is

---

[1] See, for instance, the furnishing silk with figures in something like the same kind of framework, illustrated by R. Cox, *Le Musée Historique des Tissus* (Lyons), Paris, 1914, Vol. II, fig. 118, which must date from the last quarter of the eighteenth century.

[2] Mr. Mayorcas, the London dealer who bought this silk in Paris, informs me that he had been told of another silk like this with a red ground but that, apart from this, he has never seen anything like it, either. Unfortunately, no inference can be drawn from the fact that the silk was acquired in Paris since that city has long been the chief centre of the trade in antique silks.

worth noting that Charlier is said to have supplied velvet hangings for Versailles decorated with a pattern composed by '*Le Sieur Berin*' who must surely be identical with the famous Court designer Jean Berain (1640–1711) who was of course renowned for his *portière* compositions.[1] The present design may not be by Berain but it is from the same stable. It would thus seem likely that this silk was woven in Paris during the first two decades of the eighteenth century, after a design composed by someone in close touch with the contemporary taste at the French Court, and possibly in the workshops of Mathurin Charlier.

This seems to me the only plausible explanation. If one rejects it, one must try and find a niche for this silk somewhere in the main line of development of the Lyons tradition and this, as I have tried to demonstrate, provides no very acceptable solution to this little problem. Perhaps it is salutary when, having worked out what seems to be a fairly tidy system of chronology, one or two pieces seem not quite to fit.

[1] See Savary des Bruslons, *Dictionnaire de Commerce*, 1723, Vol. II, *Velours*, p. 1848.

NOTES TO THE PLATES

The accuracy of the dating of these patterns varies considerably. When a firm date can be given to a particular material, the reason is given in the note concerned. Where no reason is given, the dating is mine and the argument in support of the date suggested will be found in the relevant chapter of the main text.

The dates of eighteenth-century silks can, for the most part, be taken as accurate to within five years or so (since I have not paid much attention to silks woven after 1770, the degree of accuracy may possibly decrease after that date). In the case of seventeenth-century silks, on the other hand, accuracy to within about ten or fifteen years is all that can be hoped for at present, unless definite information exists about a specific material.

The *dating* of Baroque and Rococo silks is the principal subject of this book. The *provenance* of such materials is much less easily determined, as has been explained in Section II of the Introduction. The attributions given below should therefore be treated with reservation. Where silks are called English, the attribution is likely to be correct because we have presumably come to recognize most of the categories of English figured silks. Certain categories of Lyons materials can probably also be recognized (see p. 44) but, beyond that, the attributions given here are largely guesswork — influenced, certainly, by our knowledge of the history of the silk-weaving centres during this period and of the trade in rich silks, but guesswork none the less. It is worth repeating, however, by way of consolation for those who may feel cheated in this respect, that virtually all silks woven in Europe during the period with which we are concerned were either French or imitations of French patterns.

The technical information given in these notes has been kept to the minimum and is only included so as to help the reader visualize the materials illustrated. The brief technical descriptions are merely intended to give an impression of the surface appearance of the material; no attempt has been made to provide a technical analysis. Technical analysis is only useful when an extensive body of analyses has been collected, and is only really necessary when other information is lacking. There seems to be little point in embarking on an extensive programme of this kind when so much other information about seventeenth- and eighteenth-century silks has survived. It would anyway tell one little about the date of a material, which is our chief aim here, although it might one day be a help in ascertaining the provenance of various groups of silks.

The various illustrations are reproduced by kind permission of the owners concerned. Their names are given in the individual notes that follow.

The following abbreviated bibliographical references are used in these notes:

S. F. Christensen, *Kongedragterne*	Sigrid Flamand Christensen, *De Danske Kongers Kronologiske Samling paa Rosenborg. Kongedragterne fra 17 og 18 Aarhundrede,* Copenhagen, 1940. [S.F.C., *The Collection of the Kings of Denmark at Rosenborg Castle. Royal Costume from the 17th and 18th centuries.*]
Slomann, *Bizarre Silks*	Vilhelm Slomann, *Bizarre Designs in Silk,* Copenhagen, 1953.
Volavkova, *Synagogue Treasures*	H. Volavkova, *Synagogue Treasures in Bohemia and Moravia,* Prague, 1949.
Geijer, *Über die bizarren Stoffe*	A. Geijer, *Über die bizarren Stoffe,* in the Festschrift für Erich Meyer, Hamburg, 1959.

COLOUR PLATES

A. About 1712–14; Probably French.   (*Facing page* 98)

The mulberry-coloured satin ground is largely covered with silver-gilt thread; details are worked in coloured silks and silver thread.

Repeat; width 12 in. (30·5 cm.), height 22½ in. (57·1 cm.).

London, Victoria and Albert Museum, No. 485–1896.

B. About 1715–20; French (Lyons).   (*Facing page* 106)

Green damask with a pattern in a yellowish green (the leaves), a salmon and a lighter pink, white and silver-gilt thread.

Width 21¼ in. (54 cm.). Repeat; height 21¼ in. (54 cm.).

Lyons, Musée Historique des Tissus. No. 1446.

The colour of the ground is not so blue as it appears to be in this reproduction.

C. About 1735; French (Lyons).   (*Facing page* 116)

Silk with a fancy blue ground, the pattern entirely brocaded with coloured silks in a large number of shades. Black is used for the darkest areas in each colour range (e.g. the leaves range from pale green to dark green and black) which produces a striking effect.

Width 21¼ in. (54 cm.). Repeat; height 17½ in. (44·4 cm.).

London, Victoria and Albert Museum. No. T.187–1922.

The design for this magnificent silk was almost certainly drawn by the famous Lyonnais designer Jean Revel.

D. From the 1750's; English (Spitalfields). (*Facing page* 128)
The fancy yellow ribbed ground has a 'sub-pattern' of leaves; the main pattern is brocaded in coloured silks and silver thread.
Width, 20½ in. (52·0 cm.). Repeat; height 24½ in. (62.2 cm.).
London, Victoria and Albert Museum. No. T.161A–1959.

MONOCHROME PLATES

PLATE 1 (See pp. 91, 136)

A. About 1500; Italian.
Cream-coloured silk damask, brocaded with silver-gilt thread.
Repeat; width 9 in. (24 cm.), height 12 in. (30·5 cm.).
London, Victoria and Albert Museum. No. 8326–1863.

B. First Quarter of the 17th Century; Probably Italian.
Red silk damask, brocaded with silver-gilt thread.
Repeat; width 3¾ in. (9·2 cm.), height 6½ in. (16·4 cm.).
London, Victoria and Albert Museum. No. 172–1893.

C. Second Quarter of the 17th Century; Probably Italian.
Red silk damask, brocaded with silver-gilt thread.
Repeat; width 5¼ in. (13·3 cm.), height 4¾ in. (12·1 cm.).
London, Victoria and Albert Museum. No. 1159–1899.

PLATE 2 (See pp. 88, 136)

A. About 1615.
Portrait of a small girl and her nurse, by Frans Hals.
Berlin, Ehemalige staatliche Museen; now exhibited at Schloss Charlottenburg.

B. Probably about 1620.
Portrait of the Doña Isabel de Borbon, first wife of Philip IV of Spain. Painter unknown.
Madrid, The Prado.

Probably painted when the lady was seventeen years old. (See F. J. Sanchez Canton, *Los Retratos de los Reyes de España*, fig. 122.)

PLATE 3 (See p. 88)

A to C. From the 1620's, not later than 1632.
Two doublets and a gown which belonged to King Gustavus Adolphus of Sweden who was killed in 1632. They were not necessarily new when he died.
Stockholm, Livrustkammaren.

A. Brocaded silk.
No. 3351.

B. Brocaded silk.
No. 3373.

C. Silk velvet.
No. 3368.

PLATE 4

A. 1639. (See p. 89)

Portrait of the Duke Frederik III of Schleswig-Holstein-Gottorp (1597–1659), dated 1639. Painted by J. Strachen.
Hillerød, The Danish National Historical Museum, Frederiksborg Castle. No. 2887.

B. ABOUT 1640; PROBABLY ITALIAN. (See p. 88)

Red satin with silver-gilt thread.
Width 20½ in. (52 cm.). Repeat; width 5⅛ in. (13 cm.), height 8 in. (20 cm.).
London, Victoria and Albert Museum. No. 123–1895.

C. ABOUT 1640; PROBABLY ITALIAN. (See p. 88)

Ribbed white silk with a red and green pattern.
Width 21½ in. (54·6 cm.). Repeat; width 7 in. (17·8 cm.), height 11 in. (28 cm.).
London, Victoria and Albert Museum. No. 143–1880.

PLATE 5

A. SECOND QUARTER OF THE 17TH CENTURY; PROBABLY ITALIAN. (See p. 91)

Ribbed red ground enriched with silver-gilt strip, the pattern in the ground being produced by a flushing weft. Brocaded with silver-gilt thread.
Repeat; width 5 in. (12·7 cm.), height 5½ in. (13·9 cm.).
London, Victoria and Albert Museum. No. T.196–1910.

B. ABOUT THE 1630's; ITALIAN. (See p. 89)

A chasuble made of a silk velvet which has a dark honey-coloured pile, cut and uncut, on an off-white ground.
Repeat; width 5¼ in. (13·3 cm.), height 5½ in. (13·9 cm.).
London, Victoria and Albert Museum. No. 583–1884.

A chasuble in the Cathedral Treasury at Pisa is made of a rather similar velvet (see I. Podreider, *Storia dei Tessuti d'arte in Italia*, Bergamo, 1928, fig. 272). It bears the arms of Giuliano di Raphaele Medici who was created Archbishop of Pisa in 1620 and who died in 1636.

PLATE 6 (See pp. 89, 103)

A. 1642.

Portrait of a daughter of Holger Rosencrantz (probably his daughter Sophie, born in 1615), dated 1642. By an unknown artist.
Hillerød, The Danish National Historical Museum, Frederiksborg Castle. No. 5677.

B. ABOUT THE 1640's; PROBABLY ITALIAN.

White satin ground, the pattern chiefly green, the flowers being rendered in two shades of pink. The pattern has a marked twill binding.
Repeat; width 7½ in. (19 cm.), height 14 in. (35·6 cm.).
London, Victoria and Albert Museum. No. T.173–1909.

C. About the 1640's; Probably Italian.

White satin ground, with a pattern in dull red, mauve and green.
Repeat; width 6½ in. (16·4 cm.), height probably about 18 in. (46 cm.). Made up of two fragments.
London, Victoria and Albert Museum. No. 882–1897.

PLATE 7

A. Second Quarter of the 17th Century; Probably Italian.   (See pp. 89, 92)

Brocatelle with a red ground and a pattern executed in yellow, white and silver-gilt thread,
    outlined with a flush effect.
Repeat; width 7 in. (18 cm.), height 16 in. (40·7 cm.).
London, Victoria and Albert Museum. No. 468–1893.

B. About 1640; Probably Italian.   (See pp. 89, 103)

Black satin ground, with a pattern executed in dull green and white, with buff and light blue
    details. The silk is actually in three fragments, photographs of which have here been reassembled
    to give a clearer impression of the pattern.
Repeat; width 5¼ in. (13·3 cm.), height 15 in. (38 cm.).
London, Victoria and Albert Museum. Nos. 1039 and A–1888, and 1142–1899.

A very similar silk is illustrated by Agnes Geijer in her *Oriental Textiles in Sweden*, Copenhagen,
1951, No. 65. It is made up as a chasuble which is dated 1639. Dr. Geijer thought the silk might
have been woven in Asia Minor but I see no reason to doubt that it is European and derived from
the standard sprig-patterns so common during the early part of the 17th century (e.g. Pls. 2A and
3A and B, here). Almost identical to the pattern of the Swedish example is that of a silk made up as
a coat for King Frederik III of Denmark which is also datable to about 1640. (See S. F. Christensen,
Kongedragterne, XLIII.) The width of the Danish example is about 21 in. (54 cm.). A not
dissimilar pattern but in velvet is illustrated by E. Flemming, *An Encyclopaedia of Textiles*,
London, 1927, Pl. 148; he attributes it to Genoa and the second half of the 17th century.

PLATE 8   (See pp. 89–90)

A. About 1655–60; Probably Italian.

Entirely a greenish brown colour. The twill ground has a marked ribbed effect. The pattern is
    formed by flushing warps. The dark details are in uncut velvet pile.
Width about 20½ in. (52 cm.). Repeat; width 4 in. (10 cm.), height 6⅞ in. (17·5 cm.).
The Danish Royal Collections, Rosenborg Castle, Copenhagen.

Made up as a suit for King Frederik III of Denmark about 1655–60. (See S. F. Christensen,
Kongedragterne, No. 26 and Pls. XXXI and XXXII.) A pair of breeches of a silk with a pattern
conceived along the same lines was found in the bombed tombs of the Landgraves of Hesse-Kassel
after the 1939–45 War. They are thought to have belonged to Landgrave Wilhelm V who died in
1663. (See Lore Ritgen and Peter Thornton, *Die Gewänder aus der Gruft der Landgrafen von
Hessen-Kassel*, Zeitschrift für Waffen und Kostümkunde, 1960, Heft 2.)

B. About 1660; Probably Italian.

A pair of so-called Rhinegrave breeches made for Edmund Verney about 1660.
The Verney Collection, Claydon, Buckinghamshire. (Victoria and Albert Museum photograph.)

(See J. L. Nevinson, *New Material for the History of 17th Century Costume in England*, Apollo xx, 1934, p. 315.)

King Frederik III of Denmark had a suit made of a somewhat similar material about 1655–60 (See S. F. Christensen, *Kongedragterne*, No. 23, Pl. XXVIIa.)

PLATE 9 (See p. 90)

A. ABOUT 1650–60; PROBABLY ITALIAN.

Pink satin ground with a white flush figure and brocaded yellow details.

Repeat; width 6¼ in. (15·8 cm.), height 18 in. (45·7 cm.).

London, Victoria and Albert Museum. No. 1297–1877.

B. ABOUT 1660–70; PROBABLY ITALIAN.

Cream-coloured satin ground with a white flush effect, the main pattern being executed in silver and silver-gilt thread.

Width 21¼ in. (54 cm.). Repeat; width 7 in. (17·8 cm.), height probably about 22 in. (56 cm.).

London, Victoria and Albert Museum. No. 450–1893.

PLATE 10 (See p. 90)

A. 1650's OR 1660's; PROBABLY ITALIAN.

Hood from a cope. The silk has an off-white ground and is decorated with a floral pattern that has green stalks and flowers in yellow, pink, blue, mauve and white.

Hood; width 20½ in. (52 cm.), height 18 in. (45 cm.).

Silk; width of repeat 6½ in. (16·4 cm.).

London, Victoria and Albert Museum. No. T.116–1941.

B. 1650's OR 1660's; PROBABLY ITALIAN.

Ribbed cream-coloured ground, with the pattern partly woven in pale green silk, the rest brocaded in yellow, purplish red, white, two shades of blue and two of pink. The binding of the pattern produces a heavy hatched effect.

Width 21 in. (53·4 cm.). Height of repeat, over 36 in. (90 cm.).

London, Victoria and Albert Museum. No. 1225–1877.

The height of the repeat makes this silk unsuitable as a dress-material but many technically similar silks exist with smaller repeats; these must be of about the same date.

PLATE 11

A. ABOUT 1665–69; VERY PROBABLY FRENCH. (See p. 90)

Ribbed striped silk in shades of brown, the wiry pattern being black while there are details in a straw colour produced by a flushing weft.

Width 22¼ in. (56·5 cm.). Repeat; width 5¾ in. (14·5 cm.), height 10½ in. (26·5 cm.).

Copenhagen; The Danish Royal Collection, Rosenborg Castle.

Made up as a coat and breeches for King Frederik III of Denmark between 1665 and 1669.

See S. F. Christensen, *Kongedragterne*, No. 28, Pls. XXXIV and XXXV. The material of which the waistcoat belonging to this suit is made is illustrated in our Plate 12B. It is thought that these silks were probably among those ordered by the Danish Queen from a certain Madame la Barre in Paris.

B. About 1660; French or possibly Dutch.   (See p. 90)
A light-weight red silk with faint white stripes, a white wiry pattern and black details.
Width 19 in. (48·3 cm.). Repeat; width 6¼ in. (15·8 cm.), height, 7 in. (17·8 cm.).
London, Victoria and Albert Museum. No. 1189–1899.

A rather similar but somewhat richer material is depicted in a portrait of a young boy by de Jongh, dated 1661, which was in the hands of Messrs. Koetser, St. James's, London, in October, 1959. It is possible that both the silk in the portrait and the one illustrated here were woven in Holland where a small industry producing mostly rather simple materials was active (see pp. 64–67 and Pl. 17A and B).

C. Third Quarter of the 17th Century; French or possibly Dutch.   (See p. 90)
Green ground with a white pattern.
Repeat; width 6½ in. (16·4 cm.), height 8 in. (20·3 cm.).
London, Victoria and Albert Museum. No. 1186–1899.

As with the previous silk, the attribution to Holland is tentative. The strapwork ornament in many ways recalls that frequently found on Dutch houses of the period.

D. Third Quarter of the 17th Century; Probably Italian.   (See p. 92)
Red silk damask.
Width 20½ in. (52 cm.). Repeat; width 10 in. (25·4 cm.), height 15 in. (38·1 cm.).
London, Victoria and Albert Museum. No. 1185–1877.

PLATE 12   (See p. 92)

A. About 1650–60.

Portrait of a young lady believed to be Hortense Mancini, Duchesse de Mazarin, painted — judging from the costume — about 1650–60. Dutch School.
New York, Metropolitan Museum of Art. No. 713.

The dress is of a greyish white silk with a silver-gilt pattern. I am indebted to Miss Edith Standen for supplying me with information about this painting.

B. About 1665–69; Very probably French.   (See pp. 90, 92)
Greenish-brown and white striped satin with a pattern executed in brocaded silver-gilt thread supported by areas of a light bronze colour produced by pattern wefts.
Repeat; width 7 in. (17·5 cm.), height 15 in. (38 cm.).
Copenhagen, The Danish Royal collections, Rosenborg Castle. (See S. F. Christensen, *Kongdragterne*, No. 28, Pls. XXXIV to XXXVI, and our Plate 11A, above.)

Made up as a waistcoat for King Frederik III of Denmark between 1665 and 1669. The silk was probably the '*Brocardt vert nouveau patron de fleurs*' which was among a batch of silks the Queen of Denmark had received from Paris.

PLATE 13

Two sheets of engraved motifs by Paul Androuet Ducerceau, a Parisian ornamentalist who was active from about 1660 and died in 1710. I have suggested that these were engraved in the 1660's or soon after (see p. 103).   (See pp. 20, 93, 103)

A. Inscribed '*Bouquets propres pour les Éstofes de Tours*'.

B. Inscribed '*Petites Fleurs Arabesques, ou Semences de Bouquets pour les Etoffes*'.
Another sheet in the series is inscribed '*Fleurs a la Persienne pour la Broderie et des Etoffes de Soye*'.

C. From about the 1660's; Perhaps French and possibly made at Tours (see pp. 103–104).
Ribbed white ground enriched with silver strip. The pattern entirely brocaded in red, two shades of pink, and yellow and green silks.
Repeat; width 7½ in. (19 cm.), height 15½ in. (39·5 cm.).
London, Victoria and Albert Museum. No. 452–1896.

PLATE 14 (See p. 104)

A. A linen damask tablecloth. Dutch (Haarlem); dated 1658. It bears the arms of Adolfus van Aggama and his wife.
Friesch Museum, Leeuwarden, Holland.

    I am very much indebted to Mr. C. A. Burgers for drawing my attention to this and a few other dated Dutch linen-damasks decorated entirely with floral patterns. Several of these have now been published by Marie-Cornelie Roodenburg in the *Album Discipulorum* dedicated to Prof. J. G. van Gelder (Utrecht, 1963) in an article entitled *Linnen Tafeldamast met de Wapens en Monogrammen van Hendrik en Amalia van Solms.*

B. From the 1670's(?); Perhaps French, possibly made at Tours. (See pp. 92, 104)
Off-white ribbed ground with a dark green pattern, the flowers being rendered in pinks, dark red, yellow and grey.
Width of material 18 in. (46 cm.). Repeat; height 6½ in. (15 cm.).
London, Victoria and Albert Museum. T.94 to c–1929.

    This silk has almost the same colouring as that shown in Plate 13c and must surely have been woven in the same place.

PLATE 15 (See p. 90)

A. From about the 1660's; Perhaps English.
Ribbed white ground entirely covered with silver thread. The wiry pattern is dark mauve. The leaves are brown, the flowers variously blue, pale yellow, puce and two shades of pink. There is no brocading.
Width 17½ in. (44·4 cm.). Repeat; width 8¾ in. (22·2 cm.), height 7 in. (17·8 cm.).
London, Victoria and Albert Museum. No. T.14–1922.

    A manuscript label originally attached to this panel described it as 'part of King Charles 1st's train . . .'. It seems more likely that, if the silk has associations with English royalty, it was used by Charles II (1660–85). The silk is perfectly well woven although the design is not particularly good. The silk may well have been made in England, since the London silk industry, although not flourishing at this time, was already active (see p. 54).

B. About the 1670's; Italian or French. (See pp. 90, 110)
Off-white damask with a brocaded silver-gilt pattern. The silk core of the silver-gilt thread is bright yellow and, although this is not in itself unusual, the yellow colour is very noticeable, not merely where the metal thread has been worn away.
Width 21 in. (53·4 cm.). Repeat; width 11¾ in. (29·8 cm.), height 19½ in. (49·5 cm.).
London, Victoria and Albert Museum. No. 536–1896.

PLATE 16 (See p. 92)

1670's; FRENCH.

Details of two pairs of breeches that belonged to King Charles XI of Sweden (1660–97). He wore the second pair at his coronation in 1675. The other pair may be slightly earlier.

A. Grey satin with stripes of silver strip. The flush pattern has silver details. The material is exceptionally magnificent.

Repeat; height about 19¾ in. (about 50 cm.).

This illustration is composed of several detailed photographs assembled to show the complete pattern.

B. Cream-coloured satin, the pattern brocaded with thick silver thread. Surprisingly enough, the weaving is not of the highest quality.

Repeat; 17¼ in. (43·5 cm.), height 7 in. (17·5 cm.).

Both are in the Royal Armoury, Stockholm (Kungl. Livrustkammaren) and are respectively numbered 3452 and 3447.

See Gudrun Ekstrand, '1600-talets vita Kröningsdräkter i Livrustkammaren', *Journal of the Royal Armoury*, Stockholm, Vol. VIII, 10, pp. 227–52, with summary in English; where the second pair of breeches is discussed.

PLATE 17

A and B. ABOUT 1678; DUTCH (HAARLEM). (See pp. 92, 105)

A. Silk with a green ground, brocaded with white silk and with metal thread.

B. Silk with a light brown ground and a pattern in dark brown, green, and pink. Some outlines have been drawn in on the photograph for the sake of clarity.

Haarlem, The Municipal Archives, Notary's Protocol No. 468.

These are among several samples of Haarlem silks attached to a document concerning some legal dispute in 1678. (See G. T. van Ysselsteyn, 'Het Haarlemse smalweversgilde', in the yearbook for 1957 of the Stichting Textiel Geschiedenis.)

C. ABOUT 1675; FRENCH OR ITALIAN. (See p. 138)

The Queen's Closet at Ham House, Richmond, outside London. (Victoria and Albert Museum photograph.)

The closet was among the additions made to the house between 1673 and 1675. The original hangings shown here are described in the Inventory of 1679 as being of 'crimson and gold stuff bordered with green, gold and silver stuff'. The borders are made up of strips of a richly brocaded silk which appears to be a dress-material. The two 'sleeping chayres' are both still covered in the same material as the main field of the hangings. The contents of Ham House are entrusted to the care of the Victoria and Albert Museum, London.

PLATE 18 (See p.110)

A. THIRD QUARTER OF THE 17TH CENTURY; FRENCH OR ITALIAN.

Ribbed pink ground with a white pattern. Some flowers are brocaded either in blue, green or orange silk. The binding of the white flush pattern forms a hatched effect.

Width 21¼ in. (54 cm.). Repeat; height 16 in. (40·25 cm.).
London, Victoria and Albert Museum. No. 131–1880.

B. 1670–1690; FRENCH OR ITALIAN.

Pink satin ground (now faded to a muddy brown), with a white pattern and certain flowers rendered in green or blue.
Width 21 in. (53 cm.). Repeat; height 19½ in. (49·5 cm.).
London, Victoria and Albert Museum. No. 305–1896.

PLATE 19

A and B. ABOUT 1680 OR 1681; FRENCH OR ENGLISH.　　　　　　　　　　(See p. 105)

　A. Long waistcoat of brown silk damask which, judging from its rather straggling pattern, may possibly be English.
　　Repeat; width 7 in. (17·8 cm.), height 11 in. (27·9 cm.).

　B. Long coat and breeches made of a white ribbed silk brocaded with silver-gilt flowers. The cuffs are of pink satin with a white pattern and silver-gilt flowers.　　(See p. 93)
　　The repeat of the white silk is — width 9¾ in. (24·8 cm.), height 7 in. (17·8 cm.).
London, Victoria and Albert Museum. Respectively 173–1900 and 175 and A–1900.

　　Both belonged to Sir Thomas Isham who died, shortly before his wedding-day, in 1681. The white suit was probably his wedding suit and the brown suit is not likely to be much earlier. (See J. L. Nevinson, 'Men's Costume in the Isham Collection', *Connoisseur*, XCIV, 1934, p. 313.)

PLATE 20　　　　　　　　　　　　　　　　　　　　　　　　　　　　　(See p. 93)

A. ABOUT THE 1680's; PROBABLY FRENCH.

　Two panels from a long waistcoat rather similar in style to that illustrated in Plate 19A. Reserved, irregular-shaped panels of the pink satin ground are surrounded by areas of closely-packed silver thread. The brocaded floral motifs are executed in silver and a shiny black metal thread.
　Repeat; width 7 in. (17·8 cm.), height 14 in. (35·6 cm.).
London, Victoria and Albert Museum. T.3 and A–1922.

B. ABOUT 1686.

　Portrait of the Markgräfin Augusta Maria von Baden-Durlach (1649–1728), with her son, attributed to J. G. Wagner, about 1686.
Baden-Baden, Neues Schloss.

　　See Gerda F. Kircher, *Zähringer Bildnissammlung im neuen Schloss zu Baden-Baden*, Karlsruhe, 1958, Pl. 25.

PLATE 21　　　　　　　　　　　　　　　　　　　　　　　　　　　　　(See p. 93)

A. ABOUT 1690–97; PROBABLY FRENCH.

　Pink satin ground largely covered with silver thread; the pattern produced with two kinds of silver and silver-gilt thread.
　Made up as a cope.
Sweden, Strängnäs Cathedral. Photograph from Antikvarisk Topografiska Arkivet, Stockholm, No. 2766.

The cope was made for the Coronation of King Charles XII in Strängnäs Cathedral in the year 1697. An inscription to this effect appears on the pendant to the hood of the cope. I am greatly indebted to Dr. Agnes Geijer for drawing my attention to this silk and for supplying me with the above details.

B. ABOUT THE 1690's; FRENCH.

Brown satin brocaded with two kinds of silver-gilt thread.
Width 21 in. (53·4 cm.). Repeat; width 7 in. (17·8 cm.), height 16 in. (40·7 cm.).
London, Victoria and Albert Museum. No. 466–1897.

PLATE 22 (See pp. 93, 105)

SMALL, RICH PATTERNS FROM THE LAST TWO DECADES OF THE 17TH CENTURY; FRENCH.
All are in the collections of the Victoria and Albert Museum, London.

A. Satin, striped in the warp brown, black and off-white. The pattern executed in white with brocaded silver and silver-gilt thread.
Repeat; width 7 in. (17·8 cm.), height 9½ in. (24·1 cm.).
No. T.71–1921.

B. Red damask, the pattern brocaded with silver thread and with black details.
Repeat; width 7 in. (17·8 cm.).
No. T.154–1932.

C. Reddish brown damask with silver-gilt thread forming a longitudinal stripe (a rare feature), the pattern brocaded in silver-gilt thread.
Repeat; width 6 in. (15·2 cm.), height 11 in. (27·9 cm.).
No. 1301–1899.

PLATE 23 (See p. 93)

A. 1684.
Portrait of Norbert Liebstejn of Kolovrat, by Jodocus Verbeeck. Dated 1684. This shows the typical small rich patterns of the period.
Czechoslovakia; Oblastní galerie, Rychnov nad Kněžnov Castle. Cat. No. 71.

B. 1690.
Portrait of an unknown man by Adrian van der Werff, signed and dated 1690. From the collection of Prince Westdorf, Haarlem. Sold at Messrs. Sotheby, London, 9th December 1959, lot 156; the photograph reproduced with their kind permission.
The silk is crimson and has a silver-gilt pattern.

PLATE 24

A. FROM THE EARLY 1690's; PROBABLY FRENCH.
A Torah mantle given to the Klausen Synagogue, Prague, by Samuel Taussig and his wife in 1694. The central panel is of a silk with a green ground, pink stripes and a silver-gilt pattern.
Prague, The Jewish Museum. No. 17.377.
See H. Volavkova, *Synagogue Treasures*, Pl. 50.

B. From the First Half of the 1690's; Probably French.   (See p. 93)

Damask with a violet colour, and silver-gilt flowers.

Width 18½ in. (47 cm.). Repeat; height 12 in. (30 cm.).

Used for repairing a mediaeval cope belonging to the Church at Norrbärke, in Dalarna (Central Sweden) probably in 1696 when the church acquired a '*gyllenduk med blå botten*' (cloth of gold with a blue ground). (See A. Geijer, *Über die bizarren Stoffe*, p. 207; I am very greatly indebted to Dr. Geijer for providing me with this photograph.)

PLATE 25   (See p. 93)

A. A Page of Watercolour Sketches, presumably for Silk-Patterns, by Lambert van Haven; About 1690.

Copenhagen, The State Collection of Prints and Drawings. (I understand from Dr. Erik Fischer, who kindly assisted me in obtaining this photograph, that there are many more designs for silks by van Haven in the collection.)

Van Haven was general architect to the Danish Court and, from 1671, *pictor primarius*. He worked on all kinds of architectural and decorative schemes. These sketches, which were among the drawings sold to the Royal Library by van Haven's widow in 1696, are probably for silks that were to be woven at the silk-factory established in Copenhagen under royal patronage in the 1680's (see p. 73, above). A suit at Rosenborg Castle, Copenhagen, worn by King Christian V about 1690, has cuffs of a silk decorated with much the same kind of pattern as another of van Haven's compositions which is not illustrated here. (See S. F. Christensen, *Kongedragterne*, No. 61 and Vol. I, pp. 128–31.)

B. A Pattern for a Stomacher from a Book of Embroidery Designs entitled *Nuovissimi Esemplare di Ricami*, published in Venice in 1694.   (See p. 105)

The areas to be worked in metal thread (usually silver-gilt) are hatched; the silk areas are engraved naturalistically.

PLATE 26

A. About 1695; French.   (See pp. 92, 110)

Light blue damask; the lining of a suit made for King Frederik IV of Denmark about 1695.

Copenhagen, The Danish Royal Collections, Rosenborg Castle. (See S. F. Christensen, *Kongedragterne*, No. 65, LXX–LXXII.)

The waistcoat of the same suit is made of a superb silver and blue silk with a 'lace-pattern'. This material would, however, not provide so good an example for our purpose. In the Victoria and Albert Museum is a silk very similar to the one illustrated here (No. 170–1896) which is extremely well woven and has detail colouring (salmon-pink and yellowish green) that suggest a Lyons provenance for this particular kind of pattern (see p. 44).

B. About 1694(?); Perhaps English (Spitalfields).   (See p. 110)

Panel from the costume of the funeral effigy of Queen Mary II who died in 1694. The drawing of the pattern is not very good and the weaving could be better. Both these points suggest that the silk was perhaps woven in England. In spite of this gawkiness, the pattern is surprisingly naturalistic, and the question arises whether this material is of the period (i.e. from the 1690's) or whether the effigy was re-dressed at a later date. In my own view the silk is original; the alternative is that the silk was woven about 1720, by which time, of course, the English weavers had become extremely skilled. That semi-naturalistic 'lace-patterns' not unlike this in conception were being woven in the 1690's is demonstrated by the existence of a silk damask panel with a comparatively naturalistic pattern, which forms the back of the waistcoat mentioned in the previous note; unfortunately this material has never been published, nor has it been photographed.

London, Westminster Abbey. (Photograph by the Victoria and Albert Museum.)

PLATE 27 (See p. 94)

A. ABOUT THE MID-1690's; FRENCH.
Off-white silk damask with a brocaded silver pattern.
Width 22 in. (55 cm.). Repeat; height 17 in. (43 cm.).
Lyons, Musée Historique des Tissus. No. 29058.

B. ABOUT 1700; PROBABLY FRENCH.
Effigy of Frances Stuart, Duchess of Richmond, who died in 1702.
London, Westminster Abbey. (Victoria and Albert Museum photograph.)

The Duchess was very much a lady of fashion and it is probable that the dress now worn by her funeral effigy dates from the last years of her life. The silk has a cream-coloured ground with a flush pattern. The main pattern is executed in silver and silver-gilt thread.

PLATE 28 (See p. 95)

A. ABOUT 1695; FRENCH.
A white damask ground, the pattern brocaded with pink, blue and green silk and silver-gilt thread.
Width 19¾ in. (50 cm.).
Stockholm, Historiska Museet. No. 32128:9.

Made up as an altar-frontal. From Eskilstuna Church. I am extremely grateful to Dr. Agnes Geijer for sending me a photograph of this silk and for allowing me to publish it here.

B. ABOUT 1695; FRENCH.
A blue damask ground, brocaded with silver thread.
Oslo, Kunstindustrimuseum. No. 749.

Now made up as a christening robe but, like so many robes of this kind, probably originally used for a smart dress (ill. Slomann, *Bizarre Silks*, Pl. XXII).

PLATE 29

A. ABOUT 1695; FRENCH. (See p. 95)
Blue damask ground, the pattern brocaded with silver thread; pink details.
Berlin, Staatliche Museen, Kunstgewerbe-Museum. No. 79.227. (Destroyed during the 1939–45 War.) (See Slomann, Bizarre Silks, Pl. XLII.)

A very similar silk at Tådene Church, Västergötland, Sweden, dated 1699, is illustrated by Geijer, *Über die bizarren Stoffe.*

B. 1695–1700; French.   (See p. 96)

Brown damask ground, brocaded with silver-gilt thread and some light-blue details.
Width 22 in. (55·5 cm.). Repeat; height 11 in. (28·5 cm.).
Lyons, Musée Historique des Tissus. No. B.1482.

PLATE 30

A. About 1700; French.   (See pp. 92, 96)

Off-white damask, brocaded with silver and silver-gilt thread, with crimson details.
Width 21¾ in. (55 cm.). Repeat, height 13¼ in. (32·5 cm.).
Lyons, Musée Historique des Tissus. No. 1449.

B. 1700–1705; French.   (See p. 96)

Off-white damask, brocaded with metal thread, with crimson details.
New York, The Cooper Union for the Advancement of Science and Art. No. 1902–1–900.

    (See Slomann, *Bizarre Silks*, Pl. XXIV.) This silk came from a Spanish collection — which, of course, does not necessarily mean it was made in Spain.

Note: Concerning the date of two silks like these, see the Note on Plate 32A, below.

PLATE 31   (See p. 96)

A. About 1699; French.

Ribbed cream-coloured ground with silver-gilt thread.
Width 20 in. (52 cm.). Repeat; width 5 in. (12·6 cm.), height 7 in. (18 cm.).
Copenhagen, The Danish Royal Collections, Rosenborg Castle.

    Made up as a dressing-gown; part of a set of informal garments made for King Frederik IV (1699–1730) early in his reign. The set can be traced back to 1705 but was probably made in 1699 or 1700. (See S. F. Christensen, *Kongedragterne*, No. 67 and Pls. LXXVI and LXXVII.)

B. About 1700; French.

Silk with its surface almost entirely covered with silver thread.
Width 20 in. (51 cm.).
Kassel, Staatlichen Kunstsammlungen.

    Made up as a skirt. Discovered in ruined tombs of the Landgraves of Hesse-Kassel in the Church of St. Martin, Kassel, which was bombed during the 1939–45 War. The skirt almost certainly belonged to the Prussian princess who, in 1700, married the Landgrave Frederick and who died in 1705. It may have been part of her wedding-dress. The silk of a robe that belonged to the same princess is illustrated in Plate 38B, below. (See two articles dealing with this find in the Journal *Waffen und Kostümkunde*, 1960, Heft 2; Lore Ritgen and Peter Thornton, *Die Gewänder aus der Gruft der Landgrafen von Hessen-Kassel.*)

PLATE 32   (See p. 96)

A. About 1700; Probably French.

Brown ribbed ground with a flush pattern, brocaded with two kinds of silver-gilt thread.
Norwich, The Castle Museum. By permission of the Norwich Museums Committee.

Nothing seems to be known about the origin of this coat other than it is 'said to have come from the Lady Kennedy Collection'. It would appear, from the cut of the coat, to date from about 1700. I am most grateful to Miss Betty Vizard for drawing my attention to this and another coat which belongs with it and which is of a silk rather like those illustrated in Plate 30, and particularly like that shown in Plate 30A.

B. About 1700; French or Italian.

Red silk damask.

Width 21¼ in. (54 cm.). Repeat; height 21¼ in. (54 cm.).

Stockholm, The Royal Palace, Kungl. Husgerådskammarens Textilsamling No. 123. (I am extremely grateful to Dr. Åke Setterwall for showing me this sample which is in a fascinating collection, preserved in the Palace, of textile fragments that have from time to time been removed from the walls and furniture in the various Swedish royal palaces.)

Little money is likely to have been spent on silk furnishing materials by the Swedish Royal household after about 1700 and until well into the 1720's when this silk would have been very old-fashioned. Soon after his accession in 1697, Charles XII became embroiled in a succession of military campaigns which were such a severe drain on the nation's finances that the state finally went bankrupt in 1710. Charles was first and foremost a soldier; his tastes were simple and he cared little for furnishings and the other trappings of material splendour with which most Baroque monarchs liked to surround themselves.

PLATE 33

A. 1700–02; Perhaps English. (See p. 96)

Yellow satin with a pattern in silver thread.

London, Westminster Abbey. (*Victoria and Albert Museum photograph.*)

Four small pieces of this rich silk material have been used for the cuffs of the coat worn by the funeral effigy of King William III (d. 1702). The present illustration shows a *montage* of detailed photographs of the cuffs which helps to make the general style of the pattern clear.

B. 1700–05; French or Italian. (See p. 97)

Claret-coloured damask, the pattern brocaded in silver and silver-gilt thread with a few yellow details.

Berlin, Staatliche Museen, Kunstgewerbe-Museum. No. 80–437.

See Slomann, *Bizarre Silks*, Pl. VIII.

PLATE 34

A. About 1695–1705; French. (See p. 110)

Silk damask with a bronze satin ground and a white pattern supported by additional weft effects in off-white silk.

Width 20 in. (50 cm.). Repeat; height 19 in. (48 cm.).

London, Victoria and Albert Museum. 593–1896.

B. About 1706; French. (See pp. 111–112)

Detail of a dressing-gown which forms part of a magnificent toilet set perhaps made for the marriage of Lord Huntingtower in 1706. (See R. Edwards and P. Ward-Jackson, *Ham House;*

A guide, London, 1951, p. 57.) The set includes a mirror, the shape of which does not permit a date for this silk later than 1715 at the very latest. Light blue and silver, the latter predominating. *Richmond, Ham House (Victoria and Albert Museum photograph).*

PLATE 35 (See p. 105)

A. About 1680–1700(?); Probably French.

A light-weight silk with a brown satin ground, and a white pattern with passages in a darker brown and dark blue.

Repeat; height 6½ in. (16·4 cm.), width 16½ in. (41·3 cm.).
London, Victoria and Albert Museum. No. 1138–1899.

The sombre colouring suggests a rather earlier date for this silk than the comparatively gay material illustrated in the adjacent plate. It is, however, possible that it too belongs to the early years of the 18th century.

B. About 1700–1710(?); Probably French. (See p. 106)

An off-white damask ground with a brocaded pattern in green, pink and white.

Repeat; height 23 in. (58·5 cm.), width 9½ in. (24 cm.).
London, Victoria and Albert Museum. No. 1205–1899.

The gay colouring suggests a date already in the 18th century but the tight, regular treatment of the pattern keeps to the 17th-century tradition. A small archway in the damask pattern (not visible in the reproduction) perhaps links this silk with the kind of pattern shown in Plate 39B of about 1708.

PLATE 36 (See p. 97)

A. About 1700–03; French.

Cherry-red damask. Made up as a chasuble, dated 1704.
Repeat; width 7 in. (18 cm.), height 18½ in. (47 cm.).
From the small church at Kårsta in Uppland, Sweden.

See A. Geijer, *Über die bizarren Stoffe*, p. 207, fig. 4. I am much indebted to Dr. Geijer for providing me with this photograph.

B. About 1705; French or Italian.

Salmon-pink satin ground, brocaded with silver and silver-gilt thread, and with details in green and two shades of blue.

Repeat; width about 18½ in. (47 cm.). Overall height, 7 ft. 7 in. (230 cm.); overall width, 5 ft 5 in. (160 cm.).
Prague, Jewish Museum. No. 12.951.

A curtain presented to the Pinkas Synagogue, Prague, by the High Rabbi Loeb Rosenberg in 1706. (See H. Volavkova, *The Synagogue Treasures*, Pls. 41 and 42.)

PLATE 37

Two English Silk-Designs by the Spitalfields Designer, James Leman. (See p. 97)

These are among a set of drawings representing Leman's early work, now in the possession of the silk-weaving firm of Messrs. Vanners & Fennell Bros. Ltd., of Sudbury. I am extremely grateful to the Director, Mr. Kipling for giving me permission to publish these designs, and those shown in Plates 39B, 43B and 45A which are from the same set. (Victoria and Albert Museum photographs.)

A. Drawing No. 18. Inscribed '*London, Novr. 9th 1706. Mr. Trenchfield's first sattin tishue figure . . . by me James Leman*'. Trenchfield was a silk-mercer. The silk was to be woven in two colours only; the pattern is here painted in yellow ochre.

B. Drawing No. 28. Inscribed '*London, Jan. 31st 1706/7* [i.e. 1707] *Brocaded flowd: sattin four colours . . . by James Leman*'. (See pp. 98, 106)

Leman was at this time still working for his father who died in 1712. He apparently inherited the family business and came to play an important part in the Spitalfields silk industry until his death in 1745. (See P. Thornton and N. Rothstein, 'The Importance of the Huguenots in the London Silk-industry', *Proceedings of the Huguenot Society of London*, Vol. XX, No. 1, a paper read in March 1959 which includes an outline of Leman's career. Other designs from Leman's establishment are reproduced below (Pls. 39B, 43B, 45A, 50B, 51A, 52A, 53B, 54A) and in *The Burlington Magazine*, August 1958, in the *Zeitschrift für Waffen und Kostümekunde*, 1960, Heft 2, and in F. Lewis, *James Leman* Leigh-On-Sea, 1954 — in the last case with somewhat misleading captions. Most of these designs are probably by Leman himself although he sometimes commissioned work from other leading Spitalfields designers.)

PLATE 38

A. ABOUT 1705–10(?); PROBABLY FRENCH. (See p. 97)

Bright salmon-pink satin damask ground, the flowers rendered in brown, green, pale blue and white. Very faded.
Width 20½ in. (52 cm.). Repeat; height 24 in. (61 cm.).
London, Victoria and Albert Museum. No. 561–1898.

The date of this silk is uncertain but it would appear to be an early example of the kind of pattern illustrated in Plate 50B.

B. ABOUT 1705; FRENCH. (See pp. 98, 106)

Brown damask ground, richly brocaded with silk and metal thread.
Width 20 in. (51 cm.).
Kassel, Staatliche Kunstsammlungen.

See Note to Plate 31B where a reference is given to an article in which this silk is discussed. It is made up as a robe and was found in the tomb of a princess who died in December 1705 when the garment was probably quite new. Fragments of an identical material are in the Musée des Tissus at Lyons.

PLATE 39

A. ABOUT 1705–12; FRENCH (PERHAPS WOVEN AT TOURS?).

Satin damask striped in the warp; brick red, gunmetal, dull green and white.
Fragment; width 16 in. (40 cm.). Repeat; height 27½ in. (68·5 cm.).
London, Victoria and Albert Museum. No. 902–1892 and A.

This silk was presented to the Museum by Monsieur Louis Roze, a member of one of the leading Tours silk-weaving families. It may possibly be a Tours weave. The dull colour-scheme of this silk strengthens this supposition, since that would seem to have been a feature of many Tours silks in the 18th century. (See p. 36 and Notes on Plates 75, 82A and 91A.)

B. A silk-design by James Leman inscribed '... *London, Aprill 3rd 1708. This pattern for an orrace Tissue brocade with gold and silk ... For my father. James Leman'.* (See p. 98)
In the collection of Messrs. Vanners & Fennell Bros. Ltd., Sudbury. Drawing No. 45 (see Note to Plate 37).

An orrace tissue was apparently a silk woven with silver thread that ran right across the whole width of the material (i.e. the silver was not confined to patches that were brocaded). In this instance, as the inscription indicates, details were also to be brocaded in silver-gilt thread, as well as in coloured silks — of which there were to be six different colours.

PLATE 40 (See p. 98)

A. About 1708; French: or English.
Grey and claret-coloured damask, brocaded with silver thread and coloured silks.
Boston, Massachusetts; Museum of Fine Arts. No. 59.306.

I am greatly indebted to Mr. Adolph Cavallo for drawing my attention to this interesting silk and for providing me with a photograph of it. Judging from the English designs, this silk was probably woven about 1708.

B. About 1709.
Portrait of Count Valetti by Vittore Ghislandi.
Venice, Accademia.

Tassi, Ghislandi's biographer, wrote that one *'né veder certamente potrannosi, panni più veri e naturali di questi'* (Ugo Ojetti and others, *Il Ritratto Italiano* ..., chapter on 'Il Ritratto a Bergamo nel Seicento e nel Settecento', by Ciro Caversazzi, p. 150). Italian authorities tend to date the portrait about 1710. Comparison with English silk-designs indicates a date about 1709 for the waistcoat material. Illustrated in colour in *Abbigliamento e Costume nella Pittura Italiana*, Rome 1964 (ed. F. C. Bentivegna), fig. 267.

PLATE 41

A. About 1700–10; French or Italian. (See pp. 98, 105, 140)
Brocaded satin, with an ivory-coloured ground and pattern in salmon-pink, green, pale yellow and pale blue.
Width 21 in. (53·5 cm.). Repeat; height 30 in. (76 cm.).
Copenhagen, Kunstindustrimuseum. No. A66–1927.

B. About 1705–12; French. (See pp. 98, 105)
White damask ground, the pattern executed in coloured silks and silver-gilt thread.
Width 19¾ in. (50 cm.). Repeat; height 10½ in. (26·5 cm.).
Berlin, Staatliche Museen, Kunstgewerbemuseum. No. 99,35.

PLATE 42

A. 1705–10; French. (See pp. 97–98)
The silk is almost entirely covered with silver and silver-gilt thread. There are details worked in coloured silks.

Overall height 38½ in. (97 cm.), width of silk 20¾ in. (52·5 cm.).
Prague, Jewish Museum. No. 12.665.

    A Torah mantle from the Pinkas Synagogue, Prague. The inscription indicates that it was given by the Rabbi Abraham Ellbogen and his wife in 1710. The silk has been mounted upside down in the mantle. (See H. Volavkova, *The Synagogue Treasures of Bohemia and Moravia*, Pls. 37–39.) A design dated 1710 which has much the same rhythm and rather elongated forms is reproduced in Plate 43B, below.

B. About 1710; French.   (See p. 97)

Green damask, brocaded with silver and silver-gilt thread, and with pink silk details.
Width 21 in. (53·4 cm.). Repeat; height 28½ in. (71·8 cm.).
London, Victoria and Albert Museum, T17–1956.

PLATE 43

A. About 1710; French or Italian.   (See p. 98)

The silk is a red damask, brocaded with silver-gilt thread, and with yellow and green details.
Width of the silk about 20¼ in. (51 cm.).
Prague, The Jewish Museum. No. 924.

    Part of a curtain presented to the Lipnik Synagogue in 1811. The fragments of this silk have here been assembled and re-photographed to show the full pattern. (See H. Volavkova, *The Synagogue Treasures of Bohemia and Moravia*, Prague, 1949, Pls. 28–30.) A chasuble of the same material bearing the embroidered date 1710 is in the Ferdinandeum, Innsbruck (illustrated by A. Geijer, *Über die bizarren Stoffe*, in the *Festschrift für Erich Meyer*, Hamburg, 1959, fig. 5).

B. English Silk-Design by James Leman (see Note on Plate 37).   (See pp. 97–98)

Inscribed 'London, June 13th 1710. This pattern for an orrace tissue brocaded with silk [and] gold.
    For my father Peter Leman. James Leman'.
Collection of Messrs. Vanners & Fennell Bros. Ltd., Sudbury. No. 79.

PLATE 44   (See p. 114)

A. About 1705–10; Probably French.

Green and white damask ground with an additional white effect in the pattern.
Width 19¾ in. (50 cm.), length of the fragment 28½ in. (72 cm.).
Dresden, Museum für Kunsthandwerk. No. 16364.

B. About 1710–15; Probably French.

Red and white damask with an additional white effect in the pattern.
Overall width of the chasuble, about 30 in. (76 cm.). Repeat; height 18½ in. (47 cm.).
Gothenburg, Historiskamuseet. No. 74–1924. From Roasjö Church, Västergötland.

PLATE 45   (See p. 99)

A. English Silk-Design by James Leman (see Note on Plate 37); 1711.

Inscribed 'London, July 3rd 1711. This pattern for an orrace tissue brocaded with silk of 2 or more
    colours... For my father Peter Leman. By me James Leman'.
Collection of Messrs. Vanners & Fennell Bros. Ltd., Sudbury. No. 36.

B. Engraving of a Silk-Design by Daniel Marot; about 1711. (See p. 99)

Marot was not a silk-designer but he must have understood the general principles of repeating patterns suitable for weaving when he drew this and two other compositions, all three of which are supposed to have been published in Holland before 1712. He may of course have consulted a Dutch silk-designer (see p. 65) and he must have studied contemporary silk-patterns. Marot's three designs would have been entirely up-to-date in 1711–12 (as a comparison with English silk-designs shows) but with these designs he was probably not breaking fresh ground in this specialized field even though he was a brilliant designer of ornament in general. (See P. Jessen, *Ornamentwerk*, 1892, Pls. 199, 204 and 205.)

PLATE 46

A. About 1712; French or Italian.

Dalmatic of a silk damask brocaded with silk and silver thread.
Pisa Cathedral Sacristy. (Allinari photograph).

B. About 1714; French. (See pp. 99, 107)

Dress of a silk with a damask ground brocaded with silver-gilt thread.
Width 20¾ in. (53 cm.). Repeat; height 24 in. (61 cm.).
Copenhagen, National Museum. No. 802/1922. (See the Commemorative volume published by
the National Museum in 1957 on the occasion of its bi-centenary, p. 130, where this dress is
illustrated in colour.)

The dress comes from Valdemarslot, the seat of the Juel family, and is thought to have been worn by Christine Elisabeth Juel (1675–1738) who was first married in 1695 and then again in 1714. The dress was perhaps made for her second wedding.

PLATE 47

A. 1710–15; French.

Yellow damask ground, brocaded with silver and silver-gilt thread and with coloured silks.
Paris, Musée des Arts Décoratifs. No. 2600.

B. About 1712–15; French. (See p. 98)

Claret-coloured damask ground, brocaded with silver and silver-gilt thread and with silk —
principally pink and dark green.
Width 21 in. (53·4 cm.). Repeat; height 27½ in. (69·8 cm.).
London, Victoria and Albert Museum. No. T.130–1938.

PLATE 48

A. About 1713; French. (See pp. 98, 107)

Cream-coloured silk damask brocaded with coloured silks and metal thread.
Cologne, Schnütgen Museum.

According to information kindly supplied by the Cologne City Archivist, the arms embroidered on this chasuble are those of the von Codone and the von Groote families. Johann Jacob von Codone married Maria Anna von Groote in August 1713; it seems probable that the chasuble is of that date or that the bride's wedding-dress was later made up into a chasuble, as was often the practice. I am indebted to Miss Natalie Rothstein for drawing my attention to this silk.

B. About 1715; French (Lyons?). (See p. 107)

Green damask ground. The foliage is yellowish green; there are details in pink, white and silver-gilt thread.

Width 21 in. (54 cm.), height of fragment 23 in. (58 cm.).

Lyons, Musée Historique des Tissus. No. 1655.

PLATE 49 (See p. 99)

A. About 1714; English or French.

Waistcoat of silk with a blue satin ground largely covered by silver-gilt thread, decorated with small brocaded silk flowers.

London, Westminster Abbey. (Victoria and Albert Museum Photograph.)

The waistcoat is that worn by the effigy of Robert Sheffield, Marquess of Normanby, who died in February 1715 at the age of three.

B. About 1714.

Portrait by Alexis-Simon Belle (1640–1734), thought to be of Matthew Prior.

In an English private collection. (I am greatly indebted to Mr. Richard Kingzett of Messrs. Thomas Agnew & Sons for obtaining the owner's permission for me to reproduce this splendid portrait here.)

PLATE 50

A. 1715–20; French (Lyons?). (See p. 107)

Green damask brocaded with coloured silks and silver-gilt thread.

Width 20¼ in. (51·5 cm.)? Repeat; height 28¼ in. (72 cm.).

Paris, Union Française des Arts du Costume.

Detail of a magnificent dress of the *Régence* period which came from a collection that belonged to the Heurtault, Du Quesne and Bonneval families. (The whole dress is illustrated in colour in R. König and P. W. Schupisser, *Die Mode in der menschlichen Gesellschaft*, Zürich, 1958, Plate opposite p. 174. I am much indebted to Monsieur François Boucher for providing me with this photograph and the above information.)

B. English Silk-Design; Probably Drawn in 1717. (See p. 106)

Width 10 in. (25·4 cm.), height of drawing (torn) 18 in. (45·7 cm.).

London, Victoria and Albert Museum. E.4481–1909.

This comes from a set of designs from the establishment of James Leman, an important Spitalfields silk manufacturer, which range in date from 1717 to 1722. Since this drawing is numbered '1' and is badly torn, it may have been the first in the set and is therefore probably from the year 1717, although this is not certain. This date would, however, fit our present theory about the date of such patterns and the drawing can anyway not be later than 1722. Leman may have composed this pattern himself but since he also commissioned work from independent designers, this too is not certain. Other designs from Leman's establishment of this period are shown in Plates 51A, 52A, 53B, 54A. Leman's early work has already been discussed (see Note to Plate 37).

167

PLATE 51 (See p. 99)

A. English Silk-Design Dated 'May 19th 1718'.

Width 10½ in. (26·6 cm.), height 28 in. (71·2 cm.). The width of the silk would thus have been about 21 in. (53·4 cm.).

London, Victoria and Albert Museum. No. E. 4451–1909.

This is from the same set of drawings as that illustrated in Plate 50B.

B. About 1718; English or French.

Silk with a red satin ground largely obscured by silver and silver-gilt thread and with details executed on a dull blue-grey, dark green, pink and yellow silks.

London, The Spanish and Portuguese Synagogue, Bevis Marks.

Made up as a Torah Mantle embroidered with the cipher AMDC for Abraham Mendes da Costa who is known to have commissioned a Torah Scroll in 1720. This mantle must belong to the scroll. The silk has a pattern very similar to the design shown in the adjoining plate.

PLATE 52 (See p. 107)

A. English Silk-Design, Dated May 22nd, 1718.

Width 10¼ in. (23·5 cm.), height 18¼ in. (46·3 cm.). The silk would thus have been about 20½ in. (52 cm.) wide.

London, Victoria and Albert Museum. E.4466–1909.

This is from the same set of drawings as that illustrated in Plate 50B.

B. Detail from a Painting by Antoine Watteau, *La Danse*, or *Iris, c'est de bonne heurre ...*

Berlin (Dalem), Gemäldgalerie der Ehemals Staatlichen Museen.

This painting is thought to date from about 1719 (see H. Adhemar, *Watteau; sa vie — son œuvre*, Paris, 1950, Cat. No. 208). Compare the pattern on the silk of the dress with the design in the adjoining illustration.

PLATE 53

A. About 1720; English (Spitalfields). (See p. 111)

Brocaded damask with a cream-coloured ground. The brocaded colours are a pinkish purple coupled with a flesh-pink, and a dull dark blue linked with a light blue. The purple and the dull blue are typical of English silks and silk-designs of this period.

Width 21⅛ in. (54 cm.). Repeat; height 24¼ in. (61·6 cm.).

London, Victoria and Albert Museum. No. 688–1899.

The pattern is very similar to several designs from James Leman's collection (see Note to Pl. 50B).

B. English Silk-Design, Inscribed 'London, May 12, 1721'. (See pp. 110–111)

Stated to be a design for a 'paduasoy' (*pou de soie*), brocaded with gold and one colour. We are not absolutely certain what a paduasoy was but the indications are that it was a rich and heavy silk with a tabby ground and a self-coloured pattern, also in tabby weave. They were usually brocaded as well, as in this instance.

London, Victoria and Albert Museum. No. E.4446–1909.

From the same collection as the design illustrated in Plate 50B. The designer has only drawn one half of the pattern which would have been symmetrical about a vertical axis, in this case represented by the left-hand margin of the drawing.

PLATE 54

A. ENGLISH SILK-DESIGN, DATED APRIL 28TH, 1721.   (See pp. 107, 111)

Width 10 in. (25·4 cm.), height 22¾ in. (57·8 cm.). The width of the silk would thus have been 20 in.

London, Victoria and Albert Museum. E.4519–1909.

This design would have been symmetrical and should be read like that illustrated in Plate 53B.

B. ABOUT 1721; ENGLISH.

Brocaded damask with white ribbed and blue satin stripes, the pattern in white and green with bluish-red details.

Width of the material 19 in. (48·3 cm.), height 21 in. (53·4 cm.).

London, Victoria and Albert Museum. No. T.14–1945.

This striking pattern is closely related to some of the designs woven by James Leman about 1721 (see Note to Pl. 50B). The style of the dress suggests a date between 1715 and 1725. There was an undated portrait of a girl wearing a dress of this material in the Hengrave Hall Sale in 1952 (lot 1786), probably painted by J. Worsdale (c. 1692–1767).

PLATE 55

A. ABOUT 1720–25; FRENCH.   (See p. 111)

Crimson damask with a pattern in two kinds of silver thread.

Width 20½ in. (52 cm.). Repeat; height 21 in. (53·4 cm.).

London, Victoria and Albert Museum. No. T.128–1938.

B. ENGLISH SILK-DESIGN; DATED 1725.   (See p. 112)

Inscribed '. . . For Mr. Lekeux. March the 11, 1725 . . .'.

Width 10 in. (25·4 cm.); the full design would thus have been 20 in. wide. Repeat; height 20¼ in. (51·4 cm.).

London, Victoria and Albert Museum. No. 5973–11.

Designed by Christopher Baudouin, a prominent English silk-designer. Information about Baudouin, together with a reproduction of the inscription on the back of a drawing related to the present design which enables one to attribute both of them to him, will be found in an article by P. Thornton and N. Rothstein, 'The Importance of the Huguenots in the London Silk-industry', *Proceedings of the Huguenot Society of London*, Vol. XX, No. 1, pp. 66–69 and Pl. VI, 1. Mr. Lekeux was a prominent Spitalfields weaver of brocaded silks.

PLATE 56   (See p. 114)

A. ABOUT 1715–20; FRENCH.

Pink ground with a pattern mainly in white but with secondary effects in ivory-coloured silk (*frisé*).

Width of fragment 19½ in. (49·5 cm.). Repeat; height 24 in. (61 cm.).

Krefeld, Gewebesammlung der Textilingenieurschule. No. 00529/F954a.

B. FRENCH SILK-DESIGN; DATED 1725. (See p. 114)

Inscribed '*nouveau de l'année 1725*'.
Paris, Bibliothèque Nationale, Cabinet des Estampes, Vol. Lh.44a.

This is one of several designs in the French collections bearing the date 1725. No earlier date has yet been found on a *French* silk-design. Comparison with the design illustrated in Plate 58B suggests that this may also be by 'Ringuet', who can almost certainly be equated with the famous Lyonnais designer, Jean Ringuet (see Note to Pl. 58B).

PLATE 57

A. 1725–30; FRENCH. (See p. 112)

This dress is preserved at Lysekloster in Norway and is traditionally supposed to have been worn by a member of the Forman family at her wedding in 1755. This seems unlikely as the silk appears to date from the second half of the 1720's and would have been very old-fashioned in 1755. There was apparently another wedding in the family in 1730 and it seems much more likely that the dress was made for that occasion. (I am deeply indebted to Mrs. Kielland of the Kunst-industrimuseum, Oslo, and to Dr. Robert Kloster of the Vestlandske Kunstindustrimuseum, Bergen, for information about this fine dress and for supplying me with this photograph.) When the photograph was taken it was generally believed that such silks all belonged to the 1690's, which is probably why the lady has been furnished with a *fontange* head-dress of the kind that went out of fashion about 1708. She would of course not have worn such a head-dress in the 1720's. The photograph shows very clearly the way the material has been made up so as to display the formal pattern to the best advantage.

B. ABOUT 1725–30; FRENCH(?).

Fawn-coloured satin ground with a pattern rendered in off-white silk bound in two different ways to produce two effects.
Width about 21 in. (53·4 cm.). Repeat; height 13¾ in. (34·5 cm.).
London, Victoria and Albert Museum. No. 1232–1877.

PLATE 58

A. FRENCH SILK-DESIGN; DATED 1726. (See pp. 110, 112)

Inscribed '*Persienne en deux dorures ... de Mr. Molon, de l'année 1726. Fond de moisayque, la moisayque continuee*'.
Paris, Bibliothèque National, Cabinet des Estampes, Vol. Lh. 44a.

A *persienne* was a silk with a satin ground; this material was to have a pattern executed in two kinds of gold thread. The ground was to be diapered (*mosaïque*); a single repeat of the ground pattern is shown in the top left-hand corner. '*Mr. Molon*' was almost certainly the famous Lyonnais designer, Jean Monlong, whom Joubert de l'Hiberderie praised in his *Dessinateur pour les Fabriques d'étoffes d'or, d'argent et de soie* (Paris, 1764, p. x) as an artist who '*possédoit parfaite-ment la composition de l'Étoffe qu'il traitoit noblement*' (see Chapter IV).

B. FRENCH SILK-DESIGN; DATED [17]28. (See pp. 110, 112, 113)

For a rich silk with two kinds of silver and two kinds of silver-gilt thread, and with coloured flowers, stated to be by '*Mr. Ringuet ... nouveau du mois de 7bre ... 28*'.
In the same volume as the Monlong design here illustrated with it.

Ringuet is also mentioned by Joubert, who credits him as having *'indroduit le premier les fleurs naturelles sur l'Étoffe.'* (See Chapter IV, here, and P. Thornton, 'Jean Revel, dessinateur de la Grande Fabrique, in the *Gazette des Beaux-Arts*, July–August, 1960, where a silk with a very similar pattern to this is illustrated in fig. 11.)

PLATE 59
(See pp. 107, 113)

A. Portrait of the Princess Frederike Luise of Prussia with her Betrothed, the Margrave of Brandenburg-Ansbach, Painted by Antoine Pesne, Probably in 1729.
Berlin, Schloss Charlottenburg.

See G. Poensgen, *Antoine Pesne*, Berlin, 1958, fig. 90 and No. 106c. The couple were married in May 1729.

B. *'The reading from Moliere'*, Painted by Jean-François de Troy.   (See pp. 113, 141)
In the collection of the Marquess of Cholmondeley, Houghton Hall, Norfolk, by whose kind permission this photograph is reproduced.

On the left-hand chair is the date 1710 but everything points to a date in the late 1720's. The silk worn by the lady on the left has a pattern rather like that illustrated in Plate 58B which was composed by Ringuet in 1728. The whole question of the date of this painting is discussed by J. Cailleux in a supplement to the February 1960 issue of *The Burlington Magazine*.

PLATE 60

A. French Silk-Design; Dated 1729.   (See pp. 110, 112)
For a rich silk with two kinds of gold thread. Inscribed *'de Mr Molon de 1729'*.
Paris, Bibliothèque Nationale, Vol. Lh. 44a.

See note to Plate 58A where another design by Monlong is discussed.

B. About 1730; French (Lyons).   (See pp. 108, 113, 114, 116)
Bronze-coloured satin with a pattern executed in off-white, shades of pink ranging through to brown, yellow, shades of green, and light and dark blue.
Width about 21¾ in. (55 cm.).
Lyons, Musée Historique des Tissus. No. 25–703. (See R. Cox, *Le Musée Historique des Tissus*, Paris, 1914, Vol. I, Pl. 27, where this silk is called *'Louis XIV'*.)

There is a design for a silk rather like this in the Library of the Paris Musée des Arts Décoratifs. This is illustrated in that Museum's repertoires of ornament and designs (Série XXI, published in 1912, Pl. 46) where it is wrongly, I believe, attributed to Tours. Reasons for tentatively attributing this pattern to the famous Lyonnais designer Jean Ringuet, are given in the Note on p. 113.

PLATE 61

A. About 1729–31; English or French.   (See p. 116)
Dark green ribbed silk ground, the foliage rendered in white and grey; the flowers yellow and in shades of pink, blue and mauve.
The London Museum. No. 33. 40–1.

Made up as a dress. The silk is very well woven and, if it is English, as seems probable, is a very good imitation of a contemporary French silk. It even has a dark ground which is more typical of French than English silks of the period. The dark green of the ground, however, is a colour commonly found in English silks of the time but more normally used for the foliage (e.g. see Pl. 65B).

B. ABOUT 1730–31; PROBABLY FRENCH. (See p. 115)

Pink satin brocaded with two kinds of silver-gilt thread. Trimmed with silver-gilt lace.

Copenhagen, The Danish Royal Collections, Rosenborg Castle. (See S. F. Christensen, *Kongedragterne*, No. 72, Pl. LXXXI and LXXX.)

Detail of a suit worn by King Christian VI of Denmark at his Coronation in 1731. The rich lace trimming makes it difficult to distinguish the pattern but close inspection shows it is a member of the 'lace-pattern' group.

C. 1736; FRENCH. (See p. 115)

White taffeta (tabby) with a bronze-coloured pattern, the details executed in silver, green, yellow and purple thread.

Paris, Bibliothèque Nationale, Cabinet des Estampes, Richelieu Collection, Vol. Lh.45b, No. 1319.

This fragment is pasted onto a page inscribed '1736'. It is presumably part of a symmetrical pattern, a late example of the typical 'lace-patterns' of the 1720's.

PLATE 62

A. ABOUT 1731–32; FRENCH (PROBABLY LYONS). (See pp. 116–117)

Brocaded satin, the ground light yellow, the leaves shaded green to white, the flowers in shades of pink and mauve. Black details.

Width 22 in. (56 cm.). Repeat; height 26 in. (66 cm.).

Lyons, Musée Historique des Tissus. No. 25.642.

The colouring is typical of a large group that is probably associated with Lyons. The rather ponderous floral composition in which considerable use is made of black and white suggests that this may be an early example of the work of Jean Revel, here still working within the rather rigid, symmetrical convention typical of the 1720's.

B. LATE 17TH CENTURY(?). (See p. 114)

Silk with an off-white ribbed ground and a pattern in blue and white with details in shades of pink, light green, buff and mauve.

Width 22 in. (55·9 cm.). Repeat; height 14 in. (35·6 cm.).

London, Victoria and Albert Museum. No. 626–1890.

This and the silk illustrated in Plate 77B are probably examples of the kinds of material woven at Lyons during the late 17th and first half of the 18th century for the 'second-class' market. The materials are never brocaded and the patterns are somewhat formalized and simplified versions of the current fashionable designs at each stage. They must have been rather less expensive to produce than their more ambitious counterparts. The colour-changes in the pattern are sometimes abrupt and the pattern-wefts often produce shadowy bands across the material. Until about 1740, the patterns are always symmetrical (point repeats) and the central floral motif usually springs from a vase. Numerous examples of this class of materials have survived. As in the two cases illustrated here, the pinks and the greens are of shades that I associate with Lyons and, while similar materials were no doubt made elsewhere, it seems likely that many of them came from Lyons. Lacking the subtlety of the finer silks, these patterns tend to be rather gaudy but are, for the most part, quite effective.

PLATE 63 (See p. 117)

A. French Silk-Design; Dated 1733.

For a silk with a wine-coloured gros de Tours ground, brocaded with silver and coloured silks.
Paris, Bibliothèque Nationale. Vol. Lh. 44d.

In Chapter V reasons are given for tentatively attributing this striking design to the Lyonnais silk-designer Courtois.

B. About 1733; French.

Brown satin ground, the pattern executed in brownish pinks, black, a straw-colour, yellow and grey-green. The small white leaves have been embroidered on the finished silk and are therefore not part of the original design.
Width 21½ in. (54·6 cm.). Repeat; height 16½ in. (41·9 cm.).
London, Victoria and Albert Museum. No. 112–1880.

In spite of the added embroidery, it is still possible to see the similarity between this pattern and that of the design shown with it. The similarity of this pattern to another design, obviously by the same hand and of about the same date, and also in the Bibliothèque Nationale (Vol. Lh.44d, No. 29), is even more marked.

PLATE 64

A. About 1730–33; French (Lyons). (See p. 120)

Dark green satin; the temple chiefly white; the flowers in shades of red through pink to white; the leaves yellow shaded through green to white; the whole shadowed in black.
Width of fragment 18¾ in. (47 cm.), height 19½ in. (49 cm.).
Lyons, Musée Historique des Tissus. Vol. 19, no. 31.930.

The free use of black and white, made by the designer of this impressive silk, produces a startling effect, almost as if the extraordinarily naturalistic motifs were being seen in a thundery light. This is very probably the work of the Lyonnais designer, Jean Revel, produced just before he introduced the *points rentrés* technique of shading (see Chapter V).

B. English Silk-Design; Dated 1733. (See p. 117)

Width 10⅝ in. (the final width would thus have been 21¼ in. or 54 cm.). Repeat; height 28½ in. (72·4 cm.).
London, Victoria and Albert Museum. No. 5972–6.

By the Spitalfields designer, Anna Maria Garthwaite, who was to become one of, if not the, principal supplier of high-class designs to the London silk industry during the 1740's and early 1750's. A large body of her designs has survived: they are all in the Victoria and Albert Museum, London (see Note 4, p. 19 and Chapters V and VI).

PLATE 65 (See p. 118)

A. About 1734; English (Spitalfields).

Ribbed white silk ground, the pattern rendered in shades of green, blue, pink and mauve.

Width 21 in. (53·4 cm.). Repeat; height 23 in. (58·5 cm.).
London, Victoria and Albert Museum. No. T.99–1912.

    Mr. John Nevinson has very kindly drawn my attention to a portrait by Violante Siries (c. 1709–1783) of a lady wearing a dress of this material and dated 1736. The picture was sold at Christie's on 9th February 1951 (lot 144).

B. ABOUT 1734; ENGLISH (SPITALFIELDS).

Off-white ribbed silk ground, the pattern dark green with details in shades of pink and blue.
Width 16½ in. (41·9 cm.); this is an unusually narrow silk. It will be remembered that there were
    no regulations governing the widths of silks in force in England (see p. 58). Repeat; height
    16½ in. (41·9 cm.).
London, Victoria and Albert Museum. No. T.719–1913.

    This silk is typical of an easily recognized group of English silks whose chief characteristic is the dark green used for the main sections of the pattern. They belong to the late 1720's and the 1730's.

PLATE 66

A. ENGLISH SILK-DESIGN; ABOUT 1734.

Width 8½ in. (21·5 cm.); the silk would thus have been about 17 in. wide. Repeat; height 17¼ in.
    (43·8 cm.).
London, Victoria and Albert Museum, No. 5971–22.

    By Anna Maria Garthwaite. Its date has been established by comparison with the many dated designs in the set to which it belongs (see Note to Plate 64B).

B. ABOUT 1734–35; ENGLISH (SPITALFIELDS).   (See p. 118)

Detail of a dress of a brocaded silk with a white ground.
Boston, Museum of Fine Arts. No. 43.1691. (See the Museum's Bulletin, Vol. XLIII, p. 27, where
    the whole dress is illustrated.)

    The pattern of this silk is clearly related to the design shown next to it; it is even more similar to other designs from about 1734 by Anna Maria Garthwaite in the same set (e.g. No. 5971–25).

PLATE 67

A. ABOUT 1733–34; ENGLISH (SPITALFIELDS).

Black satin ground with bright green leaves, white trees. The flowers either executed in two
    shades of pink and orange, or in shades of purple with a bronze-colour. The small berries are
    light blue.
Width about 19½ in. (49·5 cm.). Repeat; height 28½ in. (72·4 cm.).
London, Victoria and Albert Museum, No. T.9–1939.

B. ABOUT 1735; FRENCH.   (See p. 119)

Close-up of a fragment of a richly brocaded French silk showing the use of the *points rentrés*
    technique of shading in the petals of a flower. Grey ground; purple and silver flowers.
Paris, Bibliothèque Nationale, Richelieu Collection, Vol. Lh.45b.

    Not every page of samples in the Richelieu Collection bears a date but the date 1735 appears on one of the pages preceding that on which this sample is mounted.

PLATE 68 (See p. 120)

A. A French Silk-Design; About 1732–33.

Inscribed '*Revelle à vous seulle*' (partially cut away in this photograph) and presumably by Jean Revel, the famous Lyonnais designer.

Paris, Bibliothèque Nationale, Vol. Lh.44d.

My attention was drawn to this very important design by Miss Natalie Rothstein. Like the silk shown in Plate 64A and in the adjoining Plate here, this composition must date from the period just before Revel introduced the use of *points rentrés* for the modelling and shading of motifs. (See P. Thornton, 'Jean Revel, dessinateur de la Grande Fabrique', in the *Gazette des Beaux-Arts*, July 1960, where this and other specimens of Revel's early work are discussed and illustrated.)

B. About 1732–33; French (Lyons).

Dark green satin ground. The large fruit are white with shades of pink; the smaller fruit are black and purple; the flowers, black, purple, light green, pink, brick-coloured, and blue. The leaves are dark, light and very light green.

Width of fragment $22\frac{1}{4}$ in. (56 cm.), height 26 in. (66 cm.).

Lyons, Musée historique des Tissus. No. 25.642.

It is interesting to note that the Spitalfields designer Anna Maria Garthwaite had, among her collection of 'French Patterns', a French drawing of this very same composition (Victoria and Albert Museum, No. 5974–7). According to the French inscription on the drawing it was to have a yellow *gros de tours* ground, and not a green satin ground as in the silk reproduced here. The inscription is evidently in the same hand as that on the design inscribed '*Revelle à vous seulle*' (Pl. 68A), and is thus presumably also by Jean Revel. It bears the date '*1734*' inscribed on it by Garthwaite; this probably records when she received it — by which time it may have been perhaps a year old. The date of this and related patterns is discussed on p. 120 and in the article referred to under Plate 68A. Another drawing for this composition, lacking an inscription, is in the Musée des Arts Décoratifs, Paris (Galais Collection, Vol. 1, No. 32).

PLATE 69 (See pp. 120–122)

A. Fragment of a Draft (*mise-en-carte*) Inscribed '*J. Revel . . . a Lyon, 22e Dec. 1733*'.

Lyons, École de Tissage, now on loan to the Musée Historique des Tissus. (I am extremely grateful to M. F. Guicherd, past Professor at the Ecole de Tissage and now curator of the Musée des Tissus, for drawing my attention to this extremely important document and for giving me permission to publish it here.)

As far as I know, this is the only surviving signed work by Revel. A coloured design (*esquisse*) for this pattern is in the Musée des Arts Décoratifs, Paris (Galais Collection, Vol. 13) and serves to help one identify the several other drawings by this master in the same collection. A copy by a less competent French draughtsman is among the 'French Patterns' owned by the Spitalfields designer, Anna Maria Garthwaite (Victoria and Albert Museum, No. 5974–10). She inscribed the date '1735' on it, presumably recording when she received it, something between thirteen and twenty-four months after its composition at Lyons by Revel. (This and related patterns are discussed in the article referred to under Plate 68A.) I understand from Miss Natalie Rothstein that she has now found an actual silk woven from this design: this I hope she will publish in due course.

B. About 1734; French (Lyons).

White ribbed ground with a delicately brocaded pattern.
Width 21¾ in. (55·5 cm.). Repeat; height 16½ in. (42·5 cm.).
Lyons, Musée Historique des Tissus. No. 26.452.

PLATE 70

A. French Silk-Design; About 1734.　　　　　　　(See pp. 116, 120, 121)

Paris, Musée des Arts Décoratifs. (Martin Collection, Vol. I, No. i).

　This design must also be by Jean Revel; it is of the highest quality, both in composition and execution. (See the article already referred to under Plate 68A.)

B. About 1733–34; French (Lyons).

This silk has a fancy brown ground, and scenery surrounded by naturalistic flowers executed in coloured silks.
Lyons, Musée Historique des Tissus. No. 24.568.

　A design for this pattern is in the Musée des Arts Décoratifs, Paris (Galais Collection; illustrated in Série XXI of the Repertoire of Designs published by the Bibliothèque in 1912, Pl. 2A). It so closely resembles other designs attributable to Jean Revel that there can be little doubt this silk was also designed by him.

PLATE 71

A. About 1735; French (Lyons).

Made up as a chasuble. The silk has a pink ground.
Vienna, Museum für Angewandte Kunst, No. T.7053.

　This silk is almost certainly after a design by Jean Revel.

B. About 1735; French (Lyons).

Green taffeta (tabby) ground with naturalistic flowers, the large radiating leaves being worked in silver.
Width 22¼ in. (56 cm.). Repeat; height 15 in. (38 cm.).
Lyons, Musée Historique des Tissus. No. 26.168.

　A fine drawing, which is almost certainly French, of this very pattern has been pasted into the volume of James Leman's early designs which is now in the possession of Messrs. Vanners & Fennell Bros. (See Note to Pl. 37; the drawing is illustrated by F. Lewis, *James Leman . . .* , Leigh-on-Sea, 1954, Pl. 1.) This and four other French, or copies of French, designs from the 1730's have been pasted onto pages from which the original designs by Leman have been removed; it is perfectly reasonable to suppose that these five drawings also belonged to Leman who would very probably have made it his business to acquire contemporary French patterns, just as Garthwaite did (see Pl. 68B and 79B). This design must also be by Jean Revel.

PLATE 72　　　　　　　　　　　　　　　　　　　　　(See p. 121)

A. About 1735 or slightly later; French (Lyons).

Green satin with green and black foliage, gold and shaded purple *rocailles* and red and mauve fruit. The figures and birds are light blue.

Repeat; width 15¼ in. (38·5 cm.), height 26 in. (66 cm.).
Lyons, Musée Historique des Tissus. No. 31.449.

I cannot agree with the traditional view that this very pretty design is in the *style Pillement*. It seems almost certain that it was composed by Jean Revel during the 1730's — when Pillement was still a boy (Pillement was born in 1728).

B. PORTRAIT BY ANTOINE PESNE OF FREDERICK THE GREAT'S SISTER, THE PRINCESS SOPHIE OF PRUSSIA, WITH HER BETROTHED, THE MARGRAVE FRIEDRICH WILHELM OF BRANDEN-BURG-SCHWEDT. (See p. 123)

The couple were married in 1734. (See the book mentioned in the Note to Pl. 59A, fig. 91).
Berlin, Schloss Charlottenburg. Nr. 292a.

She is wearing a silk closely related to the patterns illustrated in Plate 68.

PLATE 73

A. ABOUT 1735; PROBABLY FRENCH (PERHAPS TOURS). (See p. 122)
Brown satin ground brocaded with coloured silks and silver thread.
Width 21 in. (53·4 cm.). Repeat; height 26 in. (66·1 cm.).
London, Victoria and Albert Museum. No. 600–1896.

The sombre colour-scheme, with a predominating dull purple-brown, suggests that this silk was woven at Tours. At any rate, it must be an attempt to imitate the style of Jean Revel. Note, however, that the motifs are merely reversed alternately; Revel would surely always have invented a different motif for the intervening section?

B. ABOUT 1735; ENGLISH (SPITALFIELDS). (See p. 123)
White ribbed ground, brocaded with bright colours including a strong red with a purple tinge.
    Made up as a dress.
London, Victoria and Albert Museum. No. T.193–1958.

The design of this material must be French; it resembles no known English designs except in a most general way (e.g. Pl. 74A). The colouring, however, is typically English and one is forced to conclude that this silk is a direct line for line copy of a French silk, executed in London. The French original is likely to have had a coloured and not a white ground.

PLATE 74

A. ENGLISH SILK-DESIGN; DATED 1735. (See pp. 118, 122)
Signed '*Anna Maria Garthwaite*'. See Note to Plate 64B.
Width 20 in. (50·8 cm.). Repeat; height 23 in. (58·5 cm.).
London, Victoria and Albert Museum. No. 5977–2.
This shows Garthwaite imitating the Revel style.

B. ABOUT 1735–36; ENGLISH (SPITALFIELDS). (See p. 122)
Silk with a white taffeta (tabby) ground brocaded in coloured silks and rich metal thread. Made up as a dress.
Boston, Museum of Fine Arts. 43.1642.

This dress was worn by Lydia Catherine, third wife of the Duke of Chandos, a lady reputed to have been 'worth £40,000', whom he married in April 1736. The dress must be of about that date and may perhaps therefore have been her wedding-dress. The complete dress is illustrated in the Museum's *Bulletin*, Vol. XLIII, June, 1945, p. 29.

PLATE 75

A. About 1735–40; French (probably Tours). (See p. 122)

Silk with a silver-gilt ground. The fruit and flowers are white, shades of pink, reddish orange, reddish brown, dull gold, khaki, and blue. The foliage is worked in shades of blue-green and chartreuse green.

Width 21 in. (53·4 cm.). Height of fragment 20⅛ in. (50·1 cm.).

Cleveland, Museum of Art. Gift of Mr. and Mrs. J. H. Wade, No. 16.1427. (I am much indebted to Miss Dorothy Shepherd for the above information.)

The reddish brown and the blue-green shades suggest a Tours provenance for this silk. This tentative attribution is strengthened by the fact that a detail design (*esquisse*) for the pineapple motif is preserved in the Musée des Arts Décoratifs, Paris (Galais Collection, Vol. 9, p. 1: the volume mainly contains designs by the Tours designer Riffe) bears the pencilled inscription '*L.D. pinx.*'. These initials may be those of Louis Durand who, according to Bossebœuf (*La Fabrique de Soieries de Tours*, 1900, p. 460), was praised in 1768 by the Controleur General as '*un artiste distingué*' at Tours. The *esquisse* is excellent and one might easily mistake it for the work of Revel at first glance.

B. About 1735–40; French(?).

Silk with a deep golden yellow ribbed ground, silver scrollwork and polychrome flowers. The purples are very dull.

Width 20½ in. (52 cm.). Repeat; height 18 in. (45·7 cm.).

London, Victoria and Albert Museum. No. T.127–1938.

Again the dull colouring suggests this was woven at Tours. Could this perhaps also be after a design by Louis Durand?

PLATE 76

A. About 1735–40; Possibly Dutch. (See p. 122)

Brown satin; the pattern dull green and white with details in pink, blue, greenish yellow and puce.

No selvedges remain but the fragment is still 28½ in. (71·2 cm.) wide, which is unusually wide for a figured silk of this period. Repeat; height 23½ in. (59·6 cm.).

London, Victoria and Albert Museum. No. 611–1896.

The drawing of this pattern does not seem to be sufficiently good to be French and the silk does not resemble any of the familiar types of French or English materials. It may possibly be Dutch or perhaps Italian.

B. About 1736–40; French.

Off-white satin with a pattern mostly in shades of green, the two vases being shaded from pink to purple; the other vase (below) is blue.

Fragment, width 10¾ in. (27 cm.), height 16¼ in. (41 cm.).

Lyons, Musée Historique des Tissus. No. 25.251a.

A sample of a very similar silk under the date '1736' is in the Richelieu Collection, Bibliothèque Nationale, Paris (Vol. Lh.45b).

PLATE 77

A. About 1735–40; French(?).   (See p. 122)

White satin ground, the boats dark brown, the flowers shaded blue, the fruit shaded from red to black. The pattern has an engraved appearance due to fine black detail.

Fragment, width 14¼ in. (36 cm.), height 14½ in. (37 cm.).

Lyons, Musée Historique des Tissus. No. 25.251b.

Such silks — there are other specimens of the same type in various collections — may have been made at one of the smaller French centres or perhaps in Holland.

B. About 1735–45; French(?).   (See p. 114)

Off-white ground with a fancy pattern. The main pattern in shades of green (including the yellowish-green typical of many silks apparently attributable to Lyons), pink, brown, blue and touches of black. Made up as a dalmatic. The embroidery is thought to be Spanish. The arms are those of the Franciscan Order.

The central panel of silk is 16½ in. (41·9 cm.) wide. Repeat; height 15½ in. 39·3 cm.).

London, Victoria and Albert Museum. 276–1870.

See Note to Plate 62B.

PLATE 78   (See p. 123)

A. About 1733; French.

Brown and white; tabby weave.

Fragment, width 16½ in. (42 cm.), height 16¼ in. (41 cm.).

Lyons, Musée Historique des Tissus. No. 1442.

In France, this kind of silk was generally known as a '*Ras de Sicile*'.

B. About 1733; English (Spitalfields).

With a ribbed dark purple-brown ground, the pattern executed in two shades of off-white (the one in satin weave, the other in twill-bound pattern wefts).

Width 19½ in. (49·5 cm.). Repeat; height 26 in. (66·1 cm.).

London, Victoria and Albert Museum. No. T.129–1912.

This pattern is similar to designs composed by Anna Maria Garthwaite about 1733.

PLATE 79

A. About 1738–42; French (Lyons).   (See p. 125)

Green fancy ground, heavily brocaded with silver-gilt thread and with splendid colours including the rich purple which seems to be associated with Lyons materials. Made up as a cope.

Width 20 in. (50·8 cm.). Repeat; height 15 in. (38·1 cm.).

London, Victoria and Albert Museum. No. T.86–1909.

The general style of this silk suggests that it may be an example of Jean Revel's work about 1740. It can be approximately dated by reference to rather similar compositions by Anna Maria Garthwaite bearing dates in the late 1730's and early 1740's.

B. French Silk-Design; About 1738–39.   (See pp. 125, 127)

Drawn in ink on stiff, grey-blue paper and painted with strong purples, dull greens and much white.

Width 11 in. (The silk would thus have been 22 in. wide, or 54·6 cm.). Repeat; height 21 in. (53·4 cm.).

London, Victoria and Albert Museum. No. 5974–23.

One of the group of designs, all by the same hand, included among the 'French Patterns' that belonged to the Spitalfields designer Anna Maria Garthwaite. On most of them she has inscribed the date '*1739*' which presumably records when she acquired them. They are not likely to have been more than a year old when she received them from France, no doubt by a clandestine route.

PLATE 80

A. About 1738; English (Spitalfields).

White ribbed silk ground with coloured flowers. Great use is made of black. Notable is a straw-colour and a very pale mauve. Made up as a dress.

Width 20 in. (50·8 cm.). Repeat; height 21½ in. (54·6 cm.).

London, Victoria and Albert Museum. T.342–1894.

This pattern is closely similar to designs by Anna Maria Garthwaite (e.g. No. 5977–1, dated 1738) and must have been composed by her.

B. English Silk-Design; Dated 1739. (See p. 125)

Executed chiefly in green, pink and mauve on white paper.

Width 19¼ in. (48·9 cm.), height 23½ in. (59·6 cm.).

London, Victoria and Albert Museum. No. 5977–14.

By Anna Maria Garthwaite (see Note to Plate 64B).

PLATE 81 (See p. 123)

A. English Silk-Design; About 1738–40.

Design for a silk damask with a particularly large pattern (see p. 123).

Width 21 in. (53·4 cm.). Repeat; height 34¼ in. (87 cm.).

London, Victoria and Albert Museum, No. 5976–20.

B. 1735–50; Probably French.

Fancy salmon-pink ground with a pattern in white.

Selvedges now missing; width 21 in. (53·4 cm.). Repeat; height about 19½ in. (49·5 cm.).

London, Victoria and Albert Museum. No. 299–1896.

This has at some time been used as a chair covering, for which it was no doubt suitable although it was probably designed primarily as a dress-material.

PLATE 82

A. French Silk-Design; About 1740. (See pp. 126, 127)

Paris, Musée des Arts Décoratifs, Galais Collection, Vol. 9.

Signed '*J. Riffe*' with a flourish that led the 19th-century binder of the particular volume containing this and related designs to label it '*Desseins de Riffet*'. Bossebœuf, in his history of 'La Fabrique de Soieries de Tours' (*Bulletin de la Société Archéologique de Touraine*, Tome XLI, 1900, p. 460) states that Riffe was a famous designer at Tours but gives no evidence to support this assertion. Galais, who made the collection of designs in question, was a designer at Tours in the 19th century but, in a preface to the collection, he states that he also acquired many drawings from Lyons, so the fact that a design is included in his collection does not necessarily mean it was drawn at Tours. All the same, I believe Riffe did work there, because the colours are rather muddy (like those of certain silks believed to be from Tours), and because the general style seems unlike any designs that can safely be assigned to Lyons.

B. ABOUT 1742; ENGLISH (SPITALFIELDS). (See pp. 125, 127)

Brown ribbed ground, the pattern in shades of green and off-white with mauve and brown details. Made up as a dress.

Width 21 in. (53·4 cm.). Repeat; height 24 in. (62·8 cm.).

London, Victoria and Albert Museum. No. 443–1888.

The dark colour of the ground is at first glance misleading but closer inspection reveals that this was undoubtedly woven after a design by Anna Maria Garthwaite. Several of her drawings in this style, dated 1741 and 1742, are in the Victoria and Albert Museum.

PLATE 83 (See p. 126)

A. ABOUT 1742; ENGLISH (SPITALFIELDS).

Silk with a deep violet satin ground, brocaded with two kinds of silver thread. Made up as a chasuble.

Copenhagen, The Danish Royal Collections, Rosenborg Castle. No. 3329.

Part of a set of vestments, all of the same sumptuous material, one item of which bears the initials of Queen Louise of Denmark and the date 1751. The set was presumably used at her funeral in that year. The silk is, however, earlier and so closely resembles designs by Anna Maria Garthwaite drawn in 1741 and 1742 that there can be little doubt that it is of that date and English. The Queen was an English princess, daughter of George II, and married Frederik V of Denmark in 1743. Perhaps the silk was originally part of her trousseau; it may even have been used for her wedding-dress in the first place and later made into a set of vestments. It was a fairly common practice on the Continent for ladies of noble birth to have their wedding-dresses made into christening cloths or vestments.

B. ABOUT 1741; ENGLISH (SPITALFIELDS).

Pink damask; made up as a dress.

Width 21 in. (53·4 cm.). Repeat; height over 45 in. (1·14 m.).

London, The London Museum.

This silk was almost certainly woven from a design by Anna Maria Garthwaite. There are several designs very like this pattern in the Victoria and Albert Museum, dating from the year 1741.

PLATE 84

A. ABOUT 1774; ENGLISH (SPITALFIELDS). (See pp. 126–127)

White damask ground, brocaded with coloured silks. The leaves chiefly dark green, the flowers in shades of blue, pink, yellow with orange, and straw-colour with brown. Made up as a dress.

Width 20½ in. (52 cm.). Repeat; height 24 in. (61 cm.).

London, Victoria and Albert Museum, Circ. 85–1951.

This fine example of an English 'brocade with a white ground', a type of silk for which England was famous during the mid-18th century, was almost certainly designed by Anna Maria Garthwaite. There are several very similar designs by her in the Victoria and Albert Museum; for example, No. 5982–11, dated 1744.

B. ABOUT 1745–46; ENGLISH (SPITALFIELDS). (See p. 126)

Silk taffeta (tabby) with a white ground chequered with yellow lines, the flowers brocaded in naturalistic colours similar to the preceding example. The silk appears to be a lustring.

Edinburgh, Royal Scottish Museum, Loan No. L.315.2. (I am greatly indebted to Mr. Revel Oddy for obtaining the owner's permission for me to illustrate this dress and for supplying me with a photograph.)

The dress comes from a private collection in Scotland. The 'tartan' ground is interesting; the silk may have been specially woven with an eye on the Scottish market. The approximate date of this pattern can, once again, be judged by reference to the rich series of designs by Anna Maria Garthwaite from this period. Its Scottish associations and its presumed date tempt one to speculate whether the dress was worn at some festivity connected with the 'Forty-five' rebellion — perhaps as a display of patriotism or allegiance for one side or the other.

PLATE 85

A. FRENCH SILK-DESIGN; DATED 1746. FROM TOURS. (See pp. 126–127)

Inscribed '*Gros de Tours broché . . . 1746*'. This is a draught or *mise-en-carte*.

Tours, Château Plessis-lès-Tours, Museum of the Tours Silk Industry. (It was not possible to obtain a better photograph at the time of going to press.)

This is the only dated French silk-design from the 1740's that I have yet discovered. This has a certain resemblance to several other rather slight designs of the same period in the Musée des Arts Décoratifs, Paris, one of which is inscribed in pencil '*L.D. pinx.*' which may be the initials of the Tours designer Louis Durand (see Note to Pl. 75A).

B. MID-1740'S; FRENCH (LYONS).

The ground is a white, ribbed taffeta (tabby) with a flush effect; the main pattern is brocaded with coloured silks in which the salmon-pinks and leaf-greens that can usually be associated with Lyons silks predominate.

Width 21 in. (53·4 cm.). Repeat; height 17 in. (43·2 cm.).

London, Victoria and Albert Museum. No. 2028–1899.

PLATE 86

A. 1747; ENGLISH (SPITALFIELDS). (See p. 127)

Taffeta (tabby) with an off-white colour, brocaded with coloured silks (darkish green with lighter details, shades of blue, pink, dark brown and the usual yellow linked with rust-red).

Width 20½ in. (52 cm.). Repeat; height 26½ in. (67·3 cm.).

London, Victoria and Albert Museum. No. T.720–1813.

The actual design for this silk has survived. It was drawn by Anna Maria Garthwaite and bears the date '*17th April, 1747*' (Victoria and Albert Museum, No. 5985–9. See Note to Plate 64B). According to the surviving index to the volume containing her designs for that year, the silk is technically a brocaded lustring. Contemporary writers noted that lustrated silks tended to crack, since the treatment rendered the silk rather brittle. This silk is cracked in many places.

B. Late 1740's; English (Spitalfields).

Heavily ribbed white taffeta (tabby), brocaded with coloured silks.
Width now 19 in. (48·3 cm.): the selvedges have been trimmed away. Repeat; height 28½ in. (72·4 cm.).
London, Victoria and Albert Museum. No. T.18–1922.

There is a dress in the Museum of the City of New York (illustrated in A. C. Weibel, *2000 Years of Silk-weaving*, Cat. of an Exhibition held at Los Angeles Museum of Art in 1944, published in New York, 1944, fig. 388) of a silk identical to this except that the feathers are executed with silver-gilt thread. This dress is stated to have been worn by the wife of Judge William Smith at a ball in New York given in honour of the birthday of 'the Prince of Wales, later George III', in 1750. It is very probable that this silk was woven between about 1747 and 1750 but its connection with George III is, I submit, questionable because George III only came to the throne in 1760 and was not even Prince of Wales until after the death of his father, Frederick, in 1751. The association is more likely to have been with George II or with Frederick, Prince of Wales. The 'Prince of Wales Feathers' in the design may in this case be significant, although I am inclined to think the motif was purely decorative.

PLATE 87 (See p. 132)

A. Mid-18th Century; French or German.

Green silk damask.
Width 20½ in. (52 cm.). Repeat; height 22½ in. (57·1 cm.).
London, Victoria and Albert Museum. No. 623–1896.

Because there are apparently many silks of this kind in German collections, they are often thought to be German. I know of no firm evidence for this although it is quite possible that silks of this type *were* woven in Germany. Such silks must also have been woven in France (indeed, if they were woven in Germany, they were almost certainly made there in imitation of French originals) and it is even possible that many of those now in German collections were woven in France specially for the German market, which was of vital importance to the French silk-weaving industry. When hostilities prevented the holding of the great annual Fairs at Leipzig during the Seven Years War, the Lyon weavers suffered considerable hardship.

B. Mid-18th Century; Probably French.

Light blue ribbed ground with a flush effect, the main pattern being white.
Width 19¾ in. (50·2 cm.). Repeat; height 13¾ in. (34·9 cm.).
London, Victoria and Albert Museum. No. 1391–1871.

This may have been woven at any time between 1745 and 1765; the pattern gives no clue to its precise date.

PLATE 88 (See p. 127)

A. English Silk-Design; Dated 1748.

Design for 'A Silver and Silk bro[cade]' by Anna Maria Garthwaite, sold to Mr. Chaplin (a weaver) on 2nd December 1748. (See Note to Plate 64B.)
Width 10¾ in. (27·3 cm.), height 20¼ in. (51·4 cm.): drawn to half scale.
London, Victoria and Albert Museum. No. 5986–9.

B. Late 1740's; French.

White taffeta (tabby) with a flush effect, brocaded with coloured silks.
Stockholm, Nordiska Museet. No. 173.609.

The stylized motifs in the 'sub-pattern' suggest a date after about 1748; the flowers, on the other hand, are too natural to be much later.

PLATE 89

A. English Silk-Design; Dated 1751. (See p. 127)

For a 'flowered tabby' — a taffeta in two colours. Composed by Anna Maria Garthwaite and sold to Mr. Jamet, a Huguenot master-weaver, on 4th March 1751. Drawn to half scale. (See Note to Plate 64B.)
Width 9½ in. (24·1 cm.), height 18 in. (45·7 cm.).
London, Victoria and Albert Museum. No. 5988–33.

B. 1750–55; English (Spitalfields). (See p. 128)

White taffeta (tabby) ground with a flush effect, richly brocaded with silver-gilt thread and coloured silks.
Width of silk 21 in. (53·4 cm.). Repeat; height 18 in. (45·7 cm.).
Los Angeles County Museum, No. L. 2100. P2.57.8 (ex Doris Langley Moore Collection, England).

The colouring is characteristically English of the period and the style is typical of the 1750's.

PLATE 90 (See p. 128)

A. Probably from the 1750's; English (Spitalfields).

Satin with a coloured flush effect, brocaded with flowers that are typically English of the period 1750–65 or so.

I have not seen this silk and there is no record of its whereabouts now, other than that it was submitted for an opinion to the Victoria and Albert Museum by another museum. There are related silks in various collections, and similar 'compartmented' patterns are to be found among Anna Maria Garthwaite's designs from the early 1750's.

B. Portrait of Eleanor Frances Dixie by Henry Pickering.
Nottingham, The Castle Museum and Art Gallery.

From the costume, this portrait can be dated in the third quarter of the 18th century. (C. Willett Cunnington, *A Picture Book of English Costume*, London, 1960, fig. 211, dated the costume in the 1750's.) The silk seems to be from the early 1750's. The silk is white with coloured flowers.

PLATE 91

A. From the 1750's; Probably French (Tours?).
Dull green fancy ground, white and yellow meanders, flowers in dull purples and blues.
Width 19½ in. (49·5 cm.). Repeat; height 19 in. (48·3 cm.).
London, Victoria and Albert Museum. No. 1223–1899.

The compartmenting and the semi-stylization of the flowers suggests a date in the 1750's for this pattern. The dull purple and the rather narrow width suggest that it may have been woven at Tours (see p. 36).

B. About 1755–65; French. (See p. 133)

Chiné silk with a taffeta ground of a duck-egg green colour, the pattern in olive greens, pinks, yellows and purples. The silk is a lustring.
Width 17¾ in. (43·8 cm.). Repeat; height 15½ in. (39·3 cm.).
London, Victoria and Albert Museum, No. T.16–1961.

This charming summer-dress of a light-weight *chiné* lustrated silk is almost certainly French. *Chiné* silks with large patterns like this were apparently not made elsewhere, at least, not until later in the century. The French had a monopoly in this branch of silk-weaving; the smuggling of these 'clouded lustrings', as they were called in English, into this country was a profitable business, it seems. This particular dress was acquired from Paris only recently, however.

PLATE 92

A. About 1755–60; English (Spitalfields).

White ribbed ground brocaded with silver-gilt thread and coloured silks in the characteristic English colour-scheme of the period. Made up as a dress.
Width 21¾ in. (52·5 cm.). Repeat; height 24¾ in. (63 cm.).
Stockholm, Nordiska Museet. No. 143.709.

The dress is stated to have been worn at the Swedish Court during the 1760's by Charlotta Sparre who was married in 1733 and died in 1787. This very splendid silk is clearly English and ought to date from the second half of the 1750's. It seems that English silks mostly reached Sweden via Hamburg.

B. From the 1750's; French.

Light blue ground with a complex flush pattern, the pattern rendered in shades of green, red, purple and in silver-gilt thread.
Repeat; height 14¼ in. (36·2 cm.).
Photograph reproduced by kind permission of Messrs. Mayorcas Ltd., London, of a silk now in the Los Angeles County Museum.

Other fragments of the same silk are now in the Victoria and Albert Museum (T.350–1960).

PLATE 93

A. From the 1750's; French (Lyons).

Silk with an off-white ground which has a sub-pattern and is brocaded with silks in what I believe to be the typical Lyons colour-scheme of the mid-18th century.
Paris, Union Française des Arts du Costume. (I am much indebted to M. François Boucher for giving me this photograph and permission to illustrate this pretty dress from the Union's magnificent collection.)

B. Portrait of Madame de Pompadour by Quentin La Tour, Drawn in 1755. (See p. 128)

Paris, Musée du Louvre. (See A. Besuard & G. Wildenstein, *La Tour . . .*, 1928 No. 385.)

She appears to be wearing a dress of white satin richly brocaded with silver-gilt thread and with small flowers in coloured silks.

PLATE 94 (See p. 128)

A. ENGLISH SILK-DESIGN; DATED 1752.

Design for a '*Sing*[*le*] *Com*[*ber*] *Damask patt*[*ern*]' by Anna Maria Garthwaite and sold to the Huguenot master-weaver Mr. Maze (Massé?) on 19th May 1752. Drawn to half-scale. (See Note to Plate 64B.)

Width 11¼ in. (28·5 cm.), height 22 in. (55·9 cm.).

London, Victoria and Albert Museum, No. 5989–16.

B. FRENCH SILK-DESIGN; ABOUT 1754(?).

Inscribed '*de Barot*'.

Paris, Musée des Arts Décoratifs, Library, Martin Collection, Vol. 2.

Another design in the same volume and in the same style is dated 1754. In the Galais Collection, which is in the same Library, there is a complete volume of similar designs entitled '*Desseins de Baraut*', another of which is also dated 1754. All these related designs must belong to the third quarter of the 18th century. Bossebœuf (see reference given under Pl. 75A) states that there was a designer at Tours named Barrot in 1720 [*sic*] but whether this is the same man or his son, or whether Bossebœuf knew of Barot's existence solely through the designs in the Galais Collection, which was always supposed (wrongly) to contain designs from Tours only, is not clear. It is perhaps not irrelevant that in the volume containing the present design is another by a certain M. Suleau. There was a designer of this name working at Lyons in 1759 (Capitation Roll for that year, Lyons Silk Industry Archives). The rather bright colours are not typical of Tours.

PLATE 95 (See p. 129)

A. ABOUT 1760; FRENCH (LYONS).

The fancy ground is cream-coloured; brocaded with silver-gilt thread and coloured silks in shades of green, pink and blue.

Width 20¾ in. (52·5 cm.). Repeat; height 16 in. (40·5 cm.).

Lyons, Musée Historique des Tissus. No. 27.573.

The parasol-shaped flowers were probably influenced by the engravings of Jean Pillement which began to appear, first of all in London, in 1755. The pattern probably dates from about 1760. Although Pillement worked at Lyons several times during his career, there is no evidence that he ever composed designs for silks but his distinctive style may well have influenced contemporary silk-designers, as would seem to have been the case in this instance. There has been a tendency among students of historic textiles to use the term *Style Pillement* somewhat indiscriminately to cover all designs with a *chinoiserie* flavour (e.g. see Note to Pl. 72A). In this present instance, such a label would for once be justified.

B. 1760–65; FRENCH(?).

Pale lilac taffeta (tabby) with a brocade pattern; the meander white, the flowers of coloured silks including a very noticeable black.

Width 19¾ in. (48·9 cm.). Repeat; height 16¼ in. (41·3 cm.).

London, Victoria and Albert Museum. No. 595–1896.

Comparison with French dated designs shows that this kind of pattern was current about 1762 or just after. The silk is not of the highest quality and could possibly be Spanish or Italian.

PLATE 96 (See p. 129)

A. Woven in the 1760's; Swedish.

Yellow satin with a fancy pattern, brocaded with three kinds of silver and silver-gilt thread and coloured silks.

Stockholm, Nordiska Museet. Berch Collection No. 17.648.

A sample woven in Stockholm from silk produced at Kanton, a hamlet specially built for the purpose in the grounds of Drottningholm Castle outside Stockholm, probably from designs by Jean-Eric Rehn. The establishment enjoyed the special patronage and encouragement of the Queen of Sweden, Louisa Ulrica, a sister of Frederick the Great, who, like her brother, was a great admirer of French culture. Another related silk in the Collection was woven in 1768.

B. An Italian Silk-Design; Dated 1765.

Inscribed '*Primo marzo 1765. Copiato da un campione di Francia arrivo da Gaillard*' (1st March 1765. Copied from a French sample sent by Gaillard).
Paris, Musée des Arts Décoratifs, Library, Vol. DD 98.

This and its companion volume contain Italian silk-designs from the factory of the Zucchi brothers in Venice and from a factory at Vicenza. This is probably from the Zucchi establishment. Gaillard was presumably a French agent, perhaps in Milan (see p. 49) or at Lyons.

PLATE 97

A. 1765–1770; French(?). (See p. 130)

Dull grey taffeta (tabby) ground with shaded mulberry-coloured stripes; meanders produced by a flush effect in white, the flowers brocaded in colours.
Width 21 in. (53·4 cm.). Repeat; height 10½ in. (26·6 cm.).
London, Victoria and Albert Museum. No. 108–1880.

Comparison with dated designs in the collection of Messrs. Warner (see next item) shows that, this silk was probably woven in the late 1760's.

B. French Silk-Design (mise-en-carte), Dated 1771. (See p. 129)

Inscribed '*Du 26 juillet 1771. J. Gallien & Cie . . .*'. The narrow stripes in the ground are red, the wide stripes are yellow.
Collection of Messrs. Warner & Sons Ltd. Reproduced by kind permission of Sir Ernest Goodale, C.B.E.

From a set of designs by Gallien ranging in date from 1761 to 1771. Leroudier, *Les Dessinateurs de la Fabrique Lyonnaise*, Lyons, 1908, p. 25, states that Gallien was famous for his *mise-en-cartes*, of which this is an example. Leroudier mentions another set, presumably in France, dating from 1770 to 1775.

PLATE 98

A. Third Quarter of the 18th Century; English or French. (See p. 131)

Coat and waistcoat of brown velvet with a voided cut and uncut pile on a ribbed silk ground, specially woven to shape for the purpose.
London, Victoria and Albert Museum. No. 828 and A–1904.

The 'fur-trimming' resembles the fur frequently depicted on silks woven during the 1760's (e.g. Pl. 96A).

B. Third Quarter of the 18th Century; French.   (See p. 132)

Deep blue fancy ground with a small sprig pattern in red, yellow and blue; the meander is produced by a white flush effect.

Width 20 in. (50·8 cm.). Repeat; height 13¾ in. (34·9 cm.).

London, Victoria and Albert Museum, No. 297–1896.

Small-patterned silks like this were made for men's clothes. At first glance, they all seem much alike but they *do* vary considerably in detail and in their colouring. Technically these patterns are mostly *droguets de soie* by which term the whole class is now generally known (not with strict accuracy, since this kind of pattern was produced in other weaves as well).

PLATE 99   (See p. 130)

A. From the 1760's; French (Lyons?).

Mauve taffeta (tabby) ground with a blue flush effect, brocaded with coloured silks. The greens are yellowish, the pinks a salmon colour — both pointing to a Lyons provenance.

Width 21 in. (53·4 cm.). Repeat; height 12½ in. (31·7 cm.).

London, Victoria and Albert Museum. No. 313–1896.

A design for a pattern almost exactly like this in the Museum of Fine Arts, Boston, Massachusetts (56.B44.7) is attributed to Jean-Pierre Ringuet. Like his father, Jean Ringuet (see Pl. 58B and Chapter IV, Note 1, p. 112), he was a Lyonnais designer. He was born in 1728 and died between 1769 and 1771 so he would have been active during the third quarter of the 18th century. Since this silk obviously dates from that period, the attribution is likely to be correct. Moreover, it is unlikely that anyone would invent such an attribution since Jean-Pierre Ringuet's name is now hardly remembered by anyone.

B. Probably Woven in the Late 1760's; English (Spitalfields).

White fancy ground of ribbed taffeta (tabby) with a flush effect, richly brocaded with coloured silks in typical Spitalfields colours.

Width 19¾ in. (50·2 cm.). Repeat; height 13 in. (33·0 cm.).

London, Victoria and Albert Museum. No. 124–1901.

Made up as a dress which, by the cut of the back, cannot be dated much before 1770. The informal scattering of small flowers is typical of Spitalfields silks from about 1742 until well into the third quarter of the century but the rather formal wreath and the stiff St. Andrew's cross inside it seem to be concessions to the taste for classical forms which was fast gaining the ascendancy over the Rococo idiom by about 1770.

PLATE 100

A. About 1770; French(?).

Fancy off-white ground with a pattern in two shades of blue and silver thread, the latter being brocaded.

Width 21 in. (53·4 cm.). Repeat; height 10 in. (25·4 cm.).

London, Victoria and Albert Museum. No. 717–1864.

The rigidity of the curves in this pattern suggest that this represents a late phase in the development of the typical ribbon-meander patterns of the 1760's.

B. About 1770; English (Spitalfields).

Off-white fancy ground with narrow red stripes and a pattern in coloured silks.
Width 20 in. (50·8 cm.). Repeat; height 8 in. (20·3 cm.).
London, Victoria and Albert Museum, No. 839–1884.

The cut of the dress does not permit one to date this pattern much before 1770.

PLATE 101

A. Probably from the 1770's; French (Lyons?). (See p. 131)

Cream-coloured taffeta, the flowers rendered in pinks and greens, the imitation engravings in purple silk.
Width 21 in. (53·4 cm.). Repeat; height 13 in. (33·0 cm.).
London, Victoria and Albert Museum. No. T.845–1919.

B. From the 1770's or Later; Probably French. (See p. 130)

Silk with a taffeta ground chequered with a weft effect and with a pattern of brocaded coloured silks.
Width 19 in. (48·3 cm.). Repeat; height 20 in. (50·8 cm.).
London, Victoria and Albert Museum. No. 537–1896.

The organization of this pattern is obviously derived from the ribbon-meanders of the 1760's but the less robust treatment and the small scale of the floral motifs indicate that this silk is of a later date and represents the airiest kind of *Louis Sieze* late-Rococo.

PLATE 102

A. About 1775–80; French or English.

Light purple satin with a white pattern supported by details in bright red, dark green, yellow and a puce-colour. Made up as a dress.
Width 20 in. (50·8 cm.).
London, Victoria and Albert Museum. No. T.188–1953.

B. From the 1780's; English (Spitalfields). (See p. 130)

White taffeta (tabby) with blue-grey stripes and small coloured flowers, brocaded.
Width 19½ in. (49·5 cm.). Repeat; height 12 in. (30·5 cm.).
London, Victoria and Albert Museum. No. T.333 and A–1913.

The bright red colour used in the brocading suggests the silk is English, as does the white ground which was always so popular in this country during the last two-thirds of the 18th century. The tiny flowers are typical of the late Rococo phase; several pattern books of the 1780's and early 1790's have survived which contain numerous examples of silks in this general style.

Note: *The following were specifically made as furnishing materials*

PLATE 103 (See p. 136)

A. From the 1640's; Italian(?).

Red with a yellow pattern; tabby weave.
Width 21 in. (53·4 cm.). Repeat; height 41 in. (1·03 m.).
London, Victoria and Albert Museum. No. 282–1880.

B. Mid-17th Century; Probably Italian (Genoa?). (See p. 136)

Silk velvet with a voided pattern in cut and uncut crimson pile on a ribbed yellow ground.
Width 23½ in. (59·6 cm.). Repeat; height 35½ in. (90·1 cm.).
London, Victoria and Albert Museum, No. 4069–1856.

In the same collection is another velvet with a similar but much less well-drawn pattern which may be a Milanese or French imitation of this successful furnishing design that probably originated at Genoa and of which many examples survive (see Chapter VII, Note 1, p. 137).

PLATE 104

A. Mid-17th Century(?); Italian (Genoa?). (See p. 137)

Silk velvet with cut and uncut crimson pile and a voided pattern revealing the ribbed yellow ground.
Width 21 in. (53·4 cm.). Repeat; height 34 in. (86·4 cm.).
London, Victoria and Albert Museum, No. 5662–1869.

B. From the 1670's(?); Probably Italian. (See p. 139)

A very rich material with a cream-coloured satin ground that was originally almost entirely covered with silver strip. The pattern is executed in several types of silver and silver-gilt thread. Much attention has been paid to the binding of the brocaded pattern in order to produce many subtle variations in the hatching which is so typical a feature of silks from the third quarter of the century. A patch of untarnished metal thread near the top still gives some idea of how this splendid 'cloth of gold' once looked.
Width 21¾ in. (55·3 cm.). Repeat; height 32 in. (81·3 cm.).
London, Victoria and Albert Museum. No. T.122–1911.

PLATE 105

A. About 1689; Italian (Genoa). (See p. 139)

Crimson damask.
Width 21 in. (53·4 cm.).
London, Victoria and Albert Museum. T. 43–1937.

Removed from the walls of one of the Presence Chambers in Hampton Court Palace, furnished in 1689. The accounts show that it cost 24/- a yard. (See F. J. Rutherford, 'The Furnishing of Hampton Court Palace for William III', *Old Furniture*, October 1927, Vol. II, pp. 15–33, and George Wingfield Digby, 'Damasks and Velvets at Hampton Court', *Connoisseur*, Vol. CIII, January–June 1939, p. 248, fig. 1.)

B. Last Quarter of the 17th Century; Italian. (See p. 137)

Crimson damask with details brocaded in gilt thread.
Width 26½ in. (67·3 cm.). Repeat; height 51¾ in. (1·31 m.).
London, Victoria and Albert Museum. No. 275–1880.

It is improbable but not impossible that this was woven early in the 18th century.

PLATE 106

A. About 1685; the Chair is English, the Velvet presumably Italian. (See p. 138)

Crimson velvet with a voided pattern in cut and uncut pile on a satin ground. The material seems to be the original covering; it was no doubt usually protected by a loose cover from the very beginning.

Present owner, unknown; formerly at Kimbolton Castle, Huntingdonshire. (Photograph, Copyright Country Life.)

B. 1685–88. (See p. 139)

The upholstery of this fine bed is carried out in a silk velvet with a white ground, the pattern being predominantly inky dark blue with purple flowers and vases, supplemented by some olive green and dull yellow. The velvet has both cut and uncut pile.

London, The London Museum.

The bed bears the cyphers of James II (1685–88) and his queen, Mary of Modena. I am extremely grateful to Mr. Martin Holmes for supplying me with information about this bed which is mentioned in Pyne's *Royal Residences* (section devoted to St. James's Palace, State Bedroom). The dark blue is unusual. Genoese velvets normally have a dark green pattern. This makes one speculate whether this velvet may not have been woven elsewhere — possibly at Lyons. It may merely be a coincidence that a certain well-known class of late 17th-century French embroidery is worked largely in a similar dark blue colour.

PLATE 107

A. About 1695; the Settee English, the Velvet Italian (Genoa). (See p. 138)

The covering of this particularly magnificent settee bearing the cypher of the first Duke of Leeds (created in 1694, died in 1712), appears to be original and is of a polychrome silk velvet which is mainly green, red and yellow.

Formerly at Hornby Castle. (Photograph, Copyright Country Life.)

B. Early 18th Century(?); Probably Italian (Genoa). (See p. 140)

Silk velvet with voided cut and uncut pile in red and green on a yellow ground.
Width (i.e. the depth in this case) $25\frac{1}{2}$ in. (69·8 cm.), Length 50 in. (1·27 m.).
London, Victoria and Albert Museum. No. T.80–1941.

PLATE 108 (See p. 140)

A. About 1705–10(?); Perhaps Italian.

A rich silk with the ground covered in silver thread and with a pattern executed in silver-gilt thread and coloured silks.
Width $21\frac{3}{4}$ in. (55 cm.), height of fragment about $37\frac{3}{4}$ in. (95 cm.).
Present owner unknown. The piece was sold in 1907 at the Helbing Galerie, Munich. (See J. M. Schmidt, Catalogue of the Spengel Sale, No. 223.)

B. About 1709; Probably English.

Yellow silk damask.
Width 21 in. (53·4 cm.). Repeat; height 50 in. (1·27 m.).
London, Victoria and Albert Museum. No. T.58–1937.

Said to have come '*from bedhangings traditionally connected with Peter the Great of Russia's visit to London in 1709 (or 1696)*'.

I have found no evidence that Peter the Great visited England in 1709 (he came in 1697), but comparison with designs for English silks in the Vanners & Fennell Collection (see Note to

Pl. 37) suggests that 1709 would be the approximate date of this pattern. It is not, in my view, likely to date from the 1690's. The hangings are said to have come from the house of a London merchant, an ancestor of the donor of the hangings to the Museum; perhaps he really did entertain Peter the Great on his visit in 1697 and there is no connection with the hangings, or perhaps some other high-born Russian was his guest in 1709 — which was the year of the Russian defeat at Poltava, when Peter was fully occupied with his military commitments although he may well have sent emissaries to many European capitals in search of allies, and help.

PLATE 109

A. About 1710; Probably Italian. (See p. 140)

Brocatelle; the pattern executed in red satin on a yellow tabby ground. An extra series of linen wefts gives additional strength to the material, making it specially suitable for furnishing.
Width 25 in. (63·5 cm.). Repeat; height 56 in. (1·42 m.).
London, Victoria and Albert Museum. No. T.852–1892.

B. About 1711; The Velvet probably Italian (Genoa). (See p. 139)

The velvet has red cut and uncut pile on a yellow ground. It is made up rather curiously as a central panel of a synagogue curtain, the panel being about $32\frac{1}{4}$ in. across (82 cm.) and 42 in. (1·11 m.) high.
Prague, Jewish Museum. No. 916. (See H. Volavkova, *The Synagogue Treasures of Bohemia and Moravia*, Prague, 1949, Pl. 27.)

The curtain was presented to the Lipnik Synagogue by Moses and Fegele Lippmann in 1711. The same velvet is found in various other collections, for instance, on a sofa at Houghton, Norfolk, England (E. Edwards and P. Macquoid, *Dictionary of English Furniture*, Vol. III, p. 97, 1st edn. only.)

PLATE 110

A. About 1714; Probably English. (See p. 139)

Silk velvet with a cream-coloured satin ground and a pattern in a dull red and a yellowish brown or tawny colour.
Reproduced by gracious permission of Her Majesty The Queen and now at Hampton Court Palace, Kingston-upon-Thames.

The velvet is used for the hangings of a state bed and the covering of some accompanying furniture, all of which were transferred from Windsor Castle. The original bill dated 10th May 1714, shows that '321 yds. $\frac{1}{8}$ of white, crimson and yellow figured velvet' were ordered at a cost of 42/- a yard. (See F. J. Rutherford, The Furnishing of Hampton Court Palace: 1715 to 1737', *Old Furniture*, 1927, Vol. II, pp. 76–86; also G. F. Wingfield Digby, 'Damasks and Velvets at Hampton Court', *The Connoisseur*, Vol. CIII, p. 252; and R. Edwards, *Dictionary of English Furniture*, 2nd edn., London, 1954, p. 56.) A chair covered with the same material is in the Victoria and Albert Museum (W.15–1931) and there is also a fragment of this velvet in the Museum's collection of historic textiles (T.107–1930). (Photographed from the illustration originally reproduced in *The Connoisseur* article referred to above, the original negative having been destroyed during the last war.)

B. First Quarter of the 18th Century(?); French (perhaps Paris). (See p. 144)

The pattern in silver and dull green on a ribbed light blue ground.

Width 21 in. (53·4 cm.), height of fragment 49 in. (1·24 m.).

London, Victoria and Albert Museum, No. T.265–1958.

The arguments of dating this silk in the first or second decade of the 18th century are set out on page 145.

Plate 111

A. About 1710–15; French (Lyons?). (See p. 140)

White ribbed ground, the pattern mainly executed in light green, supported by details in rusty
   pinks, a cyclamen pink, silver and silver-gilt thread.

Width 21¼ in. (54·0 cm.). Repeat; height 26 in. (71·2 cm.).

London, Victoria and Albert Museum. No. 329–1989.

The date and provenance of this silk are discussed under the next entry. While the two materials
are of about the same date, this silk is likely to be the earlier of the two.

B. About 1715; French (Lyons?). (See pp. 139, 140)

Red silk velvet with cut and uncut pile on a cream-coloured ground enriched with silver thread
   (the latter now largely worn away).

Width about 21 in. (53·4 cm.), height of fragment 26 in. (66·1 cm.).

London, Victoria and Albert Museum. No. 631–1883.

Although technically different, it seems reasonable to suppose (although it is far from certain)
that this velvet and the brocaded silk shown alongside it were woven at the same place and within
a few years of each other. The brocaded silk has the salmon pinks and grass green colours that
probably indicate a Lyons provenance and I think it therefore possible that both these materials
were made there. 'Genoa velvets' were certainly being made at Lyons during the first half of the
18th century. The approximate date of such patterns is established by a chair in the Victoria and
Albert Museum (W.62–1935; ill. *Picture Book of English Chairs*, 1957 edn. No. 52), bearing the
arms granted in April 1717 to Sir William Humphreys, Bart., which is covered in a rather poor but
presumably original imitation of the present velvet. The velvet on the chair may well be an English
copy (Sir William Humphreys was Lord Mayor of London in 1714–15) of this successful pattern
of which examples are to be found in several collections including that in the Musée des Tissus,
Lyons.

PLATE 112

A. About 1716–19; The Velvet Italian (Genoa). (See p. 140)

Polychrome silk velvet of the highest quality on the walls of the alcove in the bedroom of the
   charming little palace in the grounds at Nymphenburg, near Munich, known as the Pagodenburg.
   This was built by the Bavarian Court Architect, Joseph Effner, between 1716 and 1719.

Munich, Schloss Nymphenburg (B. Verwaltung der staatl. Schlösser, Gärten und Seen).

See Luise Hager, *Nymphenburg, Schloss, Park und Burgen*, Munich, 1955, pp. 30–34, espec.
p. 33 and Note 70. The author suggests that this velvet was woven 'about 1700', probably because
the traditional dating for all such velvets has long been 'late 17th century' or 'second half of the
17th century'. There seems, on the other hand, to be no reason to suppose that the velvet was not

of the latest pattern and, indeed, it seems to have features that actually indicate a date in the second decade of the 18th century for this material (cf. Pl. 111B). There is a cope of the same velvet at Lyons. (See R. Cox, *Le Musée Historique des Tissus*, Paris, 1914, Pl. 44.)

B. ABOUT 1725–35(?); ITALIAN (GENOA?). (See p. 141)
Cream coloured satin with a pattern in dark green, purple and yellow cut and uncut pile.
Width 22 in. (55·9 cm.). Repeat; height 39 in. (98·4 cm.).
London, Victoria and Albert Museum. No. 340–1891.

PLATE 113

A. ABOUT 1730; PROBABLY ENGLISH. (See p. 140)
A settee designed by William Kent about 1730 and covered with a contemporary velvet which has a red pile and a cream-coloured ground.
Reproduced by kind permission of the Marquess of Cholmondeley, Houghton Hall, Norfolk. (Photograph, Copyright Country Life.)

Several true Genoese velvets have been used in the furnishing of Houghton which is surely one of the most magnificent of the great English 18th-century country-houses. The present velvet has a pattern which seems to lack the easy flowing rhythm of the Genoese products, which suggests that this striking material is English. 'Genoa velvets' were being made in England at this period.

B. FROM THE 1730's(?); ITALIAN (GENOA). (See pp. 139, 141)
The Velvet Bedroom, Holkham Hall, Norfolk.
Reproduced by kind permission of the Earl of Leicester. (Photograph, Copyright Country Life.)

The building of Holkham started in 1734 and took many years to complete but the bed and accompanying furniture were probably made before 1740.

PLATE 114 (See p. 141)

A. FROM THE 1730's(?); ITALIAN (GENOA).

This pattern is found in several colours; red, yellow and green samples are in the Victoria and Albert Museum. The present piece was photographed in the Museum when it was submitted for an opinion but the present owner is unknown. Many variants of this well-known pattern exist and the length of the repeat differs quite considerably. The pattern has been, and is still being, imitated but the modern reproductions are much wider and usually have two repeats in a width, whereas the antique specimens are generally about 21 in. wide and never span more than a single repeat. A flock wallpaper of this pattern was used for the decoration of the offices of His Majesty's Privy Council about 1735. A fragment of this is now in the Victoria and Albert Museum (Cat. of Wallpapers, 1929, No. 14, ill.).

B and C. 1735–40(?); FRENCH.
Multi-coloured pattern with dull green and purple predominating and with subtle shading produced by *points rentrés* on a greyish-white ground.
The height of this pattern (164 in. (4·16 m.)) is very remarkable, width 31 in. (78·8 cm.).
London, Victoria and Albert Museum. No. T.73–1936.

Said to have come from a castle in Transylvania which belonged to the family of Queen Mary, Princess of Teck and consort of George V, who gave it to the Museum in 1936. This silk is in the style evolved by Jean Revel in the 1730's (see Pl. 72A) but seems to lack the cohesion of that master's style. The dull colouring suggests a Tours provenance. Wherever this was made, it represents a quite outstanding *tour de force* of silk-weaving.

PLATE 115 (See p. 142)

A. English Silk-Design; Dated 1741.

Width 21¼ in. (54·0 cm.). Repeat; height 30¾ in. (77 cm.).
London, Victoria and Albert Museum. No. 5979–16.

By the Spitalfields silk-designer Anna Maria Garthwaite (see Note to Plate 64B). The design is dated but bears no other inscription. It is executed in shades of brown on a white ground and was probably intended for a dress-material, like the other large-scale patterns Garthwaite designed around 1740 (see Pls. 81A, 82B and 83B) but such patterns could, of course, conceivably have been used for furnishing purposes.

B. From the 1740's(?); Italian (Genoa).

Yellow ground enriched with silver, the pile pattern (now much worn) rendered in green, pale blue, red, mauve, white, fawn and pink.
About half a width is all that survives of this specimen which is now only 10 in. wide (25·4 cm.). Repeat; height 31 in. (78·8 cm.).
London, Victoria and Albert Museum. No. 851–1894.

The easy, flowing rhythm and the high degree of naturalism of this pattern indicate a date between 1735 and about 1755 for this very remarkable material.

PLATE 116 (See p. 142)

A. 1753; Swedish (Stockholm).

Crimson damask brocaded with two kinds of silver-gilt thread.
Width 21¼ in. (54 cm.). Repeat; height 23¾ in. (60 cm.).
Stockholm, Nordiska Museet. Nos. 17–648/B and 99.092/B.345.

The pattern incorporating the three-crown emblem of the Swedish kings was woven for King Adolf Frederik's State Bedroom in the Royal Palace in Stockholm where the wall-hangings of this material may still be seen. The silk was woven in the workshops of the immigrant Frenchman, Barthelemi Peyron, almost certainly to a design furnished by Jean-Eric Rehn (see p. 29).

B. From the 1760's(?); Probably French.

The full height of the repeat is about 87 in. (220 cm.).
Vienna, Museum für Angewandte Kunst. No. T.8419.

Detail of a baldaquin of richly brocaded silk transferred to the Museum from the Hofmobiliendepot. Made up of panels with border-sections specially woven to match. It is not known when this baldaquin was ordered but it seems to belong to the 1760's and I would suggest that it may have been acquired for the Coronation of the Emperor Joseph II who came to the throne in 1765. *En suite* are two chair covers, as well.

PLATE 117

A. 1760–66(?); French (Lyons). (See pp. 44, 143)

Cream-coloured ground brocaded with a large number of colours.

Width 27¼ in. (69 cm.). Repeat; height 26 in. (66 cm.).
Lyons, Musée Historique des Tissus. No. 26.087.

Designed by Philippe de Lasalle and known as the *Tenture du Roi Stanislas*. Stanislas Leszczynski, exiled King of Poland, whose Court was at Nancy, died in 1766.

B. FROM THE 1770'S; FRENCH (LYONS). (See pp. 141–142)

With a fancy purple ground; richly brocaded in many colours.
Width 22 in. (55·9 cm.). Repeat; height 41 in. (1·03 m.).
London, Victoria and Albert Museum. No. T.187–1931.

Examples of the same design but with a yellow ground are to be found in various collections. The design is by Philippe de Lasalle.

PLATE 118 (See p. 144)

A. ABOUT 1780–85; FRENCH (LYONS).

Silk with a light blue ground richly brocaded in many colours.
Width 29¼ in. (75 cm.), height of fragment (?), 45½ in. (154 cm.).
Berlin, formerly in the Ermeler Haus, Potsdam. Said to have come from the walls of the Blaue Paradekammer in the Stadtschloss, Potsdam, which was being furnished about 1785.

The original designs for this material are still in the possession of Messrs. Tassinari & Chatel in Lyons (No. 6363). This firm still owns many of the designs executed by their predecessors, the firm of Pernon, with which Philippe de Lasalle was associated. This silk does not appear to be of quite the same high quality as the preceding two examples and it is possible that the pattern was not drawn by Lasalle himself although it is in the style for which he was famed. (R. Cox, *Musée Historique des Tissus de Lyons*, Paris 1908, Pl. 33, illustrates another fragment of the same material and also makes this attribution.) On the other hand, by this date, the quality of French silks had somewhat declined and a certain flatness is often prevalent in the compositions. Possibly even Lasalle was affected by the prevailing tendencies. (See J. H. Schmidt, 'Zwei Seidentapeten von Philippe de Lasalle und die Berliner Seidenmanufaktur', in *Berliner Museen*, LVI, 1935, pp. 26–32.)

B. FROM THE 1780'S; FRENCH (LYONS).

Sea-green coloured satin, richly brocaded in many colours.
Overall width 53½ in. (1·35 m.). Panels each about 20 in. wide (50·8 cm.). Border, 8½ in. wide (21·5 cm.).
London, Victoria and Albert Museum. No. T.357–1960.

The design for this very pretty silk may possibly have been composed by Philippe de Lasalle. If so, it is in a lighter vein than the more typical examples of his work. It is interesting to note how much the height of the repeat varies (compare the vase in the centre, top and bottom) even in such a high-class material as this. It was of course extremely difficult to weave a pattern exactly the same length in each repeat on a hand-operated loom especially when the repeat was a long one. There is a suite of furniture covered with this material, ordered from Paris about 1790, and now in the Rijksmuseum, Amsterdam (see F. J. B. Watson, *Louis XVI Furniture*, London, 1960, fig. 196).

PLATE 119 (See p. 144)

A. FRENCH SILK-DESIGN; DATED 1780.

A draft (*mise-en-carte*) on squared paper for a '*Musulmane à bordure pour meuble*', as an inscription on the back informs us, which is dated 1780. The border (on the right) specially designed to go with this material is much less ambitious than the borders of the silks shown in Plates 116B and 118B.

Tours, Château Plessis-lès-Tours, Museum of the Tours Silk Industry. No. Ch.62.15.17.

This was undoubtedly designed at Tours. Whereas the coloured designs known as '*esquisses*', which were intended to show how the finished silk would look (e.g. Pls. 70A and 74A), frequently passed from one centre to another (often illegally, of course), *mises-en-carte* like this and like that shown in Plate 69A almost always remained in the place where the designs concerned were woven.

B. German Silk-Design; About 1785.   (See p. 144)

A full-scale design painted on satin and inscribed '*Nr.67. Copie peinte d'un dessin satin large, lizere en deux couleurs a R.1772, en cramois fin travaille pour le metier, couleurs ord. B.612 environ. Les Freres Baudouin Fils*'.

The silk woven from this design was on the walls of the Yellow Paradekammer in the Stadtschloss in Potsdam. It had a yellow-green ground. The design was in the Ermeler Haus, Berlin, before the 1939–45 War but cannot now be found. The design and the silk are discussed and illustrated by J. H. Schmidt in the article mentioned in the note to Pl. 118A, above.

The firm of Baudouin Frères was active in Berlin in the 1780's. There is no connection between these brothers and Christopher Baudouin who was an eminent designer in Spitalfields during the early 18th century (see Pl. 55B) although they were all Huguenots and may all have come, or have been descended from families, from Tours.

PLATE 120   (See p. 144)

A. Late 18th Century; French.

Dark red satin with a pattern in white and pale green.

Width of fragment 20½ in. (52 cm.), height of oval 13¼ in. (33·6 cm.).

London, Victoria and Albert Museum. No. 363–1880.

This has been a chair cover.

B. Late-18th Century; Probably French.

Part of a valance from a set of bed-hangings which have never been made up. Richly brocaded in coloured silks on a white ground.

Width (depth, as shown here) 21½ in. (53·4 cm.). Diameter of roundel about 11 in. (27·9 cm.).

London, Victoria and Albert Museum. No. 1276d–1871.

The set came from Spain but I would have thought it rather more likely to be French than Spanish.

BIBLIOGRAPHY

Full bibliographical references are given throughout this book in the relevant places. It should be comparatively easy to locate these by referring to the List of Contents at the beginning or to the Index at the end of the book.

As no monograph has hitherto been devoted to the silk materials of the Baroque and the Rococo periods, there is no bibliography of the subject although a number of works touch upon it, mostly in a superficial manner. The following are mentioned because they contain a large number of illustrations. The dating and attributions given in these works are not all to be trusted. The patient reader may however be able to verify the dates in most cases by reference to the present study which is based on information that was not readily available to the various authors in their time.

COX, R., *Le Musée Historique des Tissus* (Lyons), Paris, 1914. 2 vols. Good illustrations; often strange dating.

CHRISTENSEN, SIGRID FLAMAND, *De Danske Kongers Kronologiske Samling paa Rosenborg. Konge-dragterne fra 17 og 18 Aarhundrede*, Copenhagen, 1940. 2 vols. Excellent survey of the rich collection of royal costume in Copenhagen; well illustrated.

FALKE, O. V., *Kunstgeschichte der Seidenweberei*, Berlin, 1913. 2 vols. What little this eminent authority had to say about silks of this period is remarkably accurate.

FLEMMING, E., *An Encyclopaedia of Textiles*, London, 1927.

HEINZ, DORA, *Der Paramentschatz der Stadtpfarrkirche in Linz*, Vienna, 1962. Of wider scope than the title would suggest; incorporating much recent research.

KUMSCH, EMIL, *Kunstgewerbemuseum zu Dresden, Stoffmuster des XVI-XVIII Jahrhunderts*, Dresden, 1888-95. 4 vols. Large plates.

PODREIDER, F., *I Tessuti d'arte in Italia attraversi i Secoli*, Como, 1925. Useful illustrations; not very informative text.

SCHMIDT, H., *Alte Seidenstoffe*, Brunswick, 1958. Useful as a modern summary under a single cover; little fresh information on our subject except on the German industry.

SLOMANN, V., *Bizarre Designs in Silk*, Copenhagen, 1953. Fine illustrations covering limited phase; controversial text.

SYLWAN, V., and A. GEIJER, *Siden och Brokader*, Stockholm, 1931. Excellent short survey paying considerable attention to later periods; unfortunately all in Swedish.

VOLAVKOVA, HANA, *Synagogue Treasures in Bohemia and Moravia*. Well illustrated; contains a selection from this astonishingly rich collection of silks, many well documented.

WEIBEL, A. COULIN, *2000 Years of Silk-weaving*, New York, 1944. Useful survey, with illustrations of silks in America.

Books dealing with historic costume often contain illustrations of dress materials. Silks are also frequently shown in use in contemporary portraits and views of house interiors.

Index

Note: *In many cases, particularly on pages 148–97, the reader should expect more than one reference for each page number mentioned. Where occasionally only a Plate reference is given, see* Notes on Plates.

INDEX

PLATES

1A. About 1500

1B. 1600—25

1C. 1625—50

2B. About 1620

2A. About 1615

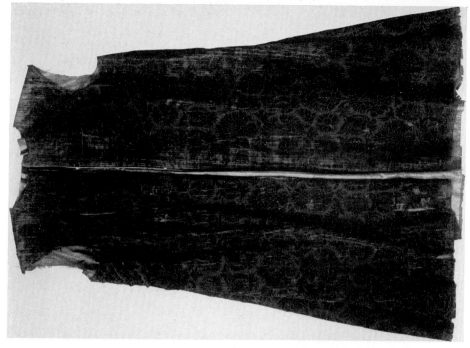

3C. 1625–32

3B. 1625–32

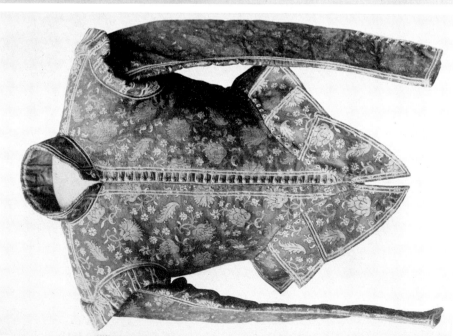

3A. 1625–32

4A. 1639

4B. About 1640

4C. About 1640

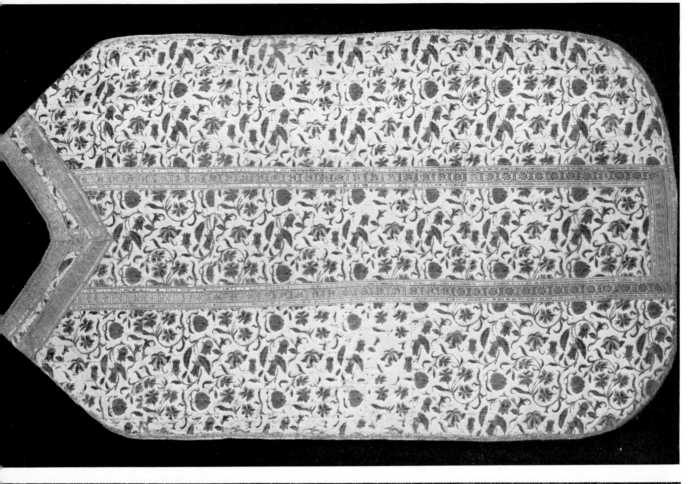

5B. 1630-40?

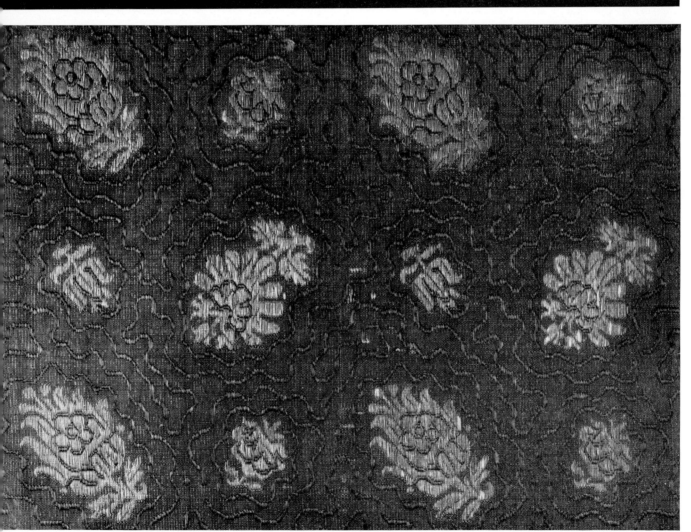

5A. 1625-50

6B. 1640–50?

6A. 1642

6C. 1640–50?

7B. About 1640

7A. 1625–50

8A. About 1655–60

8B. About 1660

9A. About 1650–60

9B. About 1660–70

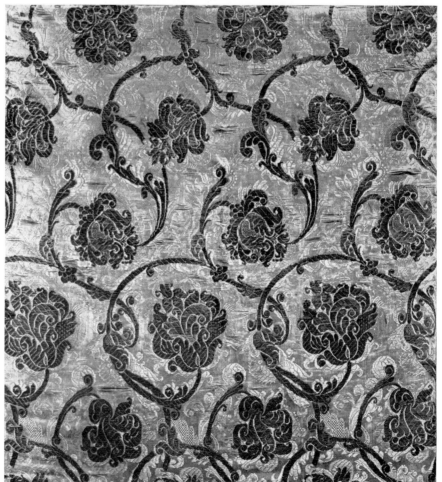

10B. About 1650—70

10A. About 1650—70

11C. 1650–75

11D. 1650–75

11A. About 1665–69

11B. About 1660

12B. About 1665–69

12A. About 1650–60

PETITES FLEURS ARABESQUES , OU SEMENCES DE BOUQUETS POUR LES ETOFFES.

A Paris Chez N.Langlois rüe St.Jacques à la Victoire auec Priuilege du Roy   3

13A. 1660–70?

13B. 1660–70?

13C. 1660–70?

Bouquets propres pour les Estofes de Tours

A Paris Chez N. Langlois

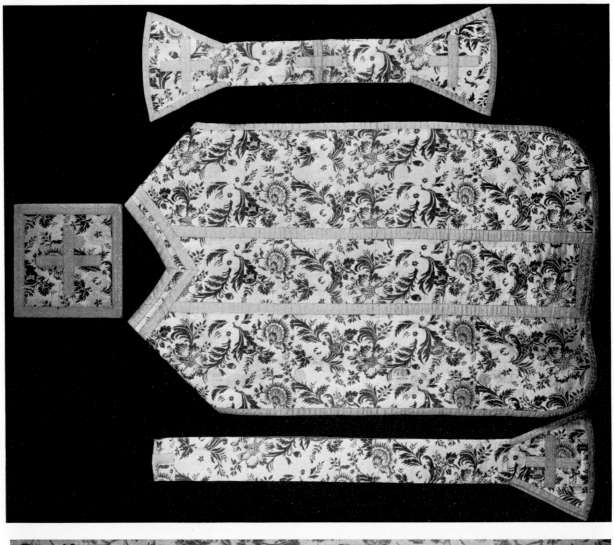

14B. 1670–80?

14A. 1658

15 B. 1670—80?

15 A. 1660—70?

16B. About 1675

16A. 1670—80

17A. About 1678

17B. About 1678

17C. About 1675

18B. 1670–90

18A. 1650–75

19A. 1680–81

19B. 1680–81

20B. About 1686

20A. 1680–90?

21B. About 1690–1700

21A. About 1690–97

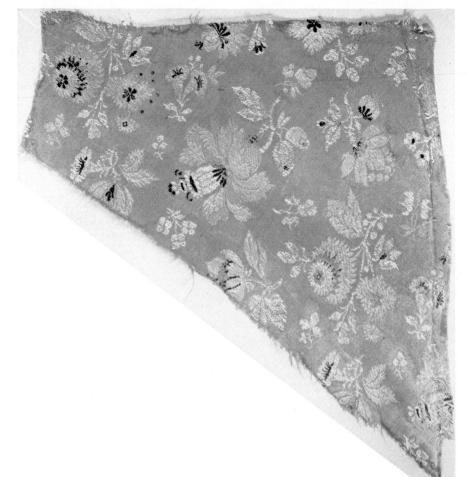

22B. 1680–1700

22A. 1680–1700

22C. 1680–1700

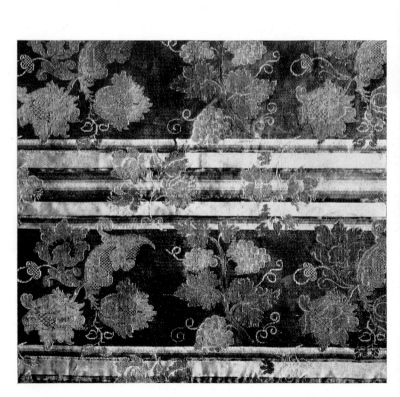

23B. 1690

23A. 1684

24B. 1690—95

24A. 1690—94

25B. 1694

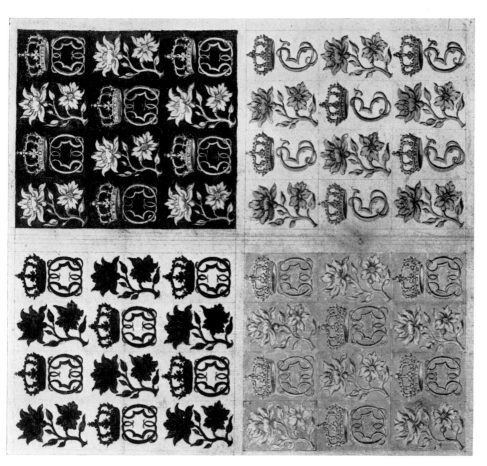

25A. About 1690

26B. About 1694?

26A. About 1695

27B. About 1700

27A. About 1695

28A. About 1695

28B. About 1695

29B. About 1695–1700

29A. About 1695

30B. About 1700–05

30A. About 1700

31B. About 1700

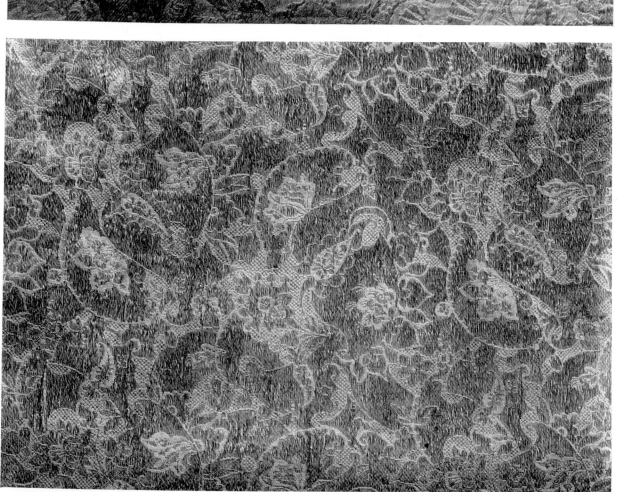

31A. About 1699

32B. About 1700

32A. About 1700

33B. 170G—05

33A. 1700—02

34A. About 1695–1750

34B. About 1706

35A. About 1680–1700?

35B. About 1700–10

36A. About 1700–03

36B. About 1705

37A. 1706   37B. 1707

38A. About 1705–10?

38B. About 170

39A. About 1705–12

39B. 1708

40B. About 1709

40A. About 1708

41B. About 1705–12

41A. About 1700–10

42A. 1705–10

42B. About 1710

43A. About 1710

43B. 1710

44B. About 1710–15

44A. About 1705–10

45B. About 1711

45A. 1711

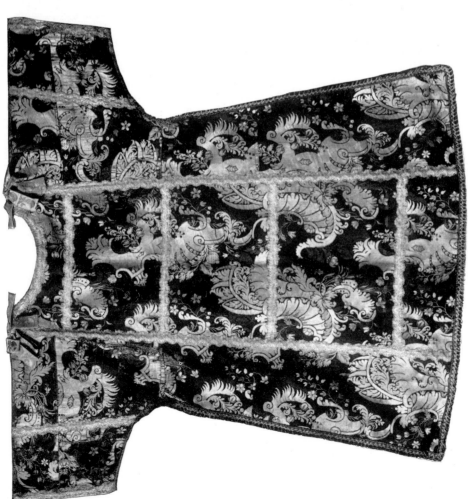

46B. About 1714

46A. About 1712

47B. About 1712–15

47A. 1710–15

48B. About 1715

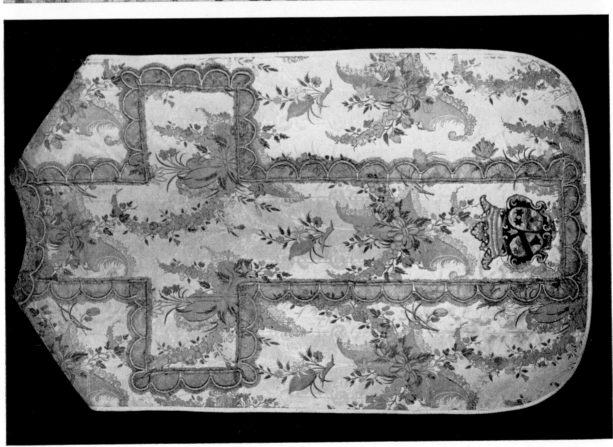

48A. About 1713

49B. About 1714

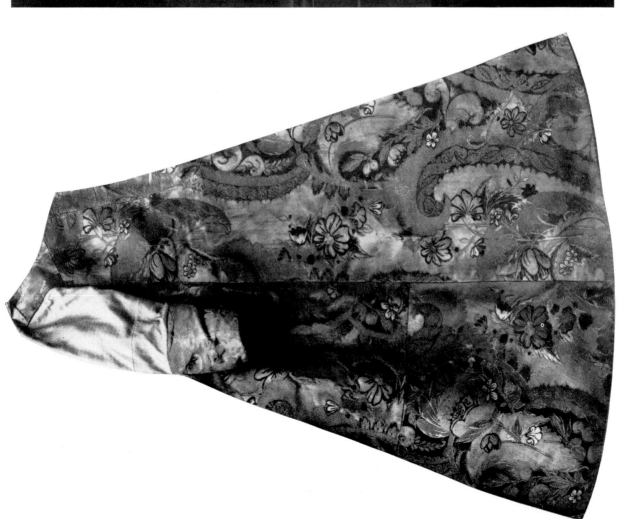

49A. About 1714

50B. 1717?

50A. About 1715—20

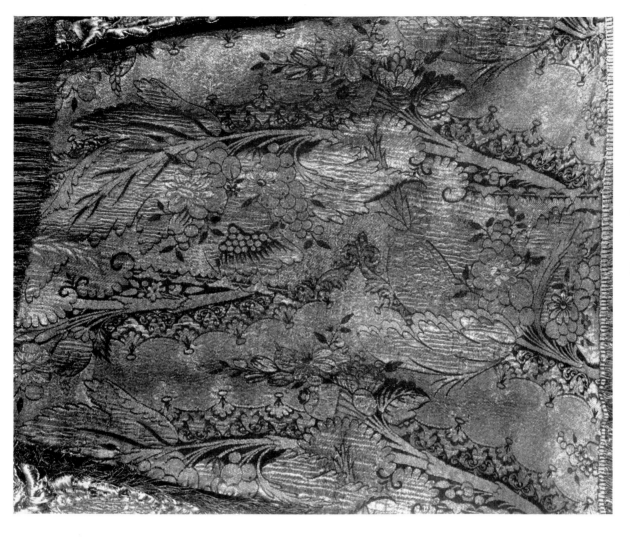

51B. About 1718

51A. 1718

52B. 1718–19

52A. 1718

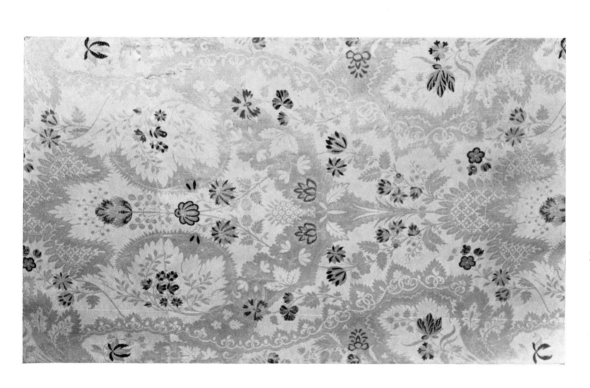

53A. About 1720

53B. 1721

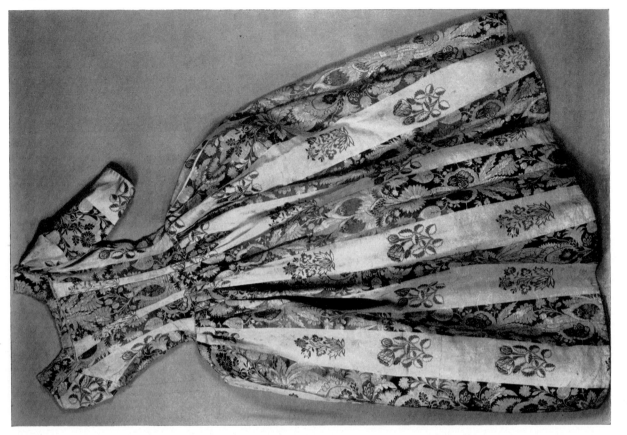

54B. About 1721

54A. 1721

56B. 1725

56A. About 1715–20

57B. About 1725–30

57A. About 1725–30

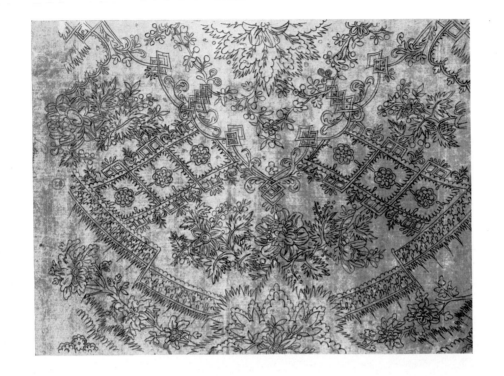

58A. 1726

58B. 1728

59A. 1729?

59B. 1728?

60A. 1729

60B. About 1730

61A. About 1729–31

61B. About 1730–31

61C. 1736

62B. Late 17th century?

62A. 1731–32

63B. About 1733

63A. 1733

64B. 1733

64A. About 1730–33

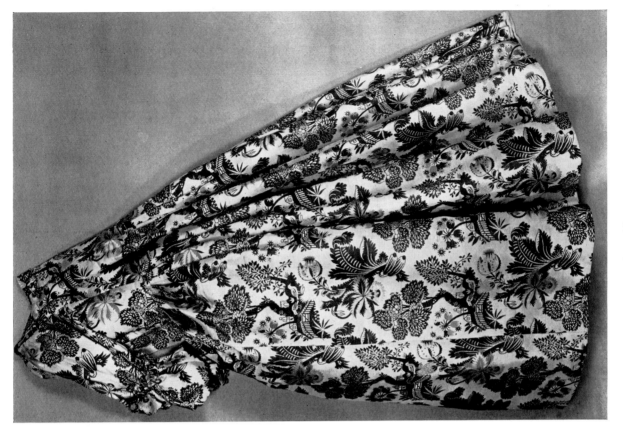

66A. About 1734

66B. About 1734-35

67A. About 1733–34

67B. About 1735

68B. About 1732–33

68A. About 1732–33

69A. 1733

69B. About 1734

70B. 1733—34

70A. About 1734

71B. About 1735

71A. About 1735

72B. 1734?

72A. About 1735-37

73B. About 1735

73A. About 1735

74A. 1735

74B. About 1735–36

75A. About 1735–40

75B. About 1735–40

76A. About 1735–40

76B. About 1736–40

77B. About 1735–45

77A. About 1735–40

78B. About 1733

78A. About 1733

79B. 1738–39

79A. About 1738–42

80B. 1739

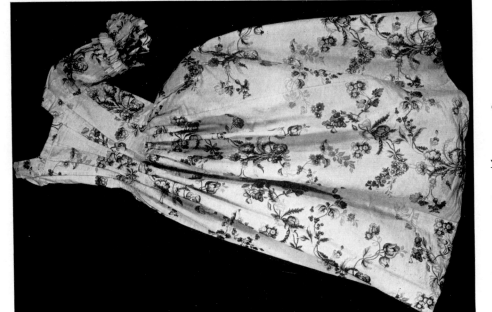

80A. About 1738

81B. 1735–50

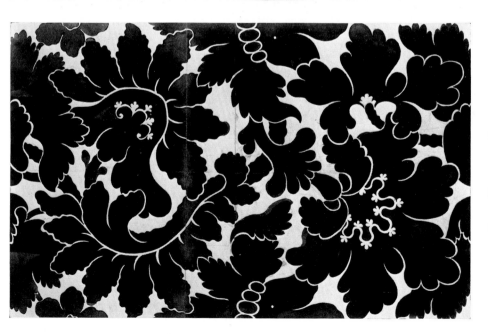

81A. About 1738–40

83B. About 1741

83A. About 1742

84B. About 1745–46

84A. About 1744

85B. About 1745

85A. 1746

86B. 1748–50

86A. 1747

87B. Mid-18th century

87A. Mid-18th century

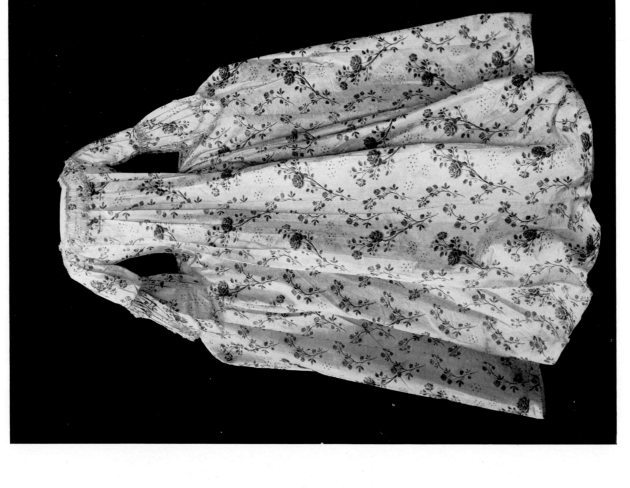

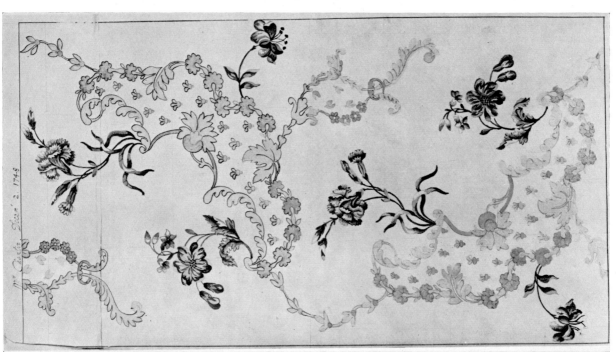

89B. About 1750–55

89A. 1751

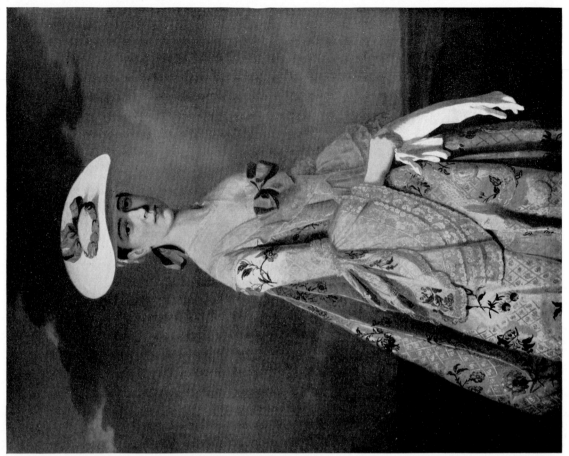

90B. 1750–60

90A. 1750–60?

91B. 1755–65?

91A. 1750–60?

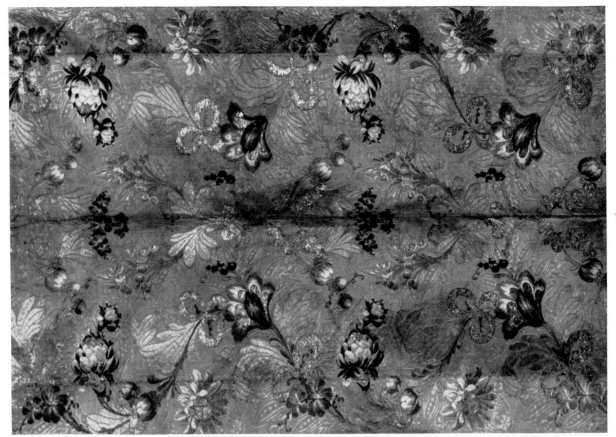

92B. 1750–60?

92A. 1755–60

93B. 1755

93A. About 1750—60

94B. About 1754

94A. 1752

95B. 1760–65

95A. About 1760

97A. 1765–70

97B. 1771

98B. 1750—75

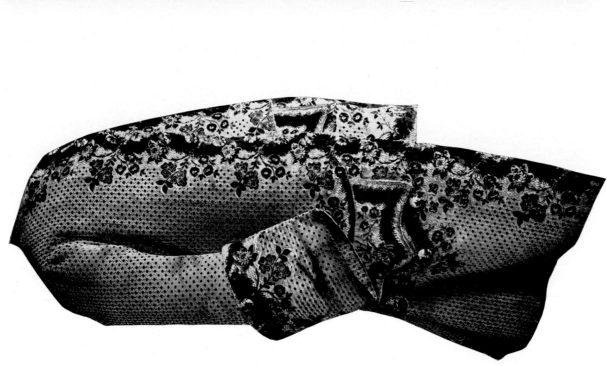

98A. 1750—75

99B. 1767–70?

99A. 1760–70

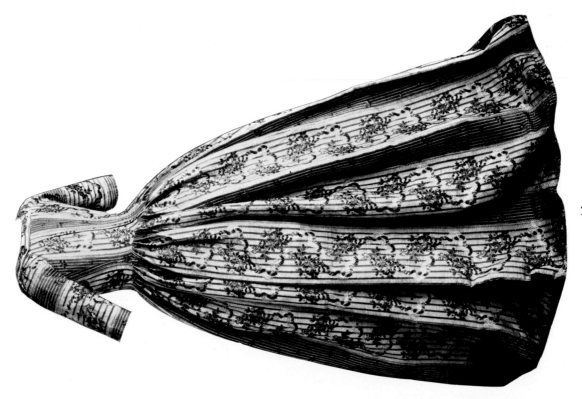

100B. About 1770

100A. About 1770

101B. 1770—85?

101A. 1770—80?

102B. 1780—90

102A. 1775—80

103B. Mid-17th century

103A. 1640–50?

104B. About 1670–80?

104A. Mid-17th century?

105B. 1575–1700

105A. About 1689

106A. About 1695

106B. 1685—88

107A. About 1695

107B. Early 18th century?

108A. About 1705–10?

108B. About 1709

109B. About 1711

109A. About 1710

110B. 1700—25?.

110A. 1714

111B. About 1715

111A. About 1710–15

112A. About 1716–19

112B. About 1725–35?

113A. About 1730

113B. 1739–40?

114A. 1730–40?

114B and c.
1735–40?

115B. About 1740–50?

115A. 1741

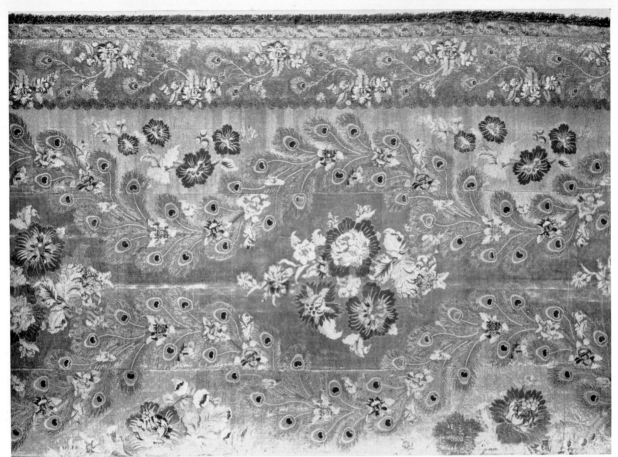

116B. About 1760–70

116A. 1753

117B. 1770—80

117A. 1760—65

118B. 1780–90

118A. About 1780–85

119B. About 1785

119A. 1780

120A. About 1780–95

120B. About 1790–1800